Nuns Behaving Badly

Nuns Behaving Badly

TALES OF MUSIC, MAGIC, ART, AND
ARSON IN THE CONVENTS
OF ITALY

Craig A. Monson

THE UNIVERSITY OF CHICAGO PRESS
CHICAGO & LONDON

CRAIG A. MONSON is professor of music at Washington University in St. Louis. He is the author of two books, most recently of *Disembodied Voices: Music and Culture in an Early Modern Italian Convent* (1995), and the editor of *The Crannied Wall: Women, Religion, and the Arts in Early Modern Europe* (1992).

The University of Chicago Press, Chicago 60637
The University of Chicago Press, Ltd., London
© 2010 by The University of Chicago
All rights reserved. Published 2010
Printed in the United States of America

19 18 17 16 15 14 13 12 11   2 3 4 5

ISBN-13: 978-0-226-53461-9   (cloth)
ISBN-10: 0-226-53461-8   (cloth)

Library of Congress Cataloging-in-Publication Data
Monson, Craig (Craig A.)
    Nuns behaving badly: tales of music, magic, art, and arson in the convents of Italy / Craig A. Monson.
        p. cm.
    Includes bibliographical references and index.
    ISBN-13: 978-0-226-53461-9 (cloth: alk. paper)
    ISBN-10: 0-226-53461-8 (cloth: alk. paper) 1. Nuns—Italy—Conduct of life—History—16th century. 2. Nuns—Italy—Conduct of life—History—17th century. 3. Convents—Italy—History—16th century. 4. Convents—Italy—History—17th century. 5. Women—Italy—Social conditions—History—16th century. 6. Women—Italy—Social conditions—History—17th century. 7. Music in convents—Italy—History—16th century. 8. Music in convents—Italy—History—17th century. I. Title.
    BX4220.I8M68 2010
    271'.90045—dc22   2010014701

CONTENTS

FIGURES

ACKNOWLEDGMENTS

Generous access to numerous archives and libraries over many years enabled me to reconstruct these histories. The research would have been impossible without the opportunity to consult the incomparable collections of the Archivio Segreto Vaticano. I enjoyed and greatly appreciated regular access to important libraries and archives in Bologna and the help of their staffs: the Archivio di Stato (dottoressa Carmela Binchi), the Biblioteca Comunale dell'Archiginnasio (dottoressa Anna Manfron and dottoressa Cristina Bersani), the Archivio Generale Arcivescovile (dottore Mario Fanti), and the Biblioteca Universitaria. I likewise received valuable assistance from the Archivio di Stato di Imola, the Victoria and Albert Museum (Revinder Chahal), the Beinecke Library (Naomi Saito), the University of California's Pacific Earthquake Engineering Research Center (Charles James), and the Newberry Library. I am perennially indebted to the library system of Washington University in St. Louis, and especially to the interlibrary loan department, which demonstrates a prodigious ability to uncover obscure volumes faster than I can get through my previous requests.

Jane Bernstein and Pamela Starr first suggested that there might be a book in all the stories they had patiently listened to, and that I would probably have a good time writing it. Early on, Kaye Coveney tactfully helped me recognize that much about early modern Italy and its convents (not to mention nuns' music) just might be unfamiliar to general readers, history buffs, or music lovers. Steve Smith responded patiently and enthusiastically to ideas and writing strategies of every sort and took great pains over elements of style and substance. Having offered abundant help and hospitality during my earlier Italian research efforts, this time, in the tenth and eleventh hours, Candace Smith willingly accepted the role of embedded agent in Bologna, following up archival loose ends (some leading to new discoveries) and leaping as agilely over and around bureaucratic hurdles as her colleague Daphne Dickey might have done. In an earlier period, Katherine Gill and Gabriella Zarri helped get me started down trails that eventually led to two chapters of the book, in ways I'm sure they have long forgotten but that I happily remember. Robert Kendrick, Anne Schutte, and Elissa Weaver generously shared information, expertise, and enthusiasm on matters linguistic, musical, iconographic, historical, and inquisitorial during the writing stage, as they have done for two decades, and critiqued anything from individual ideas to complete drafts. Lucia Marchi's help began with sorting through the vagaries of my Italian, then continued in lively discussion of historical and etymological issues. Karen Olson confronted the still unripe fruits of my high school Latin with infectious enthusiasm. The many others who kindly lent a hand include Richard Agee, Monsignor Niso Albertazzi, Antonia L. Banducci, Luisa Bedeschi, Craig Harline, Jim Ladewig, Joe Loewenstein, Beth and Hugh Macdonald, E. Ann Matter, Maribeth Payne, Dolores Pesce, Colleen Reardon, Ann Roberts, Deborah Roberts, Luca Salvucci, Michael Sherberg, Laurie Stras, Betha Whitlow, Gian Ludovico Masetti Zannini, and Anna Zayaruznaya—to whom many thanks.

From our initial contact, Randy Petilos at the University of Chicago Press offered regular encouragement, astute but tactful criticism, productive writing strategies at critical (potentially terminal) moments, and (from out of nowhere) unanticipated lively discussion of long-forgotten sixteenth-century English polyphony, from inside the notes.

And special thanks to Jimmy and Stephen for helping me achieve some salutary balance through their joyful enthusiasm, freely shared, for music worlds removed from academy and convent.

ABBREVIATIONS

AAB	Archivio Generale Arcivescovile, Bologna
ASB	Archivio di Stato, Bologna
ASI	Archivio di Stato, Imola
ASV	Archivio Segreto Vaticano
ASV, VR	Archivio Segreto Vaticano, Sacra Congregazione dei Vescovi e Regolari
BAV	Biblioteca Apostolica Vaticana
BCB	Biblioteca Comunale dell'Archiginnasio, Bologna
BUB	Biblioteca Universitaria, Bologna
Gozz.	Gozzadini
posiz.	posizione
reg. episc.	regestum episcoporum
reg. monial.	regestum monialium
reg. regular.	regestum regularium
sez.	sezione

DRAMATIS PERSONAE

SAN LORENZO IN BOLOGNA

Ambrosio da Bologna: abbot of San Giovanni in Monte; male superior of San Lorenzo

Antonia, conversa: convent servant at San Lorenzo; enthusiastic dabbler in love magic

Arcangela Bovia: subprioress at San Lorenzo; probable aunt of Laura Bovia and probable sister of Giacomo Bovio

Giacomo Bovio: primociero of San Petronio; Laura's relative and guardian

Laura Bovia (d. 1629): student and star singer at San Lorenzo; left to join musica secreta in Florence

Florentia Campanacci: singer at San Lorenzo; leading enthusiast for magical practices

Eliseo Capis: Master inquisitor of the Bolognese Holy Office of the Inquisition (1578–85)

Angelica Fava: singer at San Lorenzo; accused of stealing the missing viola

Gentile: nun organist at San Lorenzo

Panina Ghisliera: singer at San Lorenzo; owner of missing viola; aunt of Angela Tussignana

Livio da Bologna: former abbot of San Giovanni in Monte; former superior of San Lorenzo

Gabriele Paleotti (1522–1597): reforming archbishop of Bologna (1566–97)

Semidea Poggi: aristocratic enthusiast for singing and magic at San Lorenzo; in later life, a published poet

Ascanio Trombetti (1544–1590): Bolognese wind player; music teacher and magical go-between to singers at San Lorenzo

Angela Tussignana: novice at San Lorenzo, possessed by the devil

SAN NICCOLÒ DI STROZZI IN REGGIO CALABRIA

Francesco Domenico Barone: the first aristocrat from Reggio to defend the nun arsonists

Candeloro Battaglia: supporter of nun arsonists and enemy of Archbishop di Gennaro

Giovanni Filippo Battaglia: syndic of Reggio (1672–73); defender of the nun arsonists

Giovanni Domenico Bosurgi: syndic of Reggio (1672–73); defender of the nun arsonists

Matteo di Gennaro (1622–1674): archbishop of Reggio Calabria (1660–74)

Anna Monsolino: Giovanna Monsolino's sister and chief co-conspirator in setting fire to San Niccolò

Giovanna Monsolino (I): wife of Lamberto Strozzi, mother of Diego Lamberti Strozzi and Maria Maddalena Monsolino

Giovanna Monsolino (II): subprioress and chief arsonist at San Niccolò

Maria Maddalena Monsolino: sister or (more probably) half-sister of Diego Strozzi; prioress for life of San Niccolò

Maria Oliva: co-conspirator in setting the fire at San Niccolò

Maria Padiglia: exemplary nun and abbess at Santa Maria della Vittoria; founding abbess pro tem at San Niccolò

Felicità Rota: co-conspirator in setting the fire at San Niccolò

Diego Lamberti Strozzi: son of Lamberto Strozzi and Giovanna (I) Monsolino; extremely successful aristocrat in Reggio; founder of San Niccolò di Strozzi; brother or half-brother of Maria Maddalena Monsolino

Lamberto Strozzi: Florentine entrepreneur in Reggio; married Giovanna Monsolino (I); father of Diego Strozzi

Massimiano Turbulo: abbot and cantor at the duomo of Reggio;

reprimanded by Archbishop di Gennaro for dress code violations; elected vicar capitular after di Gennaro's death

SANTA MARIA NUOVA IN BOLOGNA

Girolamo Boncompagni (1622–1684): archbishop of Bologna (1651–84); distant relative of Maria Vinciguerra Malvezzi

Giulia Vittoria Malvezzi (1645–1718): musical nun; niece of Maria Vinciguerra and Vittoria Felice Malvezzi

Maria Ermengilda Malvezzi (1646–1720): pious nun, niece of Maria Vinciguerra and Vittoria Felice Malvezzi; sister of Giulia Vittoria Malvezzi

Maria Vinciguerra Malvezzi (ca. 1610–1684): chief convent patron; sister of Vittoria Felice Malvezzi

Vittoria Collalto Malvezzi (1577–1662): countess; mother of Vittoria Felice and Maria Vinciguerra Malvezzi; took up residence at Santa Maria Nuova later in life

Vittoria Felice Malvezzi (1605–1696): donor of needlework; sister of Maria Vinciguerra Malvezzi

Terentia Pulica, conversa: servant, needleworker, and donor at Santa Maria Nuova

Maria Anna Ratta (b. ca. 1650): nun donor at Santa Maria Nuova

SANTA MARIA DEGLI ANGELI IN PAVIA

Giovanna Balcona: protégée of Angela Aurelia Mogna, expelled from Santa Maria degli Angeli

Anna Domitilla Chini Langosca: Angela Aurelia's archenemy; eventually attempted various legitimate means to escape from Santa Maria degli Angeli

Angela Aurelia Mogna: nun at Santa Maria degli Angeli, who fled with Giovanna Balcona

Siro Mogni: brother of Angela Aurelia Mogna; canon at the cathedral of Pavia

Maria Montanara: poor neighbor and observer of the nuns of Santa Maria degli Angeli

Zanina Montanara: Maria's daughter

Catterina Villana: another of Angela Aurelia's protégées

La Zoppa: "the cripple," seamstress, neighbor, and observer of the nuns of Santa Maria degli Angeli

SANTA CRISTINA DELLA FONDAZZA IN BOLOGNA

Giuseppe Accoramboni (1672–1747): titular archbishop of Imola (1728–43)

Giacomo Boncompagni (1653–1731): archbishop of Bologna (1690–1731)

Christina Cavazza (1679–1751): nun singer at Santa Cristina; caught violating monastic enclosure, disguised as an abbot, to attend the opera in 1708

Domenica Colombina, "La Fuggatina": aided Christina Cavazza in her flight from Lugo back to Bologna

Antonio Giacomelli (d. 1712): chaplain of Santa Maria del Piombo; Christina Cavazza's accomplice on her secret excursions to the opera

Ulisse Giuseppe Gozzadini (1650–1728): titular archbishop of Imola (1710–28)

Prospero Lambertini (1675–1758): archbishop of Bologna (1731–40); Pope Benedict XIV (1740–58)

Valeria Rondinelli: professed nun at Sant'Agostino in Lugo; Christina Cavazza's roommate

Francesco Veronesi: sacristan of the parish church of Santa Cristina in Bologna

1

PROLOGUE

TOPO D'ARCHIVIO

I became a *topo d'archivio* (an archive mouse—or rat) by accident.

In 1986 I returned to Florence after a twenty-year absence. In the hodgepodge collections of the Museo Bardini, off the well-beaten tourist track, I happened upon a Renaissance music manuscript. Lavishly bound, elegantly hand copied, as thick as the phone book of some midwestern city, it looked significant but forgotten. I recognized an academic article waiting to be written, so I returned the following summer for a closer look.

Dusting off a few tools from the musicological toolbox (a bit rusty by then, their cutting edges dull), I studied watermarks on the paper, the musical notation, the pieces it contained, the style of the tooled and gilded leather binding, a coat of arms on the front, and an inscription on the back:

.S.

.LENA.

MALVE

CI

A.

These clues led not to Florence but to Bologna, and to Sister Elena Malvezzi at the convent of Sant'Agnese. Suor Elena had taken her vows there in the 1520s and had died, as prioress or subprioress, in 1563.

This was a surprise, because the manuscript chiefly contained French chansons and Italian madrigals. Now, in 1986 I didn't know much about nuns, but I certainly didn't expect them to be singing secular songs of this sort. I especially didn't think they'd sing one that began:

Vu ch'ave quella cosetta
Che dilletta e piase tanto
Ah lasse che una man ve metta
Sotto la sottana e[']l vostro manto.

[You who've got that little trinket,
So delightful and so pleasing,
Might I take my hand and sink it
'Neath petticoat and cassock, squeezing.][1]

Despite my brief acquaintance at this point, sixteenth-century convent music and musicians looked a lot more interesting than their twentieth-century musical equivalents—Soeur Sourire (the singing nun of the 1960s) or Maria from *The Sound of Music*. Deloris Van Cartier (Whoopi Goldberg's character) from *Sister Act* would have seemed quite another matter, but that film wouldn't be released for another five years. Why did Renaissance nuns perform such elaborate music whereas their counterparts in modern times lead such seemingly bland lives? In the 1980s most musicologists associated nuns with chant, if they thought about nuns at all. What were these sisters doing singing *this* music? I turned my back on Elizabethan England, and on "note-centered" research, and became the topo d'archivio this subject required.

My discoveries confirmed what the Malvezzi manuscript had suggested. Convent singing was a contested issue. It provoked delight and fascination (from some—but not all—nun musicians and from their audiences), but also anxiety and conflict (from the church hierarchy). Initial research in Florence and Bologna revealed that convent music required even more careful control by the Catholic bureaucracy than other aspects of its performers' cloistered lives.

So a chief place to continue searching for nuns' music would have to be the Vatican, the center of that bureaucracy, and especially the records of the Sacred Congregation of Bishops and Regulars. This Sacred Congregation, consisting of various cardinals, had been created in 1572 to oversee every facet of monastic discipline throughout the Catholic world. Because nuns' music of the sixteenth century to the eighteenth remained a "problem," the Congregation's archive should contain complaints, requests, judgments, and decrees about music.

Most such complaints and queries came from a local bishop or from his second-in-command, the diocesan vicar-general, acting in his name. In large dioceses, a specially deputized vicar of nuns (another step down in the priestly pecking order) might contact the Congregation. Sometimes it was the nuns themselves who lodged initial objections or tendered requests, though they frequently went right to the top, naively assuming that the pope himself would take an interest in their concerns. Their petitions also landed in the pile at the Bishops and Regulars. Whoever initiated the conversation, from that point on the nuns were commonly left out of subsequent dialogues, which involved prelates from their dioceses and other prelates in Rome. Much of the time the women religious who were the subject of investigation had little direct voice in discussions and deliberations about them.

Of course, one would expect any such deliberations about convent music to be buried amid hundreds of thousands of other documents treating diverse monastic matters, all tied up in some two thousand *buste* ("envelopes"—though in this case "bales" would be more accurate). Organized year by year and by months within each year, and anywhere from six to sixteen inches thick, these buste sit on block after block of shelving in the Vatican Secret Archive.

I made my way to Rome in 1989, and, after a friendly nod from a Swiss Guard at the gate, I passed through the wall into Vatican City. Diffidently proffering credentials and an elaborately signed and sealed American university letter of introduction, I negotiated the bureaucratic hurdles and landed, later that morning, in the Secret Archive's reading room. Some reading rooms—the Duke Humphrey Room of Oxford's Bodleian Library, the old British Library's central reading room, or Bologna's Biblioteca Comunale dell'Archiginnasio, for example—add inspiring elements of aesthetic pleasure to the other joys of scholarship. The Vatican Archive reading room, by contrast, seemed all business to me, sternly utilitarian and largely unmemorable.

I don't remember admiring it much during waits for my three daily manuscript requests to be filled at appointed times. I recall little about the room at all, in fact, except for a bank of tall windows to the east, plus the inevitable color photograph of a familiar preeminent prelate, keeping watch from high on the wall. Several years later I ran across an old photograph of the reading room, showing a couple of neoclassical statues in shallow niches and a few other decorative touches. They had been there all along, but they seem never to have tempered my memory's impression of the room's severity. I whiled away the wait by discreetly watching others at work.

A perpetually jovial, scratchy brown Capuchin friar, resembling an extra in some crowd behind Charlton Heston in *The Agony and the Ecstasy*, was there every day for months. He often sat in splendid isolation (at least on warm summer days), a smile on his face and a glint in his eye, too caught up in chronicling the history of his order to give much thought to bathing.

There was the young archival careerist who, rumor said, had married well into some secular branch of the Vatican bureaucracy. He came and went as he pleased, apparently on no fixed research schedule. Often he cruised around the room restlessly. Some readers allegedly never left their manuscripts open if they temporarily left their desks, imagining he might snap up an important unattended discovery of theirs as he glided past.

One young female researcher assumed a faintly defensive posture whenever a manuscript delivery clerk went by. She would apologize that she did nothing to encourage their attentions. It was just that summertime was open season on attractive young foreign women— particularly for delivery clerks in the throes of midlife crisis.

Often in residence, usually down front and happily in view, sat a tall, distinguished, aging gentleman in a dated double-breasted suit, his preternaturally black hair slicked straight back, 1930s style. Apart from his impressive bulk, he resembled the Sesame Street character who had taught many Americans in the room to count. Nicknamed "the count" by American admirers, he actually *was* a count who held court on the mornings when he showed up. How he had managed to write an unremitting stream of books and articles was a mystery. He never sat for more than half an hour and hardly untied a bundle of documents before someone, anywhere from twenty-five to eighty-five, walked up and shook hands. Then off they went to the Vatican bar.

The Vatican bar, the archive's chief concession to creature comforts, occupies a tiny cleft in the back wall of a bright, pleasant courtyard between the Vatican Archive and the Vatican Library. The bar serves up deeply discounted fare to Vatican employees. But it does not discriminate against scholars, who take carefully timed breaks within its lively, smoky haze.

The count always seemed delighted to share coffee, decades of archival experience, and batches of offprints. Any American who made the requisite self-introduction was promptly told of the count's ottocento ancestor who had served in Washington during President Lincoln's administration. The count even offered an occasional invitation, if not to his house on the Adriatic or a second in the north, at least to his pied-à-terre, not far from the Pantheon. I remember it as a caricature of a scholar's study. Dusty, dry, close, as if nobody lived there. Dimly lit by shafts of light through gaps in the heavy curtains, everything in a subtly varied palette of cappuccino, caffe latte, espresso, every surface piled with papers and stacks of the inevitable offprints. The desk, under a precarious pyramid of books, had its top drawers wide open, twin towers of volumes rising two feet or more from inside. A scholar of a decidedly old school, untroubled by deconstruction, cultural studies, and Foucault, the count had crafted a balance of affable generosity and his own brand of scholarly productivity.

Back at the archive reading room, the general anxiety level spiked around any new arrival. Tentatively wandering around the reference room, pocket dictionary in hand, submitting request forms, rebuffed if they exceeded the daily quota, reprimanded if the collocation number failed to fit the paradigm, most novices sat tensely awaiting the first items. Eyes shifted from the keeper's desk to other readers, attempting to divine the modus operandi in the absence of much official guidance.

It had always been this way. When the archive began officially to admit outsiders in the 1880s, one confused novice researcher's request for a word or two of advice drew exactly that. The comparatively benign second custodian Pietro Wenzel responded with a smile, "Bisogna pescare"— "You have to go fishing."

The "hands off" administrative attitude grew more severe by 1927: "Whoever for his own convenience needlessly avoids carrying out normal research work in the indices and habitually troubles archivists, scriptors, and ushers will render himself unwelcome." In the late 1960s Maria Luisa Ambrosini summed up the archive's daunting reputation in a book whose reprint from the 1990s included her discouraging remark on its back cover: "The difficulties of research are so great that sometimes a student, having enthusiastically gone through the complicated procedures of getting permission to work in the Archives, disappears after a few days' work and never shows up again. But for persons with greater frustration tolerance, work there is rather pleasant."[2]

Little wonder, then, that a new arrival might feel anxious. In addition, some American scholars had only a couple of weeks or so before their prebooked cheap return flights. And to top it off, the archive closes for the day at lunchtime. Hence they were first in line at opening and last to leave before lunch, with no time for coffee in the Vatican bar.

Nobody in the Vatican employ was likely to tell novices in basic training that while the archive officially closes at lunchtime, it reopens *unofficially* in the afternoon and remains open another three hours. Researchers from out of town need only request a *permesso pomeridiano* (afternoon pass). Then they can return after lunch and continue to work in the largely empty and much less frenetic reading room until early evening. But back in the 1980s you had somehow to learn about the existence of this permesso. Nobody who worked there was likely to tell you—though they would issue one if you asked.

I was lucky. From day one, I benefitted from the experienced guidance of a former student, by then a veteran of several Vatican tours of duty. She had revealed the secret of the permesso pomeridiano even before my first day, as well as other essential Roman and Vatican survival tips. How to navigate the number 64 bus, which plies the route from Central Station through town to the Vatican. Tourists trapped on bus 64 draw pickpockets who find the crush of standees easy pickings. Her most prized secret: how to visit the Sistine Chapel, even during high season, and still have the place virtually to yourself.

The archive's American veterans generally made sure other new arrivals experienced similar kindness. No need for them to squander their afternoons visiting churches, museums, and Roman ruins, lingering outdoors over a late lunch, or sipping coffee in Piazza Navona. After all, they could be slogging through a few more buste in the archive, thanks to a permesso pomeridiano of their own.

I found a seat among the music veterans, picking their way through fourteenth- and fifteenth-century papal supplications registers. They searched for the great (Du Fay, Josquin, Busnoys) and the not so great but nonetheless significant. I began sifting for nun musicians in the buste of the Bishops and Regulars. Most researchers sat in intense concentration, negotiating page after page of impenetrable text, going as fast as they dared. Silence was the rule, except for the memorable time when "Holy shit!" scorched the ears of scandalized Vatican clerks. The room waited for the color portrait to tumble from the wall. The late fifteenth century's most important composer had just emerged from hiding in my veteran friend's latest volume of papal supplications.

Such Little Jack Horner moments (pulling out a music historical plum) hardly ever happened.[3] More commonly, all endured prolonged fallow periods, a reality of archival research. One musicologist on an especially specific hunt once spent the whole summer slowly turning pages and finding nothing at all. But as I flipped documents, waiting for the odd detail of musical information to surface, I uncovered a wealth of alternative detail about sixteenth- and seventeenth-century convent life.

With pleasant regularity, something appeared that was diverting or eye-opening. Often just an amusing anecdote to relate during breaks in the Vatican bar. Nuns from Fabriano in 1650, for example, complaining about sweating youths ("most of them half naked") so bold as to play soccer right outside the convent gate. "With nothing but dirty and indecent words and execrable blasphemies, they offend their chaste ears" (though apparently the gaggle of late-blooming soccer fans who overheard the youths while discreetly peering around the convent gate to watch willingly risked such aural damage).[4] After a day or two, whenever I chuckled, my veteran deskmate began to ask, "All right. What did you find now?"

These nuns' adventures and misadventures didn't fit my 1980s musicological agenda, but they were too compelling to consign back to archival oblivion. Who knew how long it might be before someone else requested that busta? Many buste appeared never to have been opened since the secretary of the Sacred Congregation sent them off to the archive. Before the end of that first Vatican tour, my deskmate suggested that someday I should write a book retelling some of those forgotten tales.

This book offers five of the most interesting of these histories. Each relates a singular response to the cloistered life. All touch off major crises. They disrupt the convent status quo, provoking aftershocks that might continue for generations. They reveal the incapacities of hierarchically imposed systems of external oversight and control. Given these realities, they sometimes even destroy their communities.

"AUT VIRUM AUT MURUM OPORTET MULIEREM HABERE"

"A woman should have a husband or a wall."[5] This late medieval aphorism remained equally apt in sixteenth- and seventeenth-century Italy. A respectable woman's choice—actually, her father's, uncle's, or brother's choice *for* her—was either marriage or the convent. Italy had not seen such a boom in female monasticism since the late 1200s. But the old proverb might need updating for 1575: "Only one daughter should have a husband, and the rest should have a wall."

The wealth of Renaissance aristocratic families had to be kept intact. Husbands wanted bigger dowries, and too many dowries drained the family coffers. Convents wanted dowries too, and genteel families recognized them as a necessary evil. Otherwise any sort of girl might get in. But convents settled for a fraction of what a husband demanded.

So while one daughter was commonly groomed for the marriage market, the rest were regularly bound over to the cloister. Often not on their own, however. To soften the transition, aristocratic sisters went off together, usually in twos, though sometimes in threes or even fours. Rome tried to keep the lid on it by limiting sisters to a single pair per convent. This discouraged strong family ties and convent factions. Exceptions frequently proved the rule, however, especially for the powerful. The Chigi family from Siena, who sent three cardinals off to Rome after 1650 (one to become Pope Alexander VII), deposited no fewer than seven sisters at San Girolamo in Campansi. Nothing quite this extreme appears in subsequent chapters of this book.[6] But sisterhood is an important issue at San Lorenzo in chapter 2; sibling dynamics loom notably larger at Santa Maria Nuova in chapter 4; and they are an overweening factor at San Niccolò di Strozzi in chapter 3. There the cloistered community consisted entirely of sisters, aunts, and cousins from a single family.

In terms of numbers, nuns could not be called marginalized. In Bologna around 1630, nuns made up 14 percent of the population. For those who really mattered—the nobility—the percentages ran much higher. In seventeenth-century Milan, no fewer than 75 percent of genteel women lived behind convent walls.[7] Their families might contain more nuns than wives. Visiting the family could mean an afternoon before the grated windows of some convent *parlatorio* (visiting room or parlor).

The convent constituted the expected, unquestioned life option for many girls. Parents' strategies of encouragement and persuasion disguised where enticement ended and coercion began. Since cloistered aunties were delighted to see baby nieces, girls often learned about the cloister in earliest childhood. Occasionally they were even stuffed into the convent *ruota*, or "turn"—a rotating, barrel-shaped device with a pie-shaped wedge cut out, used to transfer goods from the world to the cloister without face-to-face contact—for a spin and a quick cuddle with a doting relative. This meant, technically, that they were automatically excommunicated for violating *clausura* (monastic enclosure). But it was the grown-ups who paid the price and dealt with subsequent hassles. Little girls might even become keen to join favorite relatives inside the convent. If a pair of sisters joined a pair of aunts (and sometimes also a pair of great-aunts), so much the better.

It helped if potential postulants arrived early, before experiencing life's meager alternatives for women. The church set a minimum age of seven, with the additional stipulation that monastic profession must follow by age twenty-five. Exceptions to both minimum and maximum were regularly given the blind eye. A girl's entry at the exceedingly tender age of two may have been exceptional, but it happened occasionally. Extenuating circumstances and the open arms of a childless cloistered aunt were commonly involved, when the convent became a haven in times of family crisis. The death of the girl's mother or the absence of a female guardian at home was the most common cause. Even an outspoken Bolognese opponent of forcing girls into convents recognized an unpleasant reality of sixteenth-century Italy. "Cloistering women may be necessary, so that young girls aren't left alone in their paternal home, at risk of losing their honor—not only to outsiders, but also to the servants. Or, what is worse, even to their own brothers or perhaps to their own fathers."[8]

Families also softened the transition from the world by making the convent as much like home as possible. Genteel monastic houses, especially those that did not practice the "common life" (in which everything was meant to be shared), allowed girls to bring opulent convent trousseaus. Since their monastic rule forbade nuns to own property, they would simply sign everything over to the abbess, who would then hand it all right back on loan. Several inventories from such reciprocal agreements survive from aristocratic Bolognese convents. What they record is a far cry from pallets, sackcloth, and ashes: bedsteads of hardwood, with feather mattresses, comforters, and different coverlets for summer and winter; walnut chests, chairs, and the occasional armoire; elaborate curtains, often embroidered, for windows, beds, and doorways; copper, brass, and pewter vessels; the occasional birdcage with a finch inside; paintings with gilded frames; and, for the musical, the occasional harpsichord, lute, harp, viol, violin, bass viol, or trombone (often outlawed, but useful for the bass part in convent polyphony).

Where a private chapel might have been uncommon at home, a nun's own altar might rival that of modest churches, with a painting over it, sometimes with an elaborate cover as well as a frame, candlesticks, a crucifix, a choice of altar frontals and altar cloths. Other refinements included silver and ivory thimbles, silver boxes, silver pens, silver cups, silver and ivory toothpicks. In some cases, a bedroom at home could not have been much grander.

On rare occasions, wealthy fathers provided not only furnishings but even the rooms to hold them. A daughter's new convent quarters might be built from the foundation up or reconfigured within existing buildings at family expense. Such family quarters were sometimes handed along to the next generation: a discreet form of female inheritance, usefully preserving another, less widely recognized line of the family's patrimony (or matrimony).

Commonly, after several years as an *educanda* or resident student, the would-be nun's formal acceptance was voted on by the professed nuns. The Council of Trent had stipulated this should not happen before age fifteen, though convents and parents found creative ways to secure the girl's place much earlier. A "loan" of the girl's dowry, subsequently canceled at the appropriate time, worked nicely. Ultimately, at whatever time it happened, the girl received her novice's habit and her religious name as part of a formal clothing ceremony attended by family and friends.

During her novitiate year, she was to live apart from the professed nuns while she learned the religious life according to the rule of her particular order. Then the nuns formally voted a second time, to accept her as a "choir" nun. The novice received the black veil of a professed nun and promised to live in perpetual poverty, chastity, and obedience. Nuns and their male superiors seem often to have differed in their interpretation of the first and last of these. Lavish rituals of profession came to rival secular weddings in opulence, though the church hierarchy fought a losing battle to simplify them.

With the reimposition of strict monastic enclosure after the Council of Trent, even some in the church hierarchy recognized the importance of making nuns' confined, interior world pleasant and attractive. A Milanese convent architect of the late 1500s observed, "They should have agreeable places—gardens, fields, loggias, workrooms, windows that catch the light—but all situated inside. They shouldn't be locked up like slaves. Enclosed in their convents and churches, they may appropriately enjoy large, comfortable quarters, spacious cloisters, fair gardens, and other necessities of a decent, human life."[9]

The covered arcades of a central cloister most aptly fit the architect's requirements. Enclosing a large interior space, open to air and light but cut off from the world, often with gardens and a well at the center, the cloister offered the most convenient place for fresh air and exercise, even in inclement weather.

FIGURE 1.1 The recently restored cloister of Santa Cristina della Fondazza, Bologna, 2008. Photograph: Antonia L. Banducci.

At the other extreme, contrasting with the cloister's seclusion, the parlatorio offered more suspect recreation. Nuns visited their families there, seated before large, grilled windows that separated the nuns' inner chamber from the public's outer room. The parlatorio was contested territory, the site of worldly distractions that threatened a nun's interior life, at least in her superiors' view. A signed license from the local nuns' vicar could be required for admission (though laxity about this requirement seems to have been endemic). Some bishops attempted to close down the parlatorio on church holidays. They fought a losing battle to control parlatorio shenanigans during carnival, as chapter 6 clearly demonstrates. Chapter 2 reveals the parlatorio at San Lorenzo in Bologna as an eye-opening, lively center of secularized convent culture year-round—even including cloister romance—which sent the church hierarchy to red alert.

The convent chapel was the second most significant meeting place of the cloister and the world. Its central feature was its double church: an inner chapel for the nuns, shut off from an outer public chapel,

FIGURE 1.2 A late fifteenth-century parlatorio, from rules for monastic women, included in an Italian translation of Saint Jerome's *Letters* (Ferrara: Lorenzo Rossi, 1497). Photograph courtesy of the Newberry Library, Chicago (INC 5765). A worldly woman (*left*) has uttered the unspeakable, so the nuns slam the window shutters, as their elderly nun chaperone covers her ears.

which often served as the parish church. (A floor plan of Santa Maria Nuova's inner and outer churches appears as figure 4.4.) A solid wall usually divided the two so emphatically that visitors to the public church might not even realize there were nuns close by. The barrier was pierced by a grilled window above the public church's high altar. When a priest celebrating Mass there elevated the host at the consecration, it became visible to the nuns, following the Mass invisibly in their inner chapel, whose altar backed up to the same window.

Even the priest could not enter the nuns' chapel without special license. For necessary, unavoidable contacts with the nuns, there were other breaks in the chapel wall. A smaller, curtained (inevitably) grilled window gave the nuns access to communion. Another small window might also provide a place for their confessions to be heard. A ruota was embedded in the wall of the sacristy nearby. Items such as Mass vestments could be placed in the ruota by the sacristan on the nuns' side; it could then be rotated and the items removed by the priest in the public church. A second, larger ruota, often situated in the parlatorio, was used for bulkier convent supplies. This was where visiting small children might incur excommunication by going for a ride to see their cloistered relatives face-to-face. On rare occasions a particularly diminutive nun prone to wanderlust might even stuff herself in the ruota and go AWOL.[10]

The organ window or the grilled windows of nuns' choir lofts in the inner church also penetrated the chapel walls. For the church hierarchy, these were as dangerous as the grilles of the parlatorio. They lured audiences to convent churches merely to hear the nuns sing. They tempted the nuns to sing to the world and not to heaven. Choir lofts therefore were second only to parlatorios as convent battlegrounds where musical nuns opposed their bishops.

Churchmen were responding to a rising tide of enthusiasm for nuns' singing—on both sides of the convent wall. It would crest by the 1650s, notably in such cities as Milan, Bologna, and Rome, then gradually ebb during the later 1600s and on into the late 1700s.

Nuns had been singing since the beginning, of course. In fact the primary job, the so-called *opus Dei* (work of God), of professed, "choir" nuns, had always been to sing the daily round of chapel services. One wonders, however, if anyone but God chose to listen much before 1550. Before then, convent music seems to have been primarily Gregorian chant. Some of it was artfully florid. But much Gregorian chant was extremely simple, and it involved only one melodic line—no harmony. Hence its other name, plainchant.

Judging by surviving archival and musical sources, the 1500s witnessed a striking expansion of convent singing into the realm of polyphony—choral singing in parts, similar to what men had been performing in cathedrals for centuries. This richer, more immediately attractive music, the kind associated with Josquin des Prez or Palestrina, contrasted markedly with sober plainchant.

What distinguished nuns' choral singing from that in other Catholic churches (whose choirs included no women—ever) was the character of the voices, particularly the highest voices. Sopranos, altos, tenors—all were women. Though a convent in Ferrara boasted a "singular and stupendous bass," the bass viol or (when they could get away with it) a trombone often took the bottom part in convent choirs.

In the convent there were no choirboys, who had to be trained for years and really knew what they were doing for only a year or two before their voices changed. In the meantime, the boys' lack of expertise was often apparent. Convent choirs also contained no adult male "falsettists," or countertenors, specially trained to sing the higher parts, artfully at the best of times, but hooting, straining, and "false" at the worst. There were also none of those curious novelties, castrati, who thanks to anatomical modifications before puberty combined a boy's larynx with a man's chest and lungs. Castrati began to appear in Catholic Church choirs about the same time choral singing was on the rise in convent choirs; the first castrato joined the Sistine Chapel in 1562. Yet too often parents' anatomical gamble with their musical son's future did not quite pay off. Many altered offspring landed not in the Sistine Chapel but in some provincial cathedral, and that assuming their soprano voice range survived the change. Well after 1750 the touring English music historian Charles Burney found little good to say of them: "Indeed all the *musici* [castrati] in the churches at present are made up of the refuse of the opera houses, and it is very rare to meet with a tolerable voice upon the establishment in any church throughout Italy."[11]

So convent choral singing offered a novel, exciting sonority. When the nuns were in top form, theirs could be among the best sacred singing available, sometimes even better than in the local cathedral. No wonder convent choirs were soon among Italian cities' top musical attractions, both for locals and for foreigners on grand tours. In 1602, for example, Philip Julius, Duke of Stettin-Pomerania, suggested that Milanese singing nuns rivaled Queen Elizabeth I's choirboys. And 150 years later, Charles Burney willingly risked offending his Milanese hosts by skipping out before the second course at dinner, lest he miss even the beginning of services and any of the fine singing at the Convent of Santa Maria Maddalena.[12]

For an aspiring female musician, the convent choir offered the only realistic opportunity for stardom that did not bear the stigma associated with public performance and the public stage. Any respectable girl, and certainly any respectable parent, knew that whenever a woman willingly lifted her voice in public song, she must have other, disreputable skills on offer too. As the early seventeenth-century English tourist Thomas Coryat put it when describing music's place in the amorous arsenal of Venice's notorious courtesans, "Shee will endevour to enchaunt thee partly with her melodious notes that shee warbles out upon her lute, and partly with that heart-tempting harmony of her voice."[13]

With public singing clearly off-limits for women of any quality, there were few options. Only the rarest supremely talented but also ultra-respectable female singer might hope to find employment in certain elite female ensembles at such courts as Ferrara, Mantua, and Florence. These were vigilantly and jealously guarded under the watchful eyes of their dukes. Such elite singers' performances were so closely protected, respectable, and emphatically private that they became known as *musica secreta*. Young Laura Bovia in chapter 2, after being snubbed by the court of Mantua, eventually abandoned the convent of San Lorenzo in Bologna to join just such a group at the Florentine court.

The convent choir was also respectably "private," since after all the nuns were singing behind the wall, in their own inner church. But their alluring voices echoed through the windows in the wall to music-loving audiences in their public church. These women may have been heard much more widely than any court songstress. All in all, then, the convent proved an attractive career option for the respectable girl with musical talent. Her parents—let's face it—were unlikely to find her a husband in the world anyway, if another sister seemed riper for the marriage market.

When the professed "choir" nuns were not singing and praying in chapel several times during the day, they occupied themselves with useful work and recreation. The nature of it depended on the social standing of the house, but it was not of the ruder, manual sort. Refined houses (e.g., San Lorenzo, Santa Cristina, and Santa Maria Nuova in Bologna) concentrated on edible delicacies, realistic artificial flowers, or artificial fruit. Less socially exalted, more observant houses (Bologna's San Gabriele or Santa Maria degli Angeli, for example) might sew religious habits or altar furnishings. Near the bottom of the pecking order, Bologna's Convertite (reformed prostitutes) did fancy laundry (starching and pressing collars, ruffs, and fancy cuffs).[14]

Lofty aristocrats—two generations from the Malvezzi family in chapter 4, for example—excelled at the most refined silk embroidery (not for sale, of course, but as their charitable chapel adornments). The aristocrats at San Niccolò di Strozzi (chapter 3) also kept indolence at bay by working in silk—but on the other end of production: raising the silkworms.

The nuns' superiors might praise these various activities as laudable work. Not so music. One week an archbishop praised the good works of the Malvezzi nuns' obsessive embroidering (chapter 4), with no suggestion that it might ever distract them from their prayers; the next, he might condemn, even punish, the singing nuns of Santa Cristina (chapter 6) for the fruits of their own dedicated chapel labors. Such suspicion and disapproval remained an abiding, fascinating incongruity of convent "work."

A separate class of nuns, so-called *converse*, freed professed nuns for their chapel duties and for these more refined pursuits. Converse came from respectable lower-class families ("of honest parents," as their convent obituaries commonly put it). They paid much smaller dowries and had no chapel responsibilities (except, of course, to keep it clean and take communion as required) and no voice in convent government. Their labors, involving all the menial work in the kitchen, chapel, fields, and gardens, made possible their superiors' artistic, creative, and spiritual preoccupations. Each conversa also looked after three or four nuns' day-to-day personal needs.

Converse have tended to be eclipsed by professe in convent historical studies, but the convent way of life absolutely could not have gone on without them. Several of these tales reveal that converse were at the center of convent life, though often invisible to those around them. The kitchen conversa Anna, at San Lorenzo (chapter 2), crops up repeatedly, and embarrassingly, because of her successful love magic. Another kitchen conversa, the generous but uppity Terentia Pulica (chapter 4), demonstrates the great divide between conversa and professa when she incurs the wrath of Maria Vinciguerra Malvezzi for her upstart behavior. The converse at San Niccolò di Strozzi (chapter 3) become key witnesses in the archbishop's case against their betters, the nun arsonists.

True religious vocations, while by no means uncommon, were not the norm in the religious environments of several of these tales. Only one of the four aristocratic Malvezzi nuns at Santa Maria Nuova (chapter 4), for example, was remembered for outstanding religious devotion. It appears unlikely that any sister at San Niccolò di Strozzi (chapter 3) felt much sense of religious vocation. But many convent women seemed to construct lives for themselves that were tolerable, sometimes pleasant, and occasionally clearly "fulfilling." Such fulfilling lives often did not fit the Vatican paradigm of single-minded spirituality, separation, and subordination. They might follow intellectual, creative, or imaginative paths—paths that would have remained closed to their sisters in the world or would have been harder to navigate there. Convent necrologies (which, admittedly, tend to say something good or nothing at all) suggest that cloistered communities found ways to recognize, accept, and make the best of such individual paths, so long as they did not exceed the bounds of convent culture as currently and internally defined by the nuns themselves.[15] For the male church hierarchy, on the other hand, responses to such exceptional life paths were often quite another matter. The collisions between the two responses account for much of our present story.

TELLING TALES OUT OF ARCHIVES

It is difficult to imagine a group of nun musicians conjuring up the devil, or a haughty nun philanthropist tearing down, ripping apart, and burning another nun's chapel donation—not to mention an entire community of nuns deciding to burn down their convent. But documents in the Vatican Secret Archive and other Italian ecclesiastical and state archives show that these and the other extraordinary tales in following chapters "really happened."

The first hints of these stories were revealed to the Sacred Congregation of Bishops and Regulars in Rome in much the same way as they emerge for a modern-day archival researcher. A provincial prelate's initial, often arresting communication, which first appeared on the desk of the Congregation's secretary, resurfaces centuries later in a bundle of documents on the archivist's desk. It first calls attention to a crisis and may briefly describe it. The Sacred Congregation followed up by requesting additional information from the relevant bishop; latter-day researchers go searching for such information on their own. Both investigators wait for additional facts to surface, often for a good long time. The piecing together of the resultant story, whether in the sixteenth century or today, invariably requires investigation into the history that preceded and precipitated the crisis and prompted that first tantalizing document. Subsequent history of the crisis may continue to unfold long after that first document appeared on a Vatican bureaucrat's desk—for months, years, even decades. Aftershocks of a singular event may continue for centuries. The same may be true of the paper trail the crisis left behind, which the archival sleuth tries to uncover, often for months, years, even decades.

I could not resist telling these tales in the way I recovered and experienced them myself. Judging by my sources, this often also reflected how cardinals in Rome or churchmen in the dioceses dealt with them. The resulting histories rarely lead down a clear linear path. Many intriguing cases vanish without further archival traces; others peter out after yielding only the odd additional detail in the buste of the Sacred Congregation. Sometimes additional documents that should appear in records for a particular month and year aren't there. Cardinals in the Sacred Congregation were not immune to similar frustrations. Minutes of meetings occasionally complain about their own inability to recover records from previous deliberations, lost somewhere in previous decades' voluminous paperwork.

The five tales told here were, of course, among the most interesting, but they also happily left perhaps the most complete paper trails. I hope my narratives convey more of the suspense I experienced in searching out and picking my way through their details, sidetracks, and dead ends and less of the confusion they frequently provoked along the way.

To lessen the confusion somewhat, I have limited the dizzying profusion of similar Italian names when they seemed likely to befuddle modern readers. Rather than relegate minor, unnamed players in these dramas to the same anonymity they experienced in their own day, however, I have included their names in the notes when they are quoted directly, but anonymously, in the text. In the interest of clarity, a list of dramatis personae cataloging the chief players in each chapter appears at the beginning of the book.

The singular stories often emerge in vivid detail, with extensive "eyewitness testimony" and firsthand accounts. Their events are "true" to the extent that the sources document their details. Whether everything "really happened" as I tell it is difficult to say. These tales were largely filtered through male clerics. That had long been true for the voices of religious women, of course, both the paradigmatically holy ones and the sort who populate these pages.[16]

In some of the following chapters, the effect of a prelate's own point of view about the story becomes immediately obvious. The archbishop of Reggio Calabria in chapter 3 carefully chose his witnesses to create the most damning impression of the nun arsonists, whom he silences totally, for reasons I try to tease out from between the lines. Angela Aurelia Mogna, whose flight from Santa Maria degli Angeli in Pavia initiates the saga in chapter 5, may have been interviewed briefly at the beginning of the vicar-general's investigation of her misadventure, but then she virtually disappears. We never hear directly from her again, by contrast with all the other chief protagonists in her story, many of whom quote her alleged remarks. The haughty and impatient Donna Maria Vinciguerra Malvezzi of chapter 4 exceptionally takes some initiative by writing to Rome in her own defense, but we nevertheless hear her side chiefly from the Bolognese archbishop. He seems most interested, however, in justifying his own possible negligence. The opera-loving Christina Cavazza of chapter 6 has no voice of her own for the first several years of her misadventures. We know her through a Bolognese archbishop with whom she already had a "history" and through her female superiors who, I suggest, were following agendas of their own. When Donna Christina eventually takes the bold step of speaking up for herself, the offended Archbishop Boncompagni washes his hands of her. During the last two decades of her story, however, her own voice grows louder, more independent, and quite eloquent as she negotiates her life journey among and around several powerful priests.

It may surprise some readers that Maestro Eliseo Capis, the Bolognese master inquisitor in chapter 2, should convey most directly the voices of the women whose devilish conjuring he was obliged to investigate. Does that mean that what his scribe recorded was closer to the "truth"? Some witnesses may simply have believed things happened as they later recounted. Others may have bent their truths to suit the circumstances. Episcopal visitors or inquisitors of the Holy Office chose their questions carefully to fit their own objectives, as several chapters illustrate.[17] Witnesses called before them might be only as candid as they dared, or as their quick wits counseled them to be. They may have helpfully embroidered their responses, picking up threads dropped encouragingly by their priestly interrogators.

On the other hand, convent chroniclers, composing their narratives in less constrained circumstances, nevertheless had vested interests in showing their houses in the best possible light. If my own extremely well-churched spinster great-aunt was willing in her records of our family to shift an occasional younger relation's marriage date back a few months to accommodate a respectable nine months before the inevitable "blessed event," I wouldn't really expect convent chroniclers to resist making similar historical improvements on what "really happened."

In recounting these stories, I suspect I have indulged in less embroidery than some of my historical witnesses. The original sources can be extraordinarily vivid without additional help from me. For example, all the soggy details of Sister Angela Aurelia Mogna's escape from Santa Maria degli Angeli (chapter 5), hand in hand with the young Giovanna Balcona, and the sorry condition of their bedridden lower-class nosy next-door neighbors come from primary sources. On rare occasions when, admittedly, I may sail dangerously into less clearly charted waters, I take readers into my confidence in the notes. No source documents the Bolognese master inquisitor's early morning visit to the external church at the convent of San Lorenzo (chapter 2) before beginning his (documented) investigation in the parlatorio, for example. But various sources *do* document the appearance of the convent, its chapel and altars, the probable character of its organ, and its altarpiece, which he observes in that (undocumented) brief side trip I send him on.

Since these women have been forgotten and silent for so long, I have let them speak at length, as often and for as long as I thought modern readers' patience would tolerate. Language that seems charming when heard in *Masterpiece Theater* costume dramas may turn tedious rather more quickly on the page. It is also important to recognize that the constrained circumstances in which the nuns speak, whether in formal written petitions to their male superiors or in testimony before interrogators of the church hierarchy, affect what they say and how they say it. They tend to join clause after clause for page after page with few breaks. I have separated these unremitting run-on sentences into more clearly comprehensible units, trimmed reiterations and repetitive phrases, and omitted text that did not seem absolutely essential to the narrative. In the resulting translated quotations, I have suppressed the ellipses that would have peppered similar extracts in the most scholarly discourse. In some cases a moderate-length paragraph in my quoted extract might have stretched over a page or two of the original manuscript. I have often simplified syntax (avoiding the strings of gerunds so popular in the original documents, for example). Successions of such regularly repeated formulas as "Your Most Reverend and Illustrious Lordship" have sometimes been simplified or replaced with "you." In the interests of clarity, I have occasionally sorted successions of confusing third-person pronouns into their equivalent proper names.

In re-creating dialogue or scenes involving direct quotation, I have had to modify the originals in other significant ways. Scribes recorded the words and comments of inquisitors of the Holy Office in the third person, for example, with witnesses' responses in the first person. In my translations, I have reconstructed both sides in normal dialogue form, closer to what happened on the spot. Where witnesses described another person's words, I have occasionally reinstituted first person and quotation marks (which my sources never include, even when quoting directly) in my telling.

For serious poetry, as well as for frivolous verses such as "Vu ch'ave quella cosetta" quoted above (where my translations may reflect the spirit as much as the letter of the original), the Italian original precedes my translation. Scholars will also find citations of my original sources for my other translations in the notes, should they be concerned that my own ventriloquism might rival that of the priests who are rarely far removed from the surface of these narratives.

Nuns Behaving Badly was inspired in part by the writings of Carlo Ginzburg and Natalie Davis, whose *The Cheese and the Worms* and *The Return of Martin Guerre,* in the subdiscipline of "new history" dubbed "microhistory," have captured the imagination of readers well beyond the academy.[18] But the present narratives may call to mind much older traditions of telling tales, most familiar from Chaucer and Boccaccio. The book's episodic character is perhaps more akin to that approach than to the more focused, penetrating view of most microhistory. I confess to having been keen to reconstruct and retell stories from a little-known corner of Italian history in a comparatively uncomplicated way. If the rhythms of the little book's organization and its less theoretical approach encourage it to be deposited on bedside tables, atop toilet tanks, or, particularly, inside a travel bag on an overnight flight to Milan or Rome, it will perhaps have found an appropriate berth.

> And with that word we ryden forth oure weye,
> And he bigan with right a myrie cheere
> His tale anon, and seyde as ye may here.
> —Prologue, Chaucer's *Canterbury Tales*

2

DANGEROUS ENCHANTMENTS: WHAT THE INQUISITOR FOUND

San Lorenzo (Bologna, 1584)

On October 20, 1584, Maestro Eliseo Capis da Venezia, master inquisitor for the Holy Office in Bologna, made his way to the Lateran canonesses of San Lorenzo. His black-and-white Dominican habit—every Bolognese inquisitor came from the Dominican order—could still parry earliest hints of impending winter. Winter might well be over before this was finished.

Like several of his predecessors, Maestro Eliseo may have followed his religious calling through much of Catholic Europe. We know it had taken him to the Council of Trent, at least in its final days. In the later 1560s he had served as the Inquisition's adviser to the Venetian Council of Ten on possible heresies in books awaiting publication. Unlike many of Bologna's previous master inquisitors, he never rose to high office at his order's mother house of San Domenico in Bologna, a few blocks away, though he had been named regent of the *studium* at San Domenico the previous year.[1]

The Holy Office's business in Bologna had remained quiet since he moved from Ferrara to the monastery of San Domenico six years before. Heresy here had been largely stamped out in the 1560s and early 1570s. Still, he had been forced to send three to the fire. The last one, well past seventy, who taught children their numbers, had somehow survived repeated investigations over forty years. In the end, his perversity and obstinacy won him a few extra days of life, for it took three days to persuade him to accept the sacraments.[2]

This business at San Lorenzo might be Maestro Eliseo's last case. He would lay these burdens down the following year.

An elegantly simple facade of reddish-brown brick, its roofline set off with geometric lozenges and a crisp row of dentils. No opulent molded terra-cotta or stone frieze. The expansive arches of the portico—an ever-present feature in this city—seemed to balance delicately on brick columns, enhancing, not hiding, what might have been a forbidding exterior. Perhaps a bit antiquated by now—the sisters had moved in almost 150 years earlier.

The inquisitor turned off into via Castellata, looking for the public church's side door. He shouldered it open gently and slipped through the narrow gap. He paused to rest as his eyes gradually cleared dimness from the corners of the deserted interior. Again, rather understated for an exclusive house. Only a single pair of shallow side altars midway along the walls, balancing each other. A burnished luster overhead caught his eye. A tall, flat tower of large organ pipes, flanked by smaller turrets of slender pipes, dominated the wall below the ceiling vaults. A heavy frame contained the towers, with acanthus, highlighted in gold, trailing along its edges.

That was where they had sung, packing the nave with enthusiastic throngs, there only for music. Little thought about the Holy Sacrifice, eyes turning to the grilles of the organ loft in anticipation. The worst of the problem singers was gone by now, at least.

Ahead the Madonna and her infant son observed him in cool serenity, commanding his attention. The morning brightened through broad windows rising high in the side wall and delicately lit them, as Saint Lawrence and Saint Jerome watched and two angels played below. Maestro Eliseo climbed the broad steps to the altar, acknowledging the Presence, signaled by the flicker of a single lamp. Behind the tabernacle, a window stretched the length of the altar. The gilded bars of its grille, spaced so closely that a hand could not pass between them, partially screened wooden shutters on the other side—the nuns' private chapel. The shutters were closed, as they should be.

Once again the Madonna calmly met and held his gaze. He paused in quiet contemplation—whether of her or of Francesco Francia's artistic mastery, who could say? (Some say that two generations later Cardinal Archbishop Ludovico Ludovisi found Francia's Madonna so

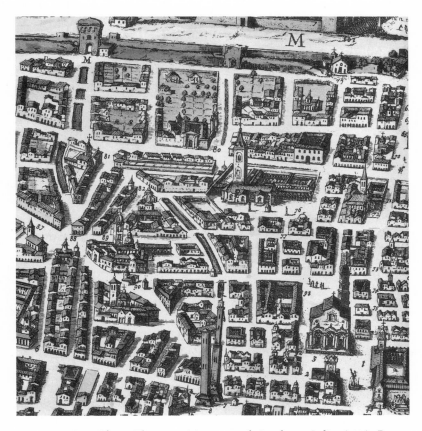

FIGURE 2.1 Joan Blaeu, *Theatrum civitatum et admirandorum Italiae* (1663). Reproduced with permission of the Biblioteca Comunale dell'Archiginnasio, Bologna. San Lorenzo stands at number 81, San Giovanni in Monte at number 89, San Domenico and the offices of the Inquisition at number 76, and San Petronio at number 3.

irresistible that he carried her off, shipped her to his collection in Rome, and hung a copy above San Lorenzo's altar.)[3]

The Curia would have to decide what to do about the other singers. All the rumors seemed ridiculous, of course, but many would readily believe them. Such behavior couldn't continue. Not in a convent of nuns, of all places.

A hollow knocking high overhead sounded the hour. Maestro

Eliseo turned reluctantly after another lingering look. He acknowledged the Presence once again, then made his way out through the front door into via Castiglione. Odors beginning to rise from the canal that bounded the convent to the east presaged a warm morning. He proceeded along the portico, by now quite bright, on his way to the convent parlatorio.

The convent facade was handsome, suggesting cultured humility, unlikely to put off families of quality. None of the severity and rough, towering exterior of the convent of Corpus Domini, about the same age, across town. San Lorenzo cared less about inspiring awe. Then again, the austere sisters of Corpus Domini, with their founder still sitting among them, her body uncorrupted 120 years after her death and the fiddle she had played to honor God alone still close at hand, were Bologna's models of sanctity and monastic propriety. These Lateran canonesses, it seemed, were not.

The appearance of Maestro Eliseo's dark figure, though intentionally early and discreet, would have provoked an uneasy stir and ripples of curiosity under the porticos along via Castiglione. A community of nuns was the last place neighbors expected to encounter the Holy Office. Others were less surprised: the Lateran canons of San Giovanni in Monte; Cardinal Gabriele Paleotti, archbishop of Bologna; Monsignor Giacomo Bovio, chief canon at the basilica of San Petronio. Maestro Eliseo's arrival was only the latest, most melodramatic scene in a musical drama that had been unfolding at San Lorenzo for two decades.

The Lateran canons of San Giovanni in Monte, just a short walk north, claimed to have done all they could to control these canonesses, particularly those obsessed with music. The canons had taken charge of them only in the early 1500s. San Lorenzo was much older, one of eleven local convents dating back to the 1200s, when the professed nuns had numbered only twenty. By the 1470s they had increased to sixty. Hemmed in by the canal, with no room to expand, San Lorenzo had acquired buildings of a struggling convent across the street, together with its church of Santa Maria del Castello, where the nuns subsequently also sang on important feast days. The Lateran canonesses passed to and fro through an underground pas-

FIGURE 2.2 The exterior of the former convent of San Lorenzo as it looks today. Photograph: Luca Salvucci.

sageway beneath the street, safely within the defined boundaries of monastic enclosure.[4]

Almost a century later, the abbot of San Giovanni in Monte could point to a long paper trail demonstrating responsible convent oversight. The Catholic Church's reforming Council of Trent had scarcely adjourned when, in summer 1564, the canons had commanded their charges to observe its new decrees. The copies of soon-to-be saint Carlo Borromeo's published convent reforms for Milan, which the canons consulted and carefully preserved in their archive, further attested to their seriousness of purpose.

As for music, the nuns' superiors initially took Trent's moderate line, which had simply prohibited "lascivious" music in church and left it at that. San Giovanni in Monte soon added more specific requirements. Their nuns might sing and play sacred music privately, so long as they did not disturb their sisters. Most important, no men could be present. And they could not play the lute. They might also sing and play in the convent chapel on important feast days.

The nuns' earliest response did not bode well. In August 1570 almost all the canonesses had to petition the abbot of San Giovanni in Monte to absolve them of their automatic excommunication for violating monastic enclosure. They had taken a short field trip, en masse, to San Lorenzo's public church, outside the cloister, "to admire the splendid and sumptuous organ—we were all curious and keen to see with our own eyes what everybody else has praised and extolled." This would be the first of many times willful independence and passion for music got the best of them.[5]

By the mid-1570s, all Bolognese convents confronted a crackdown on their music, led by stern reformer Cardinal Archbishop Gabriele Paleotti. Paleotti had nothing against music. As a youth he had learned to sing, while accompanying himself on the lute, from a local composer, Domenico Maria Ferrabosco. Paleotti repaid the favor by saving his teacher's son from the Inquisition in 1580. The younger Alfonso Ferrabosco had fallen into the Inquisition's net when he returned to Italy after lingering too long, without papal permission, in service to the heretic Elizabeth I.[6]

To Paleotti's mind, nuns' music was quite another matter. It lured the outside world to nuns' chapels, sometimes in such unruly numbers that the officiating priest could not get through the clogged street. The service had to be held up for his arrival. All this singing also lured the sisters away from their interior life of prayer. "While their bodies remain within the sacred cloisters, it causes them to wander outside in their hearts, nourishing within them an ambitious desire to please the world with their songs," as one Bolognese clergyman put it.[7]

"HERE ON EARTH, THEY SEEM TO TASTE HEAVENLY HARMONY"

Even as Paleotti's anti-music campaign intensified, San Lorenzo's singing nuns entered the musical spotlight, chiefly thanks to a student of "star quality," brought up and trained there. Laura Bovia's singular musical skills were described as "something very nearly miraculous."

Her local notoriety had become the center of controversy as early as April 1578, when the prioress complained that Laura's uncle, Monsignor Giacomo Bovio, had removed the girl because of convent musical improprieties. "It wasn't enough for him to forbid her to play prohibited instruments; he wanted to root up entirely that worthy plant. Against our wishes, the girl was chased off, who for more than eight years had been in our convent, destined to become a nun."[8]

This Monsignor Giacomo Bovio, the girl's uncle, was chief among the canons at the renowned Bolognese basilica of San Petronio, which even today overshadows the city's cathedral. The nuns' superiors must have placated Monsignor Bovio. By late summer Laura resurfaces at San Lorenzo, but with her uncle's strict command to neither sing nor play. His command apparently went unheeded.

Local perceptions of musical misbehavior at San Lorenzo, and of abiding feuds with the archbishop, only got worse over the next two years. Even this could not stifle Bovia's musical career. Before long her fame spread beyond the city. In 1581 Guglielmo Gonzaga, Duke of Mantua, was looking Laura over for one of those rare musical plums for women: a job as musical lady-in-waiting to his future daughter-in-law. In March the duke's agent wrote, "The girl is presently in the convent of San Lorenzo, where during the offices of Holy Week many thronged to hear her sing and play."

The Mantuan negotiations ultimately fizzled, however. Uncle Giacomo played too hard to get. He claimed Laura would prefer the convent, at little cost to him, since music would be her meal ticket. But hints of longtime musical improprieties cast shadows over Laura's good name. As the ducal sleuth put it, "The multitude and dubious quality of musicians Monsignor Bovio had summoned to teach the girl, and their evil ways, together with Bovio's own excessive indulgence and tenderness toward the girl, have caused sundry disorders and a lot of talk."

But the bishop of Osimo bluntly revealed the primary obstacle: "That girl is the daughter, not the niece, of Monsignor Bovio." Bolognese archbishop Gabriele Paleotti tried to reassure the duke about Laura's good name. But the duke may have realized that the prelate would be delighted to hear one less siren calling from San Lorenzo's choir loft. Guglielmo Gonzaga was unconvinced. By June 1581, he dropped Laura Bovia.

Late in 1582, she returned to the limelight as the dedicatee of a published music collection. Not of a collection of sacred music, which might have been marginally acceptable, but of the decidedly secular *First Book of Madrigals* by Bolognese composer Camillo Cortellini, nicknamed Il Violino ("The Violin"). Il Violino's hyperbolic praise publicly alluded to Bovia's earlier flirtation with Mantua while hinting that she had caught the eye of other courts as well. "She is transcendently versed not only in composition, but on every musical instrument. She composes such rare and novel works, so marvelously accompanied, that she melts the hearts of her audience. She transports their souls so high that, here on earth, they seem to taste heavenly harmony." Likewise inappropriate to the cloister's virginal modesty, one of Il Violino's madrigals even exalted Bovia's physical beauty.[9]

Getting word of serious trouble in store (most likely from the convent's subprioress, Arcangela Bovia, probably his cloistered sister), Monsignor Bovio reconsidered the wisdom of Laura's convent career. Courtly service, even at a price, looked better and better. By early 1584 Laura Bovia had turned her back on her convent home to make her way to Florence. Once her "uncle" acknowledged her paternity, legitimized her, and lent the court a substantial sum, she joined the exclusive *musica secreta* of Grand Duke Francesco de' Medici. It was none too soon, for the situation at San Lorenzo had taken another turn for the worse.

"SOWN BY THE DEVIL IN THIS FIELD OF VIRGINAL PURITY"

Paleotti decreed that in the future, Bolognese convent music could employ only one solo voice, accompanied by the organ. San Lorenzo's singing nuns simply did an end run not only around the archbishop, but also over the heads of their superiors at San Giovanni in Monte, whose cooperative spirit flagged under pressure. In summer 1583, the organist went directly to the father-general of the entire order of Lateran canons, who was then left to smooth his Bolognese subordinates' ruffled feathers:

> Yes, Donna Gentile, the convent organist, petitioned me for permission to perform on their feast day. I was inclined to allow her to per-

form some motets—with one or two voices at most, and with no other instrument besides organ. I make the laws; I can make exceptions to them. I had a look in the illustrious Paleotti's decrees, where he now permits nuns to sing with only one voice to the organ. If I was satisfied with two voices, well, it's not a sin in the Holy Spirit.

The father-general of the Lateran canons may also have been feeling a bit guilty. In April 1583, he had cracked down hard with his own stringent reforms, for which the malevolent enchantments of music provided the justification. "We have come to recognize how much the spiritual mind is troubled, and how much damage done to the religious life and to regular discipline, by permitting music at the convent of San Lorenzo. We understand how much dissension results from singing and playing, sown by the devil in this field of virginal purity."

He went on to forbid, on pain of excommunication, any use of polyphony—even sacred polyphony—and any instrument except the organ in church. Within three days all other instruments except the harpsichord had to be gone: lutes, viols, violins, double basses, harps, and wind instruments. Sisters could no longer be taught by outsiders, even those in holy orders. Nor were they to perform at the grates of their parlatorios. After dozens of other prohibitions, music resurfaces in a final, cryptic reference. "We further command, by virtue of holy obedience, on pain of excommunication, that nobody speak about the business of the viola, especially to the laity. It must be totally covered up and smoothed over." The meaning of this odd command soon became clear. The father-general had not spoken figuratively when he said "sown by the devil in this field of virginal purity."[10]

"THE DEVIL'S BUSINESS"

Just weeks earlier, on March 31, 1583, the master inquisitor Eliseo Capis had made an initial visit to San Lorenzo. Preliminary investigations were a regular part of the Holy Office's way of doing things. He seated himself near his scribe, with his back to the rear wall of the parlatorio. The shutters of the large grated windows opposite him had been left open in anticipation of his arrival. Hearing a faint

FIGURE 2.3 BCB, MS 3574, a seventeenth-century Bolognese Lateran canoness of San Lorenzo. Reproduced with permission of the Biblioteca Comunale dell'Archiginnasio, Bologna.

approaching rustle, he looked down in feigned concentration and waited.[11]

The prioress slipped in hesitantly to face him across the grates. Her habit—two long garments of white wool, with a lightweight long-sleeved, loosely gathered overdress reaching to midthigh—hid everything but the toes of her dark slippers. The black veil, framing her wimple, provided the only other contrast to layers of white.

He patiently studied his hands, listening, as moments passed, for the first anxious shifting of her body. Then he looked up and posed every inquisitor's opening gambit, "Have you any idea why you've been summoned?"

"No, Father, I don't know for certain why. But I've got an idea."

"Why, do you suppose?"

"I wouldn't want to say anything. Because I don't know anything for sure. But I heard that somebody did I don't know what with a little charm after a viola went missing. They've been saying lots of things because of that missing viola. From what I heard, Sister Angela Tussignana and Sister Semidea Poggi took a little charm and did I don't know what to find out who took that viola. But God only knows if it's true."

"Did you try to find out?"

"Yes, Father, I tried to find out the truth, but I never could discover anything for sure. One whom I questioned was Sister Arcangela Bovia, who told me the business about the charm."

"Tell me about this Semidea and this Angela."

"Oh, they're fine young ones—and very good girls. In my opinion, I don't believe these two did anything."[12]

After another question or two, Maestro Eliseo swore the prioress to silence on pain of excommunication, had her sign her testimony, dismissed her, and then summoned her own chief witness.

Subprioress Donna Arcangela Bovia—probably an aunt of the much-admired singer Laura—sailed in after the prioress, bowed perfunctorily enough to make a point, and gazed back at him.

"Have you any idea why you have been summoned?"

"I've not the slightest idea why Your Reverence has summoned me. But I couldn't be more surprised if the Grand Turk himself stood there in front of me."

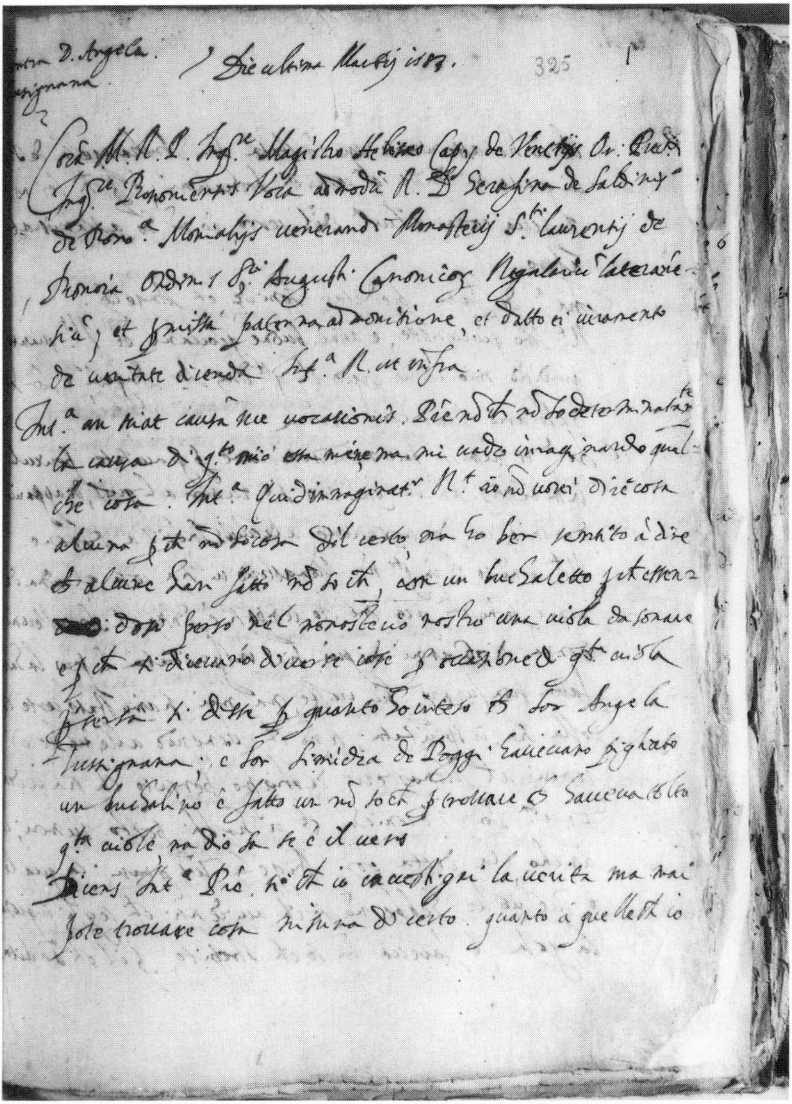

FIGURE 2.4 BCB, MS B1877, fol. 325. Reproduced with permission of the Biblioteca Comunale dell'Archiginnasio, Bologna. Maestro Eliseo begins his preliminary investigation of devilish conjuring at San Lorenzo. The bewitched Angela Tussignana and the enthusiastic singer and future poet Semidea Poggi, named immediately as chief protagonists, appear five lines up from the bottom of the page; the missing viola first crops up two lines earlier.

He took a few moments to regard her impassively, from under a carefully furrowed brow, as if pondering her thinly veiled effrontery.

"You must have some idea."

"Well, after a viola went missing in the convent, there was all sorts of fuss about somebody using a bowl of water, and somebody else tracing some figure on the floor to find the missing viola. But I don't believe anybody cast lots or used bowls of water. Nor do I know for sure who told me this, but if you wanted to find out who's to blame for these charms and casting lots, you could ask Sister Panina Ghisliera, who owned the viola. She'd know who got blamed, and what was done to find this viola. For my part, I don't know anything. I don't accuse Sister Panina or any of the others of casting lots or using charms, because I don't know anything."

"Do you know of any among you who might be possessed?"

"I don't know anything for sure about it. But they say that Angela Tussignana was possessed—because of certain things that happened to her. But the doctors said it was women's problems."[13]

He dismissed Donna Arcangela. He should have a look at this Angela Tussignana.

It did not take long for her to appear. In her novice's habit, with a shorter white veil, she stood patiently and seemingly unperturbed. She answered his opener with none of her elders' equivocations. "Yes, Father, I believe I know why Your Reverence had me summoned. I believe it's about devilish things."

"What sort of devilish things?"

Again, disquietingly direct. "About six months ago, when I was already in this convent, I chose to draw a circle in my room with a little knife to please one of my aunts, Sister Panina Ghisliera. To try to find out I don't know what. And I made this circle twice in the convent and once in my father's house. My circles got started when I was still at home, with the girl who dresses my mother's head. A young fellow named Francesco arrived—I don't know anything else about him, neither his first name nor last name nor his business. When this Francesco saw us, he said, 'I can guess who you're talking about. Go in any room you want and chat about whatever you please, and then come back and I'll reveal what you were saying.' And that Francesco knew everything we said in private. I was so amazed I asked him to teach me his secret."

Maestro Eliseo interrupted, sternly. "You're imagining things. Or you're lying. Be well advised of the dangers in lying—there's a heavy price to pay. If you fear God, tell the truth."

"Everything I said is true, and I didn't imagine it. That Francesco really did repeat our words. So I pleaded with him to teach me his secret for discovering hidden things, and he taught it to me."

When Maestro Eliseo pressed Angela further, she finally may have sensed danger. She claimed to have forgotten most of it. But what she remembered didn't help her.

"After I'd later confessed this, and received absolution, I put it all out of mind and never recited it again."

"I order you to recite it to me."

"I think it began 'Diabolus.' And there could've been three or four Latin words."

"I order you to describe the text and rituals and the necessary instruments."

"He said I should take a knife and draw a circle with it. Then stick the knife in the center. Standing outside the circle, I should say the words he'd taught me. And then I should ask whatever I wanted to know."[14]

Maestro Eliseo made a mark beside the mention of the magic circle in the transcript. Drawing magic circles on the ground was serious business—a preliminary to conjuring up the devil. Treatises on devilish conjuring, all the way back to the *Key of Solomon the King*, attributed to King Solomon himself, included detailed diagrams for such circles. Angela still seemed to be hiding things. She had said the knife should be placed within the circle. Why had she stood outside it, unprotected? But it was late, and she had revealed enough. He dismissed her, left the parlatorio, and returned to San Domenico.

Maestro Eliseo was scarcely out the convent door before the Lateran canons scrambled to reform San Lorenzo. They ritually exorcised Angela Tussignana, and since she had yet to take final vows, they expelled her. That was the last anybody saw of her. Things could have gone much worse. Back in 1559 a nest of Bolognese witches who not only dabbled in love magic but joined the devil in a witches' Sabbath had been burned, on orders of Pope Paul IV himself.[15] The Lateran canons' list of reforms, delivered just four days after the inquisitor's departure, exhorted their nuns never again to speak about the business of the viola. The sisters would happily have complied. But Maestro Eliseo Capis was just getting started.

Modern readers often get their impressions of the Holy Office from the grand inquisitor in Verdi's opera *Don Carlos*, from nineteenth-century histories that formed the basis for Verdi's character, or more recently, perhaps, from such works as *The Inquisition* by Michael Baignent and Richard Leigh. Despite the fear it did its best to promote, the courts of the Roman Holy Office held to a high standard compared with judicial proceedings in the rest of sixteenth- and seventeenth-century Europe.[16] Maestro Eliseo followed strict guidelines, clearly established and carefully monitored. He kept meticulous written records, copied hastily on the spot. Not only witnesses' every word was transcribed, but sometimes also their appearance and actions. Volunteered remarks were distinguished from responses to specific questions. Defendants could be offered the benefit of defense counsel.

Maestro Eliseo also did not bring a cart full of instruments of torture to San Lorenzo. The Bolognese Holy Office was much more circumspect than many civil authorities—certainly much less cruel than the secret police of that English heretic Queen Elizabeth I. Maestro Eliseo always hoped displaying the instruments would be enough. He, for one, never used the fire, never anything beyond the strappado (that favorite method of persuasion by suspending witnesses from their wrists tied behind their backs). But when it came to nuns, Rome was very specific: "Torture: nuns are not customarily subjected to the strappado—though they may be threatened with it."[17]

In February 1584, time came for the canons of San Giovanni in Monte to face him. Maestro Eliseo awaited them on home turf, *la stanza del camino o pozzo* ("the room of the fireplace or well"), his interrogation chamber in the Company of the Holy Cross, adjoining the basilica and monastery of San Domenico. The imposing room, dominated by a large carved chimney breast, was in the south wing of a modest cloister where Dominican monks were buried, south of the choir of the great basilica. Although the rooms had been refurbished and enlarged back in the 1560s, when the Inquisition's business was brisk, in Maestro Eliseo's day the stanza del camino had yet to receive the lavish frescos that still adorn its upper walls and ceiling today. Seated in a leather-covered armchair, behind a leather-covered table, the inquisitor might pretend to contemplate an antiquated panel painting of the Last Supper, its colors still bright, showing Christ as accuser: "One of you will betray me." Saint Peter pauses, cutlery raised, as another disciple wrings his hands. John, the beloved disciple, dozes oblivious, his head in the master's lap. Maestro Eliseo might also gaze in apparent lack of interest out a window, down into the yard outside San Domenico's pharmacy. He may occasionally have caught the curious monk apothecary glancing upward. The windows, which came down below waist level, offered limited privacy. But by keeping them open Maestro Eliseo might have caught faint scents of cardamom, cinnamon, cloves, nutmeg.[18]

For more rigorous examination, out of earshot, they had to move to a better illuminated room next door. On this occasion that would not be necessary. Besides, a second Lateran canon would already be waiting there when the inquisitor finished with the first. There would also be no need to move upstairs to a chamber reserved for the most extreme forms of heightened interrogation. For that work, the windows had to be closed.

Maestro Eliseo's scribe took his place in a chair with a seat woven of rushes and set out his writing instruments on a raised wooden bench before him. There would be no need to admit the canons discreetly, through the Oratorio of the Holy Cross. It opened into a more neutral courtyard but also had an unobtrusive interior door leading to the stanza del camino. Today the canons could arrive through the monastery's regular entrance.

Don Livio da Bologna, former abbot of San Giovanni in Monte, entered uncertainly. Maestro Eliseo may have affected a bright, open look. They were colleagues, after all, sharing common goals. Perhaps because of the intimidating surroundings or a grudge nurtured since last August, when the singing nuns had gone over the canons' heads to the father-general of their order, Don Livio required no coaxing.

To clear my conscience—since Your Reverence is investigating our sisters at San Lorenzo—things are awfully bad there, so the nuns tell me. The nuns are doing all sorts of incantations and casting lots. They're using evil spells, lots, candles, and water and magic words or magic rings to find things they've lost. Sister Tussignana could tell Your Reverence about such things. Sister Panina, Lord

Carlo Ghislieri's daughter, used candles and other things to search for a lost viola. Sister Florentia had a charm to make others like her and to learn how to sing and play through diabolical arts. They also say—it's true—that the devil made something rise above the rooftop. It couldn't have been the work of man.

When Maestro Eliseo pressed him for his sources, he claimed memory loss—a common affliction, endemic to the stanza del camino, when witnesses needed to name names. But as he later rose to leave, Don Livio added, "I believe these are great evils and that perhaps some of them are possessed. So I pray Your Reverence to remedy this immediately, so we don't end up in the devil's business."

Don Ambrosio da Bologna, the current abbot, proved just as quick to indict the nuns he was charged with looking after, and to abdicate responsibility, naming names and citing incantations, fortune-telling, love charms, but also the possible use of baptized lodestones. He too spoke of the mysterious levitating object, and of baleful howling, clashing of swords, and mysterious lights in the night. Some of the sisters were possessed. But only Angela Tussignana had been expelled. Don Ambrosio closed with a parting admonition. "These are highborn ladies. To preserve their family honor, they'll keep quiet. And possibly our convent lay governors don't even know about all this—or if they do, they'll try to cover it up, because they're unaware of the peril."[19]

Maestro Eliseo knew all about the nuns' pedigrees. San Lorenzo ranked high up Bologna's female monastic pecking order. It was in the top 20 percent based on annual income and remained a common choice for aristocratic families in the market for monastic housing. Some sisters whose names already figured in the crisis came from the highest nobility. Donna Panina Ghisliera, owner of the missing viola and aunt of the expelled Angela Tussignana, basked in the reflected glory of Pope Pius V, Antonio (Michele) Ghislieri. But as sometime inquisitor-general of the Holy Office, eventually canonized in 1712 for his determined prosecution of heresy, Ghislieri would have denounced her had he lived to hear what his cloistered distant relation was up to. Panina's father, Filippo Carlo Ghislieri, had been created senator years earlier and named auditor of the Camera di Bologna. Semidea Poggi, whom the prioress singled out from the start, was the daughter of Countess Lodovica Pepoli and Cristoforo Poggi, knight of Santo Stefano, who had served among Bologna's governing Anziani in 1565.[20]

Another six months passed before Maestro Eliseo got around to summoning Don Ubaldo da Reggio, the nuns' father confessor, in early August. Though both interrogator and witness fastidiously affirmed that nothing divulged in the confessional should or would be revealed, Don Ubaldo still had plenty to offer regarding magic's utility for convent divination and romantic pursuits, and about nocturnal noises and visions, which had twice required him to bless the cloister. Interestingly enough, though he knew all about the missing viola, the confessor made no mention of the devil's direct involvement in attempts to find it.

The master inquisitor waited another three months before making his way back to the gate at San Lorenzo on that late October morning in 1584. This time he intended to stay awhile.

Anyone denounced for heresy should have been summoned to Maestro Eliseo at the Inquisition's headquarters. The knock on the door offered the first inkling, when his enforcers arrived to compel their appearance. Such secrecy was essential. And useful. A dozen years before, Archbishop Paleotti, though no great friend of the Holy Office, particularly during Maestro Eliseo's tenure, had commanded Bologna's people: "Do not dare to warn someone that they might be questioned by the Inquisition, or that they might be imprisoned, on pain of being taken as their accomplice."[21]

The Lateran canonesses of San Lorenzo could not leave their cloister, of course, so Maestro Eliseo had to come to them. They expected him. The day before, all the nuns, assembled in chapel, had heard his pronouncement read out.

We, Eliseo Capis, apostolic inquisitor-general in the city of Bologna, having just cause to undertake an inquisition to examine all of you, in service to holy faith, and by virtue of our Holy Office, we therefore command you, by virtue of holy obedience, and on pain of excommunication, totally and truthfully to disclose everything you know relevant to this Holy Office. Possessing forbidden books and those suspected of heresy. Keeping charms that enchanters or witches use. Carrying baptized lodestones in rings or other objects, knowing secrets to invoke the devil to help find lost items, to reveal men's secrets, or to make them fall in love with you by having extraordinary masses said, such as the Mass of the Passion—that is, one in which the Passion is recited secretly and for evil ends. Whoever knows anyone to have invoked the devil, worshiped him, or sacrificed to him, and, finally, whoever either has taught or recited spells created by others since they entered this convent, must reveal it in our impending investigation without any excuse, on pain of excommunication. In the name of the Father, and of the Son, and of the Holy Spirit. Amen.[22]

Following time-honored procedures, Maestro Eliseo had prepared his list of questions in advance. He would work his way down through the community, beginning with the senior nuns.

Over several months, more than a hundred nuns and converse would be called, plus the odd priest, friar, and layperson, from as far away as Cremona. Many would be recalled a second or third time. Others eventually began to reappear on their own, offering additional unsolicited information or further denials. It would all be carefully recorded. About forty-five had so little to say that their names were simply listed together with the comment, "They said they had no precise knowledge." But they had to appear—Maestro Eliseo had his procedures.

The musical Donna Florentia Campanacci, at the center of the storm, tried to shift the focus. *Older* nuns, such as Cassandra Albergati (now dead and safely beyond Maestro Eliseo's grasp) had conjured "by the sun, the moon, and the stars." Another nun even asserted that dearly departed Donna Cassandra "was infamous for her spells and for her preoccupation with fleshly matters involving men." An elder sister tried to draw safe distinctions between past and present: "You want to know about things done before the Council of Trent or after? If before the Council, I confess to having known many types of magic in this convent. But if you mean after the Council, I can tell you that such things no longer go on here in this convent."[23]

Such diversionary smoke screens quickly dissipated to reveal a remarkably rich culture of folk magic, still very much alive among the younger generation, long after Trent. The inevitable Donna Florentia Campanacci and the singer Donna Semidea Poggi confessed to dropping the names of candidates for office into a bowl of holy water during recent convent elections. As they recited the Seven Penitential Psalms, the winner's name rose to the surface.

Other nuns employed watery procedures to foretell the future or to promote romantic agendas. Several, Donna Florentia among them, described having been required as children, of unquestioned virginity, as well as more recently, to peer into bowls of holy water, sometimes laced with rat's blood (*sangue del pontega*), sometimes on their knees under a table in the dark, with a blessed candle in hand. They then recited:

Angelo bianco,
Angelo negro,
Per la tua santità,
Per la mia virginità,
Revellatemi la schiarità.

[Angel white of hue,
Angel black, you too,
By your very sanctity,
By my own virginity,
Show all to me in perfect clarity.]

For fear of the devil on these occasions, one nun claimed, "I secretly crossed myself, kept looking downward and said, 'Lord Jesus Christ, don't let me see anything!'" It worked—"and so I never saw anything."

For Eliseo Capis, these revelations offered few surprises. The *esperimento dell'inghistera* (experiment of the glass/bowl) was a familiar favorite. Some conjurers even considered it benign because of the "holy" objects involved: holy water, a blessed candle, a virginal child, sometimes a woman carrying an unborn and therefore innocent child. Pope Sixtus V would not agree. His Bull *Coeli et terrae* of 1586 specifically condemned this prayer as devil worship.[24]

The experienced inquisitor took special note of the "angelo negro" from the nuns' invocation. Like rat's blood, the black angel strongly suggested diabolical connections to anybody intent on finding them. Laypersons under inquisitorial scrutiny wisely left this embodiment of the devil out of their confessions. They also insisted that the white angel represented a guardian angel. Perhaps Maestro Eliseo concluded that these cloistered amateurs were too confident or ingenuous to dissemble.

The inquisitor must have found the enthusiastic use of the esperimento dell'inghistera in these hallowed surroundings scandalous—appalling. For it was widely associated with women fit only for the convent of the Convertite—prostitutes. Just four years earlier, his Venetian counterparts had investigated the notorious "honest courtesan," Veronica Franco. She had successfully employed the identical incantation, both as a child and as an adult. At San Lorenzo, one star witness pointed out that women of similar ill repute frequented the convent to visit Donna Florentia and the organist Donna Gentile. "I also heard—and I'd like this to be recorded in any case—that some women infamous for magic and dissolute living came to speak with Sister Florentia and Gentile. We know this because relatives who saw that sort in our parlatorios made known that we allow such disreputable women, suspected of witchcraft, to come speak with us." Perhaps they had been there to run magical errands, or worse, to collect items useful in their trade.[25]

Donna Florentia had shared with Semidea Poggi a Latin prayer to be said three times before going to bed. If she dreamed of muddy water, fire, or tempests, bad luck awaited her. But dreams of gardens and flowers promised a bright future. Another nun had cast flour on a table and drawn a crescent while reciting a spell—but she could no longer remember it. Donna Florentia had also balanced a sieve on a pair of shears while intoning, "By Saint Peter and Saint Paul, reveal to me the truth" or "Tell me if such and such will happen." When she listed names or events, the sieve would shift to signify the correct answer—Florentia insisted that the sieve really did move.

This practice was, of course, another of the most familiar magical methods for uncovering thieves and recovering missing property. The ancient *Key of Solomon the King* included detailed instructions for its use. In his treatise on incantations (1520), the Italian philosopher Pietro Pomponazzi acknowledged having tried it himself. Englishmen were still using it in the 1640s, more than a century later, as were cunning women in Brazil as late as the mid-1700s.[26]

The inquisitor took special note of Florentia's admission of having carried a prayer in elegant calligraphy, which promised to make its user an excellent musician. Here was proof for Don Livio's accusation that she had invoked the devil to improve her musicianship. A conversa, Antonia, owned up to the common, mundane practice of casting beans. She carefully stipulated that they were ordinary beans, not "baptized." Perhaps she picked them, one by one, from a random pile, "He loves me, loves me not, . . ." to discover her current love interest's true feelings. The last bean must have turned out to be an odd one, as Maestro Eliseo later discovered.

Most of this convent magic, much like its worldly equivalent, centered on romantic entrapment of men. Since their sisters in the world had to sit back and wait for love to come to them—custom denied women an active role in courtship, which fell to fathers and brothers—love magic offered women a means of discreetly encouraging it on their own. It is especially surprising for modern observers to discover that these cloistered women, who were beyond the pale when it came to the very idea of courtship, were also enthusiastically turning to magic to foster parlatorio romance, to encourage men to come to them.

Florentia, Semidea, and Gentile all confessed to keeping charms to encourage men's affections. Semidea's prayer had to be recited before an image of Santa Marta. "Prayers to Saint Martha" were widely known, from Italy all the way to Mexico, and involved varying degrees of verbal and ritual complexity. Semidea's might have resembled a simple Venetian version, to be repeated forty-five times a day before Martha's image: "Madonna Santa Marta, I pray and strongly conjure you. Go from your blessed place to a green wood tree, and find a large stick. Go to his heart and so beat and weaken him, that for love of me he will find no rest." Or it could have run to hundreds of words in verse. The inquisitor in Modena specifically forbade the sale of printed "prayers and spells of Saint Martha" in 1608. All invariably involved "hammering" hapless victims into submission, common to many forms of love magic: "If you find him face up, turn him like a millwheel, if you find him bent over, spit him [straight] like a pig, if you find him in the street, whip him like a mad dog, and so on."[27]

The bean-casting conversa, Antonia, confessed to a different hammering ritual: "I also said a prayer to my shadow, 'O my shadow, go forth so that he can neither eat, nor drink, nor sleep, nor stay awake.'" Inquisitors had encountered something very similar in the love rituals of a Venetian prostitute who disrobed, held a blessed candle behind her body, and spoke to her shadow on the wall ("Good evening, my shadow . . ."), thereby creating a link to the devil.[28] Antonia declined to say if she took her clothes off, and Maestro Eliseo declined to ask.

Donna Florentia returned to center stage because of her charmed ring, bearing the decidedly worldly device of Cupid blowing on a heart. Her ring could make whomever she touched with it immediately "be enflamed with love," provided the ring had been prayed over on Good Friday. Two other nuns were convinced that Donna Semidea and Donna Gentile had put it to good use. For the pair had discovered their brothers ardently chatting up Semidea and Gentile in the parlatorio. Another nun testified:

> One remarkable thing is that no gentleman usually comes to our convent who doesn't fall for Semidea, Florentia, and Gentile. . . . And notably Count Guido Pepoli, Sister Ginevra's brother, fell for Sister Semidea so hard during convent visits that he exclaimed to me, "I don't know which devil must have made that sister! She's so ugly and has no elegance at all. But nevertheless I can't help myself from seeing her, and if she doesn't come, I can't keep from having her called." And in fact he just left his sister standing there, to go talk to Sister Semidea. He later told me she'd asked him to lend her a necklace and a ring for a year. And he gave them to her.

The gift of a ring, even if only for a year, mirrors, of course, that most common token of betrothal between worldly lovers. Semidea must have borrowed Florentia's magic ring. Or perhaps Santa Marta had been hammering Count Guido. How else could the homely, inelegant Donna Semidea have such an effect on her eminent cousin, the young doctor of canon and civil law Count Guido Pepoli, who was busily buying up plum Vatican posts and would be made a cardinal before he turned thirty? The cause could only be supernatural.[29]

The inquisitor pounced on accusations that Florentia and Gentile wore baptized lodestones. Because of their inherent attractive properties, these were especially helpful in attracting men—but only so long as they had been "baptized." It was difficult for ordinary lay folk to stash items under an altar cloth or around the altar to enhance their magical properties. They had to resort to stratagems such as hiding them in a baby's christening blanket. But nuns, especially the convent sacristan, had ample opportunities both to hide items and to enlist an officiating priest's aid in the magic. Even worse, nun magicians might do a takeout business in baptized charms for women on the outside.

Florentia repeatedly insisted that her lodestones had not been baptized. She emphatically denied the charge that she had hidden anything on the altar. But she had to admit to participating in a ritual that suggested she had conspired to "baptize" charms. A few years earlier, Donna Florentia related, when she was chapel sacristan, an Augustinian friar—"young, scrawny, with a skimpy beard"—who occasionally said Mass at San Lorenzo had requested Mass vestments from her. At the Gospel, to everyone's astonishment, the friar had begun to recite the Passion for Good Friday. But it was not Holy Week. That much Florentia acknowledged—but she vehemently denied having hidden any magnets under the altar cloth or in the vestments before the ceremony.

Maestro Eliseo was understandably disinclined to believe her. Confronted with further aggressive questioning, Florentia shot back, "Your Reverence has such long fingers that you could easily lay hands on the friar and find out everything." The inquisitor reached out for the friar, plucked him from Soresina (Cremona) over a hundred miles away, and brought him back for interrogation. The friar confessed to magical misuse of the Mass but claimed a holy intention. He had intoned the Holy Week Passion to end his infatuation with that bean-casting conversa Antonia, already well known to the inquisitor—her ritual enlistment of her shadow to hammer the friar must have worked. He had hoped that, just as Antonia heard him reciting Christ's Passion, "to be delivered from the fleshly passions that I had for that sister, so she, hearing the Passion of our Lord, would likewise pray, by the merits of that same Holy Passion, to be freed from the passions she shared with me." Even the friar's confession to the inquisitor mirrored the "just as . . . so" language of magical invocations for romantic ends. Alas, it didn't work. The simple Antonia had utterly missed the point—judging by her follow-up testimony shortly thereafter.[30]

But what of that "business of the viola," which prompted the inquisitor's visit in the first place? Talk of diabolical attempts to recover the missing instrument eclipsed the wealth of other magic. For somebody who had previously claimed to know very little, subprioress Donna Arcangela Bovia proved surprisingly well informed. "Sister Angela Tussignana—Please God that she never returned!—she had called up the devil from hell and asked him various questions. Others who were present said that they asked her to interrogate the devil about different things, and that she answered about what they asked."

Donna Arcangela's narrative, with information from more junior members of the community, creates a detailed picture of what had come to pass. Two years earlier, the viola had gone missing. Amateur attempts at divination, with sieves, bowls of water, and such, failed to locate it. So the notorious Angela Tussignana volunteered her help. Angela was possessed—or else she must have been a witch. "She showed she was possessed almost from the beginning, when she first joined us," claimed Donna Gentile. Her face could change horribly. She would shriek and foam at the mouth. She could lift objects much too heavy for ordinary women. She had tried to throw herself out a window. She had once fallen to the floor before the crucifix and had cast it to the ground. She claimed to have spoken to bats, which also answered her. She would take off her rochet—a garment covering a nun's front and back, open at the sides—and trample on it. One sensible nun pointed out, "But that had nothing to do with incantations. It was simply out of vexation, lamenting that she had to be a nun."

The amateur magicians were getting nowhere. So Angela exclaimed, "Leave it to me—I can tell you who had it." "Dear Sister Angela, do whatever it takes to discover the truth," exclaimed Florentia. Semidea urged, "Sister Angela, if you know how to do anything to discover who stole the viola, go ahead and do it." What happened next—or what was believed to have happened next—emerged from bits and pieces offered by every member of the community with anything to say.[31]

"If you want me to help you, you must come for me during compline—but don't come get me too late. Because if just one drop of holy water falls on me, I can't do anything," Angela commanded. Compline was the last service of the night. The other nuns would then go off to bed. Before the blessing with holy water, Angela slips quietly away from the nuns' chapel, headed for the infirmary.

From all ill dreams defend our eyes,
From nightly fears and fantasies;
Tread under foot our ghostly foe,
That no pollution we may know.

The nuns' compline hymn echoes ironically behind her as she skirts the cloister.

Semidea Poggi is waiting for Angela in the infirmary, where she is on duty, together with Florentia and the curious Gentile, "the singer, and the others interested in that missing instrument, and others who were passionate about music."

Angela first solemnly removes her veil, wimple, and rochet and lays them aside. With a lighted candle in hand, she takes the knife Francesco had given her and draws a perfect circle on the floor. She carefully sticks the knife at the center point and steps gingerly out of the circle, then exhorts the devil to appear: "Diabolus pro constrictum . . ." (nobody could remember the rest later on).

They wait. Nothing happens. The room is still illuminated. So Semidea removes the lamp but is so terrified that she carefully hides outside the door.

Then a terrible, hideous voice strikes fear into the hearts of all the sisters:

"Why have you summoned me?"

"To tell us who took the viola," Angela replies.

"Sister Angelica Fava."

"No! It's not true!" Angelica exclaims (or so some said).

"You took it. You cut up the viola with a knife, and then burned up the bits." The devil was adamant.

Suor Angela may well have smiled smugly. Some knew that the esperimento dell'inghistera had already revealed Sister Angelica Fava to her: a miniature nun who looked just like Angelica had appeared in the water.

Donna Florentia prompts Angela with a different question, "Who's responsible for the banishment of Ascanio, the musician?" But the devil refuses to answer: "It's too late for that question. Go find out about it yourself."

With that, Angela begins to recite a prayer to the Madonna. The devil vanishes into the darkness.[32]

Sister Angelica would vehemently deny the devil's accusation and would continue to protest over the intervening months and years. When the inquisitor finally arrived she exclaimed, "I'm the one who can rejoice ecstatically at Your Reverence's arrival, because I've been defamed throughout the convent for three long years!" She then confessed to having tried her hand at other spells, hoping to discover for herself who was really to blame.

Much of what he heard rang true for the inquisitor. Angela's removal of her veil, wimple, and rochet, "because the infernal one wouldn't appear otherwise," recalled other witches' disrobing, letting down their hair, or removing any scapulars. Like Angela's avoidance of holy water, it helped distance her from her consecrated state. The devil usually refused to enter the light, and his voice was always terrifying to hear. But Angela's magic circle was positively primitive in its simplicity. It never should have worked.[33]

Who among the various reluctant witnesses had actually seen what? Every bit of testimony turned out to have been hearsay. One nun after another tried to distance herself from the event, to diminish any direct involvement. Perhaps someone had told them that inquisitors had orders not to rely—or to condemn—solely on hearsay evidence (at least in theory). Not only Donna Semidea but the entire company of musical nuns claimed not to have been inside the infirmary. That left Angela Tussignana on her own, conjuring and telling them what was happening in the darkened room. Could she have played the devil's part herself? Had she simply acted out "the terrible, hideous voice that struck fear in all the nuns" alone inside in the dark?

Angela was long gone, of course, by the time the inquisitor descended on San Lorenzo for the second time. Thus she could shoulder all the blame as a convenient scapegoat. For their part, the nuns who remained had years of experience honing their creative literal-mindedness. Such skills were essential for finding wholly obedient ways around the church hierarchy's steady stream of punctilious re-

FIGURE 2.5 Dr. Faustus, protected by a more complex magic circle, conjures up the devil, who appears at the lower right. From the title page of Christopher Marlowe's *The Tragicall History of the Life and Death of Doctor Faustus* (London, 1620).

strictions and prohibitions, designed to control unruly behavior. Facing Maestro Eliseo, they had listened carefully to his questions. They could swear in holy obedience and on pain of excommunication, "I heard such and such. . . . But I was not present." (In some cases, just right outside the door.)

A witness who was *not* among those right outside the door revealed that Tussignana had admitted everything after the fact. Everything except the precise words of the devilish incantation. Angela had no longer wanted to repeat those aloud, even in her impending sacramental confession, the witness claimed. Was Angela afraid because the words were unholy or because everybody knew the dangers of reciting these incantations idly, out of context? Or because the entire incantation had never actually been spoken at all? Tussignana told the witness she would have written the invocation down, but, alas, she didn't know how to write. So the nun witness had written the words down for her herself. (How Angela managed to communicate the words without speaking them aloud is another mystery.) But by the day she testified in October 1584, this cloistered witness had also managed to forget everything except the opening, "Diabolus pro constrictum."

Maestro Eliseo might well have sniffed at Angela's invocation of the devil. It was as primitive as her magic circle. He must have heard his share of devilish conjuring. They always called upon a sizable company of holy or unholy characters. No simple "Diabolus pro constrictum" plus an additional Latin word or two.

What of this "Ascanio, the musician," whose banishment the devil had refused to elucidate? He was not hard to find: Ascanio Trombetti, master wind player of the Bolognese Concerto Palatino and of San Petronio, served as the Lateran canons' own maestro di cappella. Ascanio's name echoed through the nuns' testimony. He had transmitted Donna Florentia's incantation for telling the future through dreams. Ascanio had also brought Florentia the gold ring used for love magic. Despite their father-general's earlier prohibition, "nevertheless, Sister Florentia, Semidea, and the others, as many as six, were constantly summoning musicians. And especially Master Ascanio."

No surprise, then, that Ascanio Trombetti heard a knock on his door. When called to testify in early December 1584, Trombetti first claimed to know nothing about anything or anybody having to do with magic. Of course, he knew most of the nuns. "As a musician, I've often gone to teach the sisters the trombone and the viola. More precisely, I've taught the trombone and viola to Sister Florentia, and to many others as well—Sister Semidea Poggi, Sister Angelica Fava, Sister Panina, and Sister Cecilia Ghisliera."

More pointed questions revealed Ascanio as the ecclesiastical hierarchy's worst nightmare, the perfect justification for a new round of prohibitions. He and his music had provoked every convent impropriety. One nun summed it up: "Please God that there had never been music in this convent! Because of it, countless scandals were hatched. If Your Reverence doesn't do something about that, we'll always be topsy-turvy."[34]

Long before Ascanio Trombetti's interview, and long before this insider attack on music, the inquisitor had recognized that rumors of sisterly betrayal were encouraging strife and disharmony at San

Lorenzo. On the first day of his full investigation in October 1584, the voluble subprioress, Donna Arcangela Bovia, had complained about gossip following preliminary inquiries back in 1583. "A rumor's going around that I gave up Sister Gentile to the Inquisition—something that troubled me very much." Rather more sinister, it appeared that some singing nuns might have ganged up on Donna Angelica Fava in the matter of the missing viola. The well-informed but self-styled know-nothing Donna Arcangela suggested that the disappearing instrument had passed through various hands, including those of a layperson, Sister Fulgentia, and the then prioress, Donna Serafina Saldini. "And because certain sisters wanted Sister Angelica Fava to have taken that little viola, they sought through Sister Angela Tussignana to learn if it had been Sister Angelica, by means of the infernal one—but Your Reverence needn't go to the trouble of writing this down, because Sister Angelica will tell you about it." And, indeed, shortly thereafter Donna Angelica Fava testified that "when I complained to Sister Angela, she confirmed that she'd done it at the insistence of the others"—though it remains unclear exactly what Angela Tussignana was admitting. Had the vindictive sisters insisted she perform the ritual or that she contrive its outcome?[35]

So by Christmas 1584, Maestro Eliseo must have recognized that he was stirring up more problems than he was solving. He allowed the nuns eventually to affirm their previous confessions and request appropriate penance.

Everyone, that is, except Donna Florentia Campanacci. Trafficking in baptized charms could not be easily forgiven and forgotten. Under continued, relentless questioning in mid-January 1585, she refused to cave in, vigorously denying further knowledge or culpability. Hoping to break her, Maestro Eliseo condemned Florentia to imprisonment within the convent. A month later, her tune had not changed. "Your Reverence just doesn't want to believe I'm telling the truth! Now all the more, after my month's imprisonment, to my very great distress. Not to mention the height of shame that has befallen me in the convent! So I pray Your Reverence please to finish my trial and be satisfied with my lengthy imprisonment and my tedious torment."[36]

The inquisitor would get nothing more out of Donna Florentia. He could not convict her without a confession. The strappado was

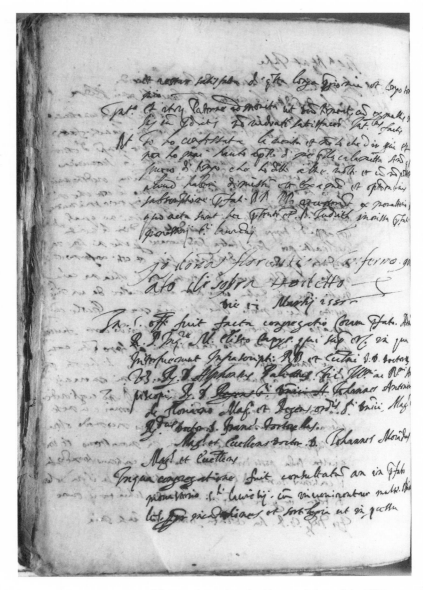

FIGURE 2.6 BCB, MS B1877, fol. 386v. Reproduced with permission of the Biblioteca Comunale dell'Archiginnasio, Bologna. "I, Donna Florentia, confirm what I said above" (middle of the page). Florentia Campanacci's affirmation in the Inquisition transcript concludes the testimony from the investigation.

unfortunately out of the question. So he told her to sign her testimony in the transcript and sent her away.

Back in October 1584, a newly elected, commonsensical (and rather less cooperative) prioress had defended herself for not taking all this witchcraft very seriously: "I would say that they're scatterbrains, these sisters. And they could have seen one thing instead of another. I didn't try to do anything more because I thought they were just little girls." Were the prioress's very sensible excuses more than self-defense? Except for the father confessor (who seems discreetly to have kept to himself what Angela Tussignana had revealed in confession) the shepherds from San Giovanni in Monte had largely abandoned their flock to Maestro Eliseo's finite mercies. Any defense had to come from the nuns' new female superior. Perhaps she recognized that such popular magic was increasingly seen as the stuff of silly girls and scatterbrains. Less than a decade earlier Cosme de Aldana had consigned it all to "certain ignorant and silly old enchantresses and charm purveyors . . . throwing flour on a polished table on St. John's Eve to forecast the husband their daughter would have."[37]

Fifteen years later, Giuseppe Passi would ride the wave of misogyny to new heights in his *I donneschi diffetti* (The Defects of Women). He cites "selecting beans, and similar folderol and vanities put to use by women. . . . If you chance to lose as much as a penny, immediately like a dog after a hare you run for the shears and the sieve to see if so-and-so stole it from you . . . with a thousand silly and vain words, thinking that the sieve will move when you pronounce your superstitious words."[38] If the ecclesiastical patriarchy took it all too seriously, were they any better than these foolish girls and scatterbrains? Wouldn't that make them a bunch of silly old ladies in cassocks?

This theory might be foisting a proto-feminist consciousness on the prioress, which would make her blink. Maestro Eliseo certainly would not fall for it, anyway. Lay intellectuals might find it all to be folderol, but the church knew better. He might have recognized a ring of truth in the nuns' endless defensive claims that it was all in jest, however. Faced with too much time on their hands and often too little of interest to engage their imaginations, this amateur magic fulfilled their desire to entertain and be entertained. But in Maestro Eliseo's view there were appropriate sorts of recreation to engage them that were not so scandalously inappropriate and dangerous to monastic propriety.

On the other hand, the ever informative Donna Arcangela Bovia had also told him the word on the street was that Franceseco Tussignani and Filippo Carlo Ghislieri "had sorted things out with the Inquisition" regarding their daughters' involvement. The Tussignani and Ghislieri clans were probably not Bologna's only powerful families lining up behind threatened female relatives. Women who suffered most at the Inquisition's hands for alleged witchcraft were the poor and the powerless. The conjurers and enthusiastic dabblers in love magic at San Lorenzo were lucky enough to hail from Bologna's most powerful, wealthy, and influential families. In large part, their heritage protected them.

Maestro Eliseo probably concluded that all this foolishness posed no threat to the nuns' salvation, though it grievously offended the dignity of holy Mother Church and offered a foul example to the laity at large. When his panel of local priestly dignitaries met on March 17, 1585, with Maestro Eliseo presiding, he may have reminded them that the last thing anybody wanted was to call any further attention to San Lorenzo as Bologna's center of folk magic, devilish conjuring, and parlatorio romance. Particularly since the Ghislieri family was starting to fret. Maestro Eliseo would still have remembered how he had provoked the hostility of the Bolognese Senate five years earlier for seeming to usurp civil prerogatives. Senators had commanded the Bolognese ambassador in Rome to appeal directly to His Holiness, who had sided with the Bolognese aristocrats.[39]

The notary of the Holy Office therefore would not perform the customary public reading of a formal sentence from the organ loft in the Oratorio of the Holy Cross. He most assuredly would not read it out from the cemetery adjoining the basilica of San Domenico. Maestro Eliseo would have cringed at the very thought of the scandal such a spectacle would provoke. He decreed, with his committee's agreement and with Rome's obligatory blessing, that the nuns should abjure their potentially heretical acts in the customary form, but in the discreet privacy of their convent—most definitely not from a stage outside San Domenico, in a heretic's hat, candle in hand, wearing a placard describing their offenses. To avoid possible scandal, they would simply swear that they had remained, and would always remain, true to their vows and to holy faith, and that they would abstain from similar bad behavior in future.[40]

Despite his role as a fomenter of more trouble and improprieties than most of his students, and despite having violated various episcopal prohibitions, Ascanio Trombetti escaped for the moment unscathed. He even kept his job at San Giovanni in Monte. But the devil, who had been so unforthcoming about him during Angela's conjuring, eventually went looking for Maestro Ascanio. On a September evening in 1590, a Bolognese book dealer returned home to discover the wind player in bed with his wife. He struck him dead with his own sword, dragged the body back to Ascanio's residence, and hung it above the doorway.[41]

"WHAT SORT OF LIFE WAS IT THAT I LIVED?"

Nothing so spectacular awaited Ascanio's former pupils. In March 1589, the nuns were forbidden, once and for all, to perform anything insufficiently spiritual. The organ could be played only during services—not even for rehearsals. The throngs who had flocked to hear San Lorenzo's singing nuns in the late 1570s and early 1580s, when Laura Bovia's star was in the ascendant, could no longer be invited to services. No special concerts could be performed for them in the parlatorio.

What of Laura Bovia, who had decamped just in the nick of time? Laura's own singing career did not survive the heyday of her cloistered sisters. After Francesco de' Medici's untimely death, the next Medici grand duke dismissed her in 1589. He reportedly feared she might whisper too many court secrets to his betrothed, Christine of Lorraine.

Laura Bovia returned to Bologna, where her uncle-become-father arranged a nice marriage for her in 1592. The former diva traded music for motherhood, producing three sons but no more music. She lived unremarkably until her death on Christmas Day 1629. She was interred at the church of San Giacomo in the village of Castelfranco, sixteen miles from Bologna. Her husband's family chapel can still be visited there, its Madonna still wearing the silver crown Laura's husband gave her four centuries ago. Any further traces of Laura have vanished.

Back at San Lorenzo, the singing nuns' superiors remarked, "They should not worry about having other spectators but the angels, ready to praise the Lord with them, to help them perform this office decorously, and to carry their prayers to heaven."[42]

But unlike Laura Bovia, who chose the world and ultimately lost her voice, Semidea Poggi, the first aristocratic enthusiast for music, magic, and parlatorio romance to be singled out on the earliest day of the inquisitor's investigation, eventually found an alternative voice. Having traded music for poetry, she composed verses and even published them in later years: *La Calliope religiosa* (1623) and *I desiderj di Parnaso* (undated, subtitled "Rhymes Born amid the Solitude of the Cloisters"). The first collection opened with twenty pages of verse by local worthies, praising Semidea's talents literally to the skies in rather hackneyed style, reminiscent of praises Laura Bovia had received forty years before. At least one aristocratic versifier, "Signor Cavaliere R.P.," contrasts the largely forgotten musical triumphs of the former singer's youth with the more salutary artistic fruits of her maturity.

> Posciache in prisca età, ne' tuoi prim'anni
> S'altr'hebbe in dolce suon glorie cosparte
> Hor scontrando stupor da le tue carte
> Altri sfugge d'Inferno ingiurie, e danni.

> [Whereas in olden days, in your tender years,
> Some had spread glories in sweet sound,
> Now others, finding amazement in your pages,
> Flee the abuses and perils of hell.]

Perusing those same pages, any cloistered sister who happened to remember the homely Semidea's alleged bewitching of the lovesick Count Guido Pepoli might have perceived a certain "do as I say, not as I did" quality in Donna Semidea's lengthy "Consiglio spirituale da fuggire il vano, e appigliarsi al vero ornamento di donna saggia" ("Spiritual Counsel to Flee Frivolity and Hold to the True Grace of a Wise Woman"):

Se poi non miri splendor nel tuo volto
    Quel di schietta beltà raggio bramato,
    A chi giamai ti volgi? . . .
    A l'empio de gli incanti inganno stolto,
    A l'arti maghe, al nemico invocato.
    Cessa per Dio. Non è quà giù permessa
    Cosa non di là sù. Cessa error, cessa.
Non l'infernal potenza, e le parole
    Con horrendi susurri, e note oscure;
    Nè già le Stelle ancor, la Luna, ò il Sole,
    Onde fingonsi ogn'hor sciocche fatture:
    Queste non pon, non pon (stimil chi vuole)
    L'amorose in altrui salde, e sicure
    Brame eccitar, ma ben con mille Danni
    A l'alme vili ordir lacci, e inganni.

[If then you see no elegance in your face,
    No longed-for glimpse of beauty unspotted,
    Whomever do you turn to? . . .
    To the wicked, foolish guile of charms,
    To magical arts, to conjuring up the devil.
    Cease, by God! Here below nothing is permitted
    That does not come from above. Stop, err no more!
No infernal power, and words
    With horrible mutterings and secret signs,
    Nor sooner by the stars, the moon, or the sun,
    By which foolish bewitchings are constantly feigned:
    These cannot, they cannot (as everyone can demonstrate)
    Arouse amorous desires in others that are solid and sure.
    But, rather, with a thousand perils
    They lay evil snares and deceits for souls.]

Reading further, a few cloistered sisters might have recognized that in "Al Santissimo Crocifisso" ("Before the Most Holy Crucifix"), a repentant Sister Semidea spoke from experience:

Signor, qual vita fu quella in ch'io vissi?
    Consumai vaneggiando i mesi, e gli anni,

Stimai carcere il chiostro, e mi soscrissi
Captiva volontaria à rei Tiranni.
Non seppi del mio ben misera, e dissi
Quei sol concenti miei, ch'eran'affanni,
Mentre invocava abissi incontr'abissi,
Voce di cataratte, horrori, e danni.
Non pensai Redentor quanto à te costa
L'alma mia, che può far sincera, e bianca
Una gocciola al fin de la tua Costa.
Hor crocifiggo à te pentita, e stanca
Qualunque iniquità, la qual s'accosta
Da la destra al ladron, non da la manca.

[Lord, what sort of life was it that I lived?
I wasted months and years being foolish.
I deemed the cloister a prison and signed on
As a willing slave to evil tyrants.
Wretched, I did not recognize my good fortune and gave voice
Only to those tunes of mine, which came from unhappiness,
While my voice, caught up in magical symbols,
loathsome sounds, and perils,
Called up abyss after abyss.
I did not consider, Redeemer, how much it costs you
For my soul, which one droplet from your side, in the end,
Could make pure and white.
So now, repentant and weary, for you I crucify
Every wickedness that may accost me—
From the right, beside the good thief, not from the left.][43]

Readers in the world may have assumed the pious nun was hyperbolically ringing the changes on that most common theme among seventeenth-century convent poets—repentance for lapses in devotion. All her religious superiors who knew otherwise were long dead. Since Cardinal Gabriele Paleotti's death in 1597, three more Bolognese archbishops had already come and gone. By 1623 another five master inquisitors had followed in Eliseo Capis's footsteps. Even the formerly lovelorn count, Cardinal Guido Pepoli, had been dead and buried almost twenty-five years. Only a few of the more venerable

Lateran canonesses inside San Lorenzo were old enough to recognize the ring of truth in Sister Semidea's repentant confession. And they weren't telling.

Long before then, choirs at other convents, most notably Santa Cristina della Fondazza (to which we return in the final chapter), had filled the void left by San Lorenzo's silenced singers. Henceforth the musical canonesses of San Lorenzo attracted only angelic audiences. During the three centuries before Napoleon's suppression of the monasteries in 1799, we hear virtually nothing more about them.

3

SPINSTERS, SILKWORMS, AND A FLIGHT IN FLAGRANTE

San Niccolò di Strozzi (Reggio Calabria, 1673)

"A CRIME WITHOUT PRECEDENT IN THE WHOLE OF CHRISTENDOM"

After a few years on the Sacred Congregation of Bishops and Regulars, its secretary would have sighed at the prospect of sifting through dozens more petitions before the Congregation's next meeting. Something less ordinary rarely relieved the tedium of dowry reduction requests and petitions to sell property or pawn altar furnishings. Perhaps convent objections to the archbishop of Naples's prohibition on nuns' keeping pet dogs, when only *male* dogs were expressly forbidden. Or an overweight Neapolitan former abbess's request to have two strong male convent servants carry her to Mass. (The "huge and gross colossus" had grown too fat to make it on her own, and the female converse had collapsed under her weight.) Otherwise, the pile of petitions had a numbing sameness.

So the secretary may have raised an eyebrow when, in early May 1673, he opened a hasty note from the southernmost region of the Kingdom of Naples, sent by Matteo di Gennaro, archbishop of Reggio Calabria. It recounted a disastrous fire at the convent of San Niccolò di Strozzi. The roof, attic, and second floor had all been destroyed, and the nuns had fled the cloister. Di Gennaro declined further comment, however, until he had time to investigate. The secretary would have to wait two weeks for details.[1]

San Niccolò di Strozzi, smoldering near the tip of the toe of the boot of Italy, was even more exclusive than San Lorenzo, up north in Bologna. The youngest of Reggio's religious houses for women, it had been established a generation earlier by a nouveau riche aristocrat, Diego Lamberti Strozzi.[2] Diego's father, Lamberto Strozzi, had joined several Florentine noblemen seeking their fortunes in the silk trade in the wilds of southernmost Italy during the late 1500s. He was so successful that he promptly bought his way into Reggio's preeminent Monsolino family. In 1586 Lamberto paid out a "dowry" of six thousand ducats (roughly six times what a genteel bride in Reggio normally paid her future *husband*) for the hand of Giovanna Monsolino.

Lamberto and Giovanna's son, Diego Strozzi, further strengthened aristocratic alliances with the locals. He strategically married Eleonora Abenavoli, daughter of Nicola, Baron of Montebello, a barony nine miles southeast of the city. To fortify the family's Monsolino alliances after Lamberto Strozzi's death, Diego's mother married her own cousin, Bernardo Monsolino (a generation her junior). For good measure, in 1608 Diego also married off his sister, Ippolita, to Bernardo Monsolino's brother (their mother's current brother-in-law).

Diego Strozzi went on to acquire extraordinary wealth and power in the city. He was appointed *regio secreto* and master of the docks in 1623 and a member of the city's governing council in 1638. Though the story is probably apocryphal, Strozzi was remembered for leading a small company of horseman against invading Turkish pirates in 1638, while his slave sounded an alarm on the trumpet. Unable to judge the size of this advancing squadron, heard but not seen through groves of mulberry trees near the shore, the pirates fled.

Diego's reputation grew even more fantastic back in Florence. A letter among the Strozzi papers in the Florentine State Archive claimed, "He was so powerful that he was the terror of the whole province. When he went around the city with thirty well-armed black slaves, accompanied by several carriages full of knights and the chief men of the city, he might well be called the great king of Reggio."[3]

Strozzi's family took up residence near several of his in-laws, in an imposing palace along strada Maestra, Reggio's main east–west thoroughfare. Palazzo Strozzi is long gone, but it probably stood near the intersection of modern via Miraglia and via Felice Valentino. It can perhaps be identified on Giovanni Battista Pacichelli's primitive en-

FIGURE 3.1 Seventeenth-century Reggio, from G. B. Pacichelli, *Il regno di Napoli in prospettiva*, vol. 2 (1703). AA marks the probable location of San Niccolò di Strozzi. BB marks the approximate location of Santa Maria della Vittoria, where the fugitive nun arsonists were confined after the fire.

graving (1703), right at city center: an agglomeration of three buildings, two stories tall plus an attic. Such palaces customarily enclosed a large courtyard with a well at the center and an exterior open staircase leading to the second floor, which contained the chief living quarters. Palazzo Strozzi's lengthy facade, extending along the south side of strada Maestra, suggested a structure as substantial as most any in the city. It rose high enough to figure in the city's modest skyline, with an unobstructed view of the battlements of the late medieval Castello Aragonese to the north. Diego subsequently incorporated the adjacent church of Sant'Angelo Piccolo (renamed the Oratorio di San Nicola da Bari) within the family compound.

Confronting his impending mortality in the early 1640s, Strozzi literally set his house in order. He had no children, but he had a spinster sister and a spinster half-sister. His mother also had a spinster sister-in-law, and his married sister already had at least four granddaughters.[4] So he resolved to confront the problem common in seventeenth-century aristocratic families: too many female offspring. Diego's will, drawn up in June 1644, stipulated that after his wife's death Palazzo Strozzi would become a convent, to house a dozen family members. In the unlikely event that Monsolino women were in short supply, other local nobles might enter, without dowries. The whole aristocratic community would be supported by Strozzi's substantial legacy. For good measure, his will further required the celebration of two thousand masses for the repose of his soul in the four months following his demise.

The palace narrowly escaped destruction during a popular uprising in 1648, when more than four hundred rampaging protesters carried off many of its furnishings but spared its occupants. On Eleonora's death later that year, the archbishop consecrated the Strozzi compound as the convent of San Niccolò di Strozzi.

Mother Maria Maddalena Monsolino, either Diego's spinster sister Porzia or (more likely) his spinster half-sister from his mother's second marriage, was installed as prioress for life. She would oversee the spiritual welfare of this handful of close relatives. That had to wait, however, until she and her future charges had all passed through the novitiate (in Maria Maddalena's case, at about age forty-five, rather than the more usual fifteen).

In the meantime, the unrelated but exemplary Sister Maria Padiglia, from Reggio's Benedictine convent of Santa Maria della Vittoria, would teach them the ins and outs of religious life. Sister Maria's family background was unassuming—she would probably never have been accepted at San Niccolò. Even though the local church hierarchy may have thought piety trumped good breeding, her genteel pupils in all likelihood did not.

In fact, Sister Maria Padiglia had her hands full with these local aristocrats, whom God had not called to the religious life. One wonders if any of them heard the faintest heavenly summons. Rather, they were heeding the will of fathers, brothers, and uncles. Because Rome had emphatic prohibitions on forcing girls into convents against their will, the bishop or his agent was required to interview every potential postulant to ensure that it was her desire, and not simply her parents'. In this case the archbishop seems to have listened mostly to genteel parents' wishes. A quarter century later, events would suggest that the girls' true feelings were not heard.

Even outside the convent, the life of a woman of quality in Reggio was well hedged in. To preserve her—and her family's—honor, she did not go out unchaperoned. Her male relatives knew she was best kept closed inside. In that way she would avoid experiencing or provoking temptation—or, equally bad, appearing to. Now, thanks to Diego Strozzi, the Monsolino women were even more definitively enclosed. They were cut off not only from the world, but also from direct contact with friends and family. Any who had grown up in the old Palazzo Strozzi may well have found the transition very disorienting. With one stroke, their familiar way of life on strada Maestra was replaced by the sterner ways of Saint Dominic's monastic rule. The palazzo's second floor became the nuns' sleeping quarters. Despite its thirteen windows—each sister presumably had a window, if not a room of her own—the restrictions of monastic enclosure now made the very walls of Palazzo Strozzi virtually impenetrable.

Over the next three years, Sister Maria Padiglia did her best to establish a spiritual lifestyle. In other convents the form of life was customarily nurtured over generations, as the company of older nuns taught the younger women how to adapt themselves to its strictures. But at San Niccolò the "older generation," as new to the religious life as the youngest novice, consisted only of the future abbess for life, Mother Maria Maddalena, and one cousin turned novice, three years her senior. The pair was outnumbered five to one by a flock of ten juniors, the oldest in her early teens, the youngest only eleven.

Sister Maria Padiglia probably shook her head in dismay at Diego Strozzi's philanthropic solution to the family's female problem. After three years there was still more spiritual work to do. So she continued to fulfill her archbishop's command, in holy obedience, for another five years, until 1656. Then she could finally turn her back on San Niccolò and return to the more suitably spiritual Santa Maria della Vittoria. Mother Maria Maddalena, the newly minted spinster turned novice turned prioress, would have to lead her relatives in the religious life as best she could.[5]

The archbishop of Reggio, Matteo di Gennaro, whose urgent message regarding the convent conflagration would land on the Sacred Congregation's desk in May 1673, was a highborn outsider who preferred to be known as "Neapolitan patrician, count of Bova, Baron of Castellace, of His Catholic Majesty's Council." He had never really found himself at home at Italy's southern tip, and in fact he stayed away from his diocese for many years. Born in 1622, he had quickly risen to the rank of *primociero* (chief canon) at the cathedral in Naples. After his predecessor's death in 1658, the see of Reggio had remained vacant for two years before the king of Spain recommended di Gennaro, still in his thirties, for the miter. He had come to His Catholic Majesty's attention for his acts of heroic charity at a hospital for the dying during a recent Neapolitan outbreak of plague, which had claimed half the city's population. Di Gennaro's good works are memorialized to this day on a plaque in the duomo of Naples, where a chapel was also dedicated to his memory.[6] As a Neapolitan aristocrat, however, jealous of the rights, privileges, and dignity of his office, Monsignor di Gennaro was not ideally suited to the social realities of the peninsula's wild southernmost region.

Calabria was infamous for violence, at the hands of God no less than man. Earthquakes regularly rolled through the province, shaking things up there in 1599 (particularly disastrous for Reggio), 1614, 1619, 1624, 1629, 1635, 1638 (with 30,000 dead, rivaling the more modern quakes of 1783 and 1908), 1640, 1649 (again causing significant damage in Reggio), 1659 (a widespread, major disaster, with 15,000 casualties), and 1660 (another major disaster). Plague was also a frequent visitor, creating not only the scourge of the 1650s (which Reggio largely escaped, thanks to a miraculous image of the Madonna della Consolazione), but an earlier one in 1636 and yet another in 1668. Famine often accompanied these afflictions or arrived on its own. And across the straits, Mount Etna restlessly waited to explode. It did so hellishly in 1669, spreading devastation as far as Catania, on Sicily's eastern coast. Lava engulfed and demolished Catania's western wall, then flowed into the city and onward to the sea—the worst eruption in Etna's history.[7]

Should natural disasters take a break, man filled the vacuum. For centuries Reggio and the Strait of Messina remained favorite targets for Turkish pirates. There had been a dozen attacks during the 1500s, followed by the legendary assault in 1638 that added luster to Diego Strozzi's reputation. When the Turks were quiet, locals stood in for them. As one observer wrote in 1570, "This region is filled with monsters, petty kings and tyrants, who despoil and tyrannize it. In the guise of Laestrygonians, they graze daily with an inextinguishable thirst and inexhaustible avarice upon the toil of mortals. They have commandeered the woods, the crags, the earth, pastures, the game, the birds. In a word, they have usurped every right of the people."[8]

Gangs of bandits and brigands found their way from the countryside into the city, scarcely controlled by the unpopular Spanish colonial government. In 1576 bandits had taken Reggio, proposing to liberate the people from the nobility. It was another such insurrection that Palazzo Strozzi barely survived in 1648. On another notorious occasion, brigands dragged a cannon into the city in broad daylight, blasted their way into a fortified house, and slaughtered all its occupants, scarcely opposed by Spanish authorities. Little wonder, then, that di Gennaro's refined sensibilities met challenges here.

In contrast to di Gennaro's obligation to protect diocesan interests, if we can believe one seventeenth-century writer, churches themselves provided convenient sanctuaries for the lawless. "Most of these criminals, enjoying the inviolable security of the churches, which they commonly call 'sanctuaries,' grow so insolent and so irreverent, so filthy, and behave so disrespectfully toward God, whose house receives them, that a Turk (the natural enemy of our faith) could not live there with greater impiety. The secular arm that comes to punish them has no authority. With shameful contempt for God and his servants, they turn churches into taverns, markets, gaming houses, and places of intolerable pollution."[9]

Even the local nobility were prone to violent rivalries and power grabs. Bitter confrontations between the Monsolino and Malgeri clans had ravaged the city since the 1560s. Using accusations of Protestant heresy as a pretext, the families spread their feud to other factions, noble and not so noble (the Monsolino family reputedly unlocked the prisons to bolster its army). The 1600s dawned before the two families finally wore themselves out.

Calabrians of all classes were thus known for rebellion and resistance—traits rarely admired by cardinals and archbishops. No wonder Monsignor di Gennaro had difficulty facing up to Reggio. He arrived in what he probably considered a poor excuse for a city, scarcely worthy of his attentions as its new archbishop. Hemmed in between the Strait of Messina, a mountain range to the north, aptly named Aspromonte ("bitter mountain"), and the river Calopinace to the east, the town hugged a narrow strip of beach and docks. An ancient, perpetually crumbling, rectangular city wall protected it. Massive battlements strengthened the harbor side of the wall, about 2,800 feet long. A dozen smaller battlements also interrupted the inland sides. But a turn around the wall's four sides would cover no more than a mile and a half, all told. These battlements sheltered a mere three thousand *fuochi* ("fires"—households), perhaps 10,000 to 13,000 souls—not much spiritual fodder for a pastor with any ambition.

Inside the city wall, Archbishop di Gennaro discovered no fewer than thirty churches, several monasteries, and a few convents, dominated by the duomo and an adjacent archbishop's residence near the castello. There was little of note beyond ecclesiastical buildings. There was no intellectual life—the city had to wait another sixty years for its first academy, the "Accademia degli Artificiosi." The better palaces, rising two or three stories along a medieval hodgepodge of irregular streets and plazas, were built of coarse local stone. With an eye chiefly toward repelling invaders, no windows were permitted on the ground floor. To an outsider like di Gennaro, the local architecture showed little trace of modern style. Less imposing structures were built of a cheaper alternative—large, crude bricks mortared with mud. These buildings simply waited to collapse in the next earthquake.

On the other hand, nature's daunting beauties might distract from these barely hospitable works of man. Rising to 6,400 feet, the rugged Aspromonte formed a rough backdrop. Its chestnut, pine, and beech forests hedged in farmers' fields carved from unyielding hillsides. Vast mulberry groves blanketed the landscape outside the city wall. These highlands contrasted with the breathtaking serenity of the strait and the ocean. The magical waters fluctuated from evanescent shades of sea green to varying cobalt blues, transformed into violet at sunset. Looking toward Messina at dawn on an especially still morning, as the sun's rays passed through lengthy stretches of oceanic atmosphere above the strait, di Gennaro may have watched incredulously as phantom castles, arches, and columns appeared to rise magically from the water's glassy surface. This bewitching phantom city, an optical illusion that locals identified as the castle of Fata Morgana, King Arthur's fairy half-sister, offered any dejected outsider one of Reggio's few consolations.

For Archbishop di Gennaro, Reggio lived up to the dubious reputation it held in the more civilized north. In 1673 events at San Niccolò

FIGURE 3.2 Reggio Calabria, Aspromonte, and the Strait of Messina in the 1600s. Giambattista Albrizzi's mid-eighteenth-century engraving, copied from earlier versions depicting a late sixteenth-century Turkish attack on the city, conveys Reggio's modest size and impressive natural setting.

would finally end the perpetually rocky pastoral relationship with his Calabrian flock. His second letter to the Sacred Congregation in Rome, dated May 16, in which he followed up on his previous notification about the fire, left no doubt about his attitude. "From the enclosed description, Your Illustrious Lordship will see how society behaves in these parts. And because their actions reached such a deplorable excess, you will realize what is the quality of people here, and will appreciate the extent of my own vexation."

To the secretary of the Sacred Congregation, Monsignor di Gennaro's narrative conveyed an air of haste. He could offer only a summary—he claimed there had been no time to copy a complete transcript of his investigation, which would have to await the next mail, and another week's delay. Having previously aroused suspicions, he now transformed them into implicitly provable accusations. He implied that the promised future evidence would prove them decisively.

Di Gennaro's second letter claimed that within hours of the blaze, he had seen to the most pressing task of collecting the fugitive nuns, who had taken refuge with relatives. For safekeeping, he deposited them at Santa Maria della Vittoria, under the watchful eye of ever-diligent Mother Maria Padiglia, who by now had risen to the rank of abbess. Immediately, the fire struck di Gennaro as suspicious. He learned that when the flames were still catching hold, before they had even spread widely, the sisters had simply fled! They had not even rung the bell or sounded any sort of alarm. He charged Mother Maria, in utmost secrecy, to keep her ears open. He was determined to discover what had really happened on the night of May 2.

It took almost no time for the truth to come out. A penitent nun revealed to the abbess at Santa Maria della Vittoria that back in February Sister Giovanna Monsolino, the founder's niece and San Niccolò's subprioress, had proposed burning the place down. She claimed that was the only way the nuns could escape the religious life and fulfill a common longing to return to their families. In fact, this bold proposal went down well among the sisters, but the plan seemed too horrible to face at that moment. But on May 2, the eve of the feast of the Invention of the Holy Cross, they torched the place and fled.

Given his estimation of the enormity of the crime, perhaps "without precedent in the whole of Christendom," di Gennaro figured he had best consult the archbishop of Messina. That would justify his developing strategy and provide someone to share responsibility should anything go awry. The prelate from across the strait declined to put anything in writing, but Reggio's vicar-general and di Gennaro's envoy to Messina, brought back his views. Di Gennaro should investigate and imprison the worst offenders—but not all twelve nuns. Recognizing the extreme gravity of the offense, the archbishop of Messina advised di Gennaro to inform the Sacred Congregation about it only "as an absolute, proven fact."

On May 12–13, di Gennaro interrogated the nun who had told all to Mother Maria Padiglia. For confirmation, he also questioned four other nuns and the convent servants. "They all testified the very same thing, with various other details, as Your Excellencies will see from the information I shall send in the next mail." In light of such overwhelming testimony, di Gennaro imprisoned Sister Giovanna Monsolino, the subprioress, "as the authoress of this evil, and most guilty of them all." He also incarcerated her sibling co-conspirator, Anna Monsolino, as well as Sister Felicità Rota and Sister Maria Oliva, "who, having participated in the crime with the others, also covered it up."[10]

A third week passed before the archbishop sent off his evidence to support this "absolute, proven fact" of arson. Di Gennaro's final installment consisted of a notarized complete transcript of his interrogation, carried out at a grilled window beside the altar in the chapel of Santa Maria della Vittoria. Matteo di Gennaro played inquisitor, while the vicar-general of Reggio carefully recorded every word.

Any good inquisitor knew that the questions he asked influenced the answers he received. To create an impression of impartiality, such interrogations ordinarily followed an established protocol, whether conducted before the Holy Office of the Inquisition or before a local bishop. First the inquisitor would draw up a list of questions. Then he would undertake interviews with the most senior members of the community. Working systematically downward through more junior members, the inquisitor asked the same questions. Finally he would end with the servants of the house. The archbishop of Reggio began his questions with the nun most ready to accuse the subprioress. Subsequently he chose witnesses selectively rather than inclusively. Acting outside the usual protocol, such a process might suggest to the onlooker that di Gennaro's conclusions would be foregone.

Predictably, di Gennaro's vague opening gambits (textbook examples for such interrogations) provoked evasive answers. "Why are you standing at the grilled windows of this convent, before me, and in the presence of my vicar-general?"

"I was summoned by the abbess, and in holy obedience, I came."

"Do you know, or could you guess, why you were summoned, and the reasons for this investigation?"

Every single witness—even those ready to tell all—answered, we must assume disingenuously, "I wouldn't know, My Lord." Equally disingenuously, di Gennaro continued, "If, as you say, you are a Dominican nun at the convent of San Niccolò di Strozzi, how can it be that you now find yourself in the Benedictine convent of Santa Maria della Vittoria?" This query finally got the ball rolling. Its obvious answer would lead to the whys and wherefores of the blaze that swept through San Niccolò.[11]

Sister Maria's original confidante wasted no words when di Gennaro commanded, "Tell me truthfully how the fire started in the convent of San Niccolò di Strozzi." She reported that the subprioress, Sister Giovanna Monsolino, had told the nuns they must burn the place down if they truly wanted to go home. Then, no longer bound by the rule of monastic enclosure, they would be able to rejoin their families. Sister Giovanna took a poll, and the ayes carried the day. "But because it seemed such an evil deed, we did nothing for the moment." Two and a half months later, on May 2, Sister Giovanna and Sister Felicità Rota bought several bundles of *deda* (an extremely flammable fatwood). They took them to the attic, where they also smeared the beams and some dried canes with oil and pig grease. That evening Giovanna told the nuns to bring their important belongings downstairs. Then she set the fire and the nuns fled, sometime between 9:00 and 10:00 p.m.[12]

The archbishop's subsequent witnesses rang the changes on this tune. When the second witness proved slightly more reluctant than the first, di Gennaro began to lead her. "*Who* torched the convent, and why?" Well, she had not actually *seen* who started the fire, but she had taken part in Sister Giovanna's preliminary conspiracy and had observed the anointing of the wood with oil and pig grease. Spinning the coda in her favor, she volunteered, "When I saw Sister Giovanna getting ready, and stuff being brought downstairs, I went into the convent's little garden, where I covered my head with a cloth, because I was very sad at the thought of the impending fire, and I said my prayers."[13]

Only after two further witnesses, whose comparative youth might have left them a bit less discreet than other sisters, did the archbishop finally call Mother Maria Maddalena Monsolino before him. He would subsequently describe her as "old, half dotty, and incapable of governing." Di Gennaro introduced a new line of questioning into this interview: "Did any nuns resist coming to Santa Maria della Vittoria?"

"Sister Giovanna Monsolino didn't want to come here. When the vicar-general called her to come along—she was a professed nun and couldn't remain outside the cloister—Sister Giovanna repeatedly clamped down on her throat to choke herself—squeezing her throat repeatedly in desperation, trying to strangle herself, because she never wanted to come here. Then, as we proceeded through the streets to this convent, she continued to cry out and weep."

Giovanna's hearsay confession to the prioress also helped build di Gennaro's case. On the day of the fire, "toward evening Sister Giovanna Monsolino told me that later that night they would do something frightful. But I shouldn't be afraid. After I'd gone to bed, around three hours after dark, the others called me and told me to get dressed because the convent was on fire. And when I was dressed I started to cry and to bang my head on the walls. And Sister Giovanna told me to calm down, because she'd set fire to the convent."[14]

Maria Maddalena's older cousin, the only other senior nun, portrayed herself as the mature voice of reason. "I said the plan didn't seem feasible, because, if our convent burned down, they'd just take us all to Santa Maria della Vittoria. But Sister Giovanna Monsolino said that wasn't so. Because we're nuns under the rule of Saint Dominic, and the nuns at Santa Maria della Vittoria are under the rule of Saint Benedict."

"Then how did the convent fire happen?"

"I was sick in bed, and Sister Giovanna Monsolino, the subprioress, came and told me that she wanted to torch the convent that evening. I pleaded with her to have pity on me for that one night. Because I was sick in bed, it would be hard for me to get up and leave with the others. Couldn't she put it off to another day? Sister Giovanna answered, 'If I don't do it today, I'll never do it!' About three hours after nightfall I heard the nuns screaming 'Fire! Fire!' The fire had already spread to the roof. I got dressed and found the other nuns waiting to leave the cloister. So I suggested that we should withdraw to another part of the convent. But they told me the fire was already catching all over. No place would be safe. And so they all left. And I left last of all."[15]

In a return to the standard protocol, Archbishop di Gennaro saved the best for last. He turned his attentions to the convent servants. Experienced investigators knew that servants, who were largely ignored by their superiors and virtually invisible to them, actually saw and heard everything. When called to testify before their betters, they apparently enjoyed their moment in the limelight. A twenty-two-year veteran servant provided an enthusiastic, matter-of-fact account. She neatly confirmed previous testimony but also described additional accelerants used in the fire: "bunches of cane that help us raise silkworms, and also some silkworm cocoons." Further, this servant illuminated the complicity of her mistresses: when the old prioress started crying and banging her head on the walls, the nuns told her, "'Don't get so upset—we're here for you. The convent belongings will all be yours. Because you're the primary and closest living relative to the founder.' And they told me, 'You don't need to confess this—it isn't a sin. Because you're a servant, required to obey whatever we command you to do.'"[16]

The second servant nun confirmed her predecessor's account almost by rote. In turn, she revealed that the nuns had gone so far as to drag their belongings downstairs back in February but then decided to postpone the deed. Her description offers a distinctly below-stairs perspective:

> To execute their plan they got their things out of the convent. But since they didn't follow through at that time, they had us carry all their stuff back inside. But on Tuesday, May 2, at around three hours after dark, they set the fire. But I didn't actually see them anoint the loft, though I did see some grease on the floor, and at first I thought that some pot full of it had fallen and broken. And that same evening we also carried stuff downstairs, before the fire started, and that day we had also carried other things down. Then, about three hours past sunset, though I still hadn't finished carrying all the stuff downstairs, Sister Giovanna Monsolino, with Sister Anna Monsolino, her sister, went up to set fire under the roof. But I didn't see them set the fire because, as I keep saying, I was still carting off all their things. And since I said that we could suffer for this deed, Sister Giovanna told me, "You can't suffer because you'll be coming home with us."[17]

Torching their convent to escape monastic enclosure is doubtless an extraordinarily audacious act. The archbishop's assessment might even be justified—truly "without precedent in the whole of Christendom." Yet, it evinced a certain logic. Acceptable justifications for breaking the rule of female monastic enclosure included war, pestilence, and fire. Some nuns at San Niccolò might have heard how the nuns of Reggio had abandoned their convents and fled to Messina in 1594 during the worst Turkish raids, which had left many buildings as smoldering ruins. In the absence of foreign invasion or pestilence in 1673, fire remained the nuns' best option.

At the same time, events after the Turkish attack confirmed the older, wiser nun's explanation for why the plot would never work. The fugitive nuns from 1594 had before long been returned to Reggio and enclosed in Santa Maria della Vittoria. But Sister Giovanna's retort—that they wouldn't be taken there because they followed a different monastic rule—also had historical justification. Santa Maria della Vittoria had originally been built to replace convents that followed a Greek monastic rule. Any nun who declined to switch religious orders had the option of returning to her family. Of the six who returned home, one had been a Porzia Monsolino.

Archbishop di Gennaro's interrogation concluded late on May 13. He immediately imprisoned the four worst offenders, Giovanna Mansolino and her sister Anna, plus Maria Oliva and Felicità Rota. All four had, of course, been ignored during the hearing that condemned them. Di Gennaro's strategy to deny the accused any voice should have elicited frowns within the Sacred Congregation. However guilty they might be, the women should have been heard. At the least, they should have been given the chance to confess. Or their denials could have been countered by others' testimony—that was standard procedure, after all. Even the much maligned Holy Office took great pains to hear the accused. Ultimately, di Gennaro's single-minded strategy probably did him harm among cardinals in Rome, who might otherwise have been naturally disposed to believe him.

"DESPERATE HOPELESSNESS CAUSED THEM TO LOSE HEART IN A SIMILARLY DESPERATE ACT"

Monsignor di Gennaro's strategy did not go unnoticed in the aristocratic houses of Reggio, where the imprisoned nuns found a voice. San Niccolò was tightly knit into the social fabric of local gentry. There is no evidence that local nobility, who took matters of honor seriously, perceived the nuns' singular behavior as a blot on family honor or on the city's reputation. They lined up squarely behind the alleged arsonists and against the clerical outsider. If local good names were sullied, he would be held accountable.

Even before the archbishop mailed off the results of his investigation, Count Francesco Domenico Barone of Reggio had written his own letter to the secretary of the Sacred Congregation. The Barone clan ranked among Reggio's prominent families. Piazza "de Barone" served as a regular public meeting place. One Francesco Domenico Barone served three terms as a syndic, in charge of city government, during this generation. Barone had in fact made a cameo appearance at the height of the present drama. The abbess testified that during the public spectacle of Sister Giovanna's attempted self-strangulation, Francesco Domenico Barone had stepped in to reassure the subprioress that "she would not be persecuted for any reason."[18]

In his letter to the Sacred Congregation, Barone proposed a brilliant alternative explanation for the conflagration. "The common report here is that these little ladies were making silkworm beds, which requires continual fires. And because these silkworm beds are made from dry canes, an extremely flammable material, at least three or four such mishaps happen here every year. So their plight has prompted only the greatest sympathy throughout the city."[19]

With this statement Barone acted as a superb defense lawyer. But for the unfortunate eyewitness testimony, the Sacred Congregation would likely have found his explanation entirely convincing. For centuries Calabria had been a leading center for raising mulberry leaves to nurture the worms that produced raw silk for export, through Messina and Naples, to the mills of northern Italy. Everyone knew that the entire local population, rich or poor, took part, including the nuns of San Niccolò. The city's economy rested primarily on this industry.

We often associate nuns with such refined aspects of silk as weaving, needlework, or embroidery (which we shall encounter in the next chapter). But the initial stage in the silk industry, sericulture, was an avocation entirely appropriate to Reggio's upper-crust women, cloistered or not. Gentry throughout Europe dabbled in raising silkworms. From the Marchioness Barbara of Brandenburg and Duchess Bianca of Monferrato in the 1400s to Zoë, Lady Harte Dyke of England in the 1930s and 1940s, sericulture remained a pastime widely pursued at exalted, as well as commoner, levels of society.[20]

Naturally the church hierarchy regularly fretted about animals within cloisters, particularly male animals, because they might encourage sensuality. But prelates could hardly object to these squirming, pale bluish white creatures, particularly since their silk generated income and sericulture occupied idle hands. Going back to Diego Strozzi's involvement in the silk business, might his monastic foundation have filled economic as well as pious needs? Perhaps not only did San Niccolò serve as a warehouse for his unmarried female relatives, but for at least four months a year sericulture made it a sanctified sweatshop, in the service of his male relations and their business interests.

As a matter of fact, the attic along strada Maestra offered an ideal space for sericulture. Some silkworm-raising families added similar attics to their dwellings specifically for this purpose. Such space provided ample room for tier upon tier of tightly packed lightweight silkworm beds; anywhere from forty to a hundred beds might be crammed into an attic. They were woven of dry cane, on which the single-minded eating machines could be fed their perpetual fare of mulberry leaves. Dried branches, on which the caterpillars subsequently spun their cocoons, stood upright against the walls or could be squeezed between the beds. In short order, masses of these dry twigs were covered with fuzzy white nests.

The enforced quiet of a monastic environment discouraged sudden noises, which many believed put silkworms off their feed. In an ironic reversal, the sound of hundreds upon hundreds of munching caterpillars—like a heavy rain on forest branches—may even have soothed their cloistered keepers during quiet breaks in their own less twiggy beds downstairs.

To maintain appropriate temperatures early in the growing season, fires in several small fireplaces around the silkworms' quarters were essential. Thus the attic at San Niccolò was well-nigh perfect for sericulture in almost every way. But it was also a conflagration waiting to happen. The outbreak of the blaze on May 2 fit conveniently into the silkworm-raising season from April to July. By May all of Reggio was so seriously engaged in the intense phase of sericulture that important government decision making was customarily postponed until June, lest too few people turn up to voice an opinion.

Perhaps it was more the season than the horrible prospect of the deed that explains why the nuns delayed putting their plan into action for two and a half months. In May the attic would be filled with the requisite flammable materials. Perhaps Cavalier Barone was not the only one to hit upon sericulture as the perfect cover for arson. If

4.
Exclusus ouo rite vermis, ocyus Texit suam moro insidens telam arbori.

FIGURE 3.3 Jan Van der Straet, *Vermis sericus* (Antwerp, 158[?]). Beinecke Rare Book and Manuscript Library, Yale University. Women raising silkworms in the 1580s: tiers of silkworm beds fill the room on the left; branches to accommodate cocoons lean against the right wall.

all the nuns had been as tough-minded as Sister Giovanna Monsolino and kept their mouths shut in the face of di Gennaro's inquiries, the explanation might even have won the day.

Having laid the groundwork for doubting the sisters' witting culpability, Barone next countered the archbishop's accusations. Barone claimed that some wrong-minded sisters, provoked by intramural dissension, had given the archbishop the misleading impression that the fire was no accident. Then the prelate overreacted so excessively against the alleged arsonists that word of his response "went around the entire city, where it is fomenting rebellion among all the nuns' relatives, for such a blot on their reputations."

In his final defense of these noble ladies, Barone shed his velvet gloves and questioned di Gennaro's own motives. He asserted that the archbishop had never forgiven the nuns for testifying against him in a suit shortly after his arrival in the diocese. The prelate might therefore have conveyed "certain dark insinuations" to the Sacred Congregation against "the reputation of twelve ladies whose families constitute our highest nobility. Considering what I have conveyed to you with utmost confidence, you may restore the reputation of an entire city."[21]

As if to confirm Barone's claim of genteel rebellion, the post also brought a letter to the Sacred Congregation from brothers of the incarcerated Maria Oliva. They seconded Barone's claim that the fire had been accidental: "The silkworm beds and canes caught fire and burned so fiercely that the nuns living there could scarcely be saved." Then the brothers launched a frontal assault. The nuns had been forced to take the archbishop to court after he had appropriated convent funds for his personal use. His selfish act had driven the starving nuns to desperation. "So the notion spread around the city that the fire, which started by accident, might have resulted from desperation, and from the ill treatment the nuns had received at the prelate's hands."

The archbishop had resorted to chains and manacles to coerce a few into incriminating the four alleged arsonists. His motivation and the brothers' coup de grace: the archbishop did so "to avoid being punished himself for having expropriated the convent's earnings for his own use, and in order to trample upon these nuns, whom he especially dislikes, and whom some say he wants to cause to die in prison."[22]

The final salvo against Archbishop di Gennaro was launched by none other than the two aristocratic syndics for 1672–73, Giovanni Domenico Bosurgi and Giovanni Filippo Battaglia. Their letter reverently addressed "the Most Eminent Lord Cardinal Altieri, Rome," which surely provoked patronizing chuckles among cardinals of the Sacred Congregation. Cardinal Altieri had indeed served as the Congregation's secretary during the 1660s. He had given up such low-level posts, however, when he was elected pope in 1670. At the time the syndics of Reggio wrote to him at the Sacred Congregation, he reigned as Pope Clement X. News apparently did not always travel fast between Rome and the hinterlands of Reggio Calabria.

Inflammatory language might naturally be expected from Maria Oliva's offended brothers. But the syndics also pulled no punches. The vehemence of the nuns' accusations in the earlier suit before the apostolic delegate had driven di Gennaro to a string of vengeful acts, they asserted. First, the archbishop forbade anyone—even brothers and sisters—to visit the convent parlatorio. He assigned the women confessors of ignoble birth and vile behavior, which drove the nuns to desperation. Like Barone, the syndics laid the blame at the archbishop's feet—at least indirectly. "Even if it might possibly be true—as some suppose—that they acted in response to Don Matteo di Gennaro's evil treatment, then it was their desperate hopelessness that caused them to lose heart in a similarly desperate act."

Repeatedly citing the dignity and reputation of the city, the syndics urged the immediate rebuilding of San Niccolò. This would free the sisters from Santa Maria della Vittoria, "where the most preeminent of them remain incarcerated, perhaps vilely locked up in chains, but also under the thumb of that abbess, their notorious antagonist (and perhaps a prime player in such embarrassments)." Sometime thereafter, any guilty parties might be appropriately punished. "In this way, not only would the public be satisfied, but great falsehoods would be laid to rest, which might otherwise cause the downfall of our entire city."[23]

The local nobility's verbal assault on the archbishop may sound exaggerated but turns out to have been grounded in fact. Di Gennaro had barely arrived in Reggio when, in June 1661, he was called to Rome to explain offenses and ill usages toward the Holy See's appointed agent in Reggio, "in contempt of this Holy See." Two years later di Gennaro ran afoul of the neighboring suffragen bishop of Bova over matters of ecclesiastical jurisdiction. The bishop of Bova accused di Gennaro of dispatching armed men to remove entrenched and defiant canons of Bova from a church whose diocesan affiliation he contested. In the aftermath of that bloody event, di Gennaro's rival attempted to have Rome excommunicate him. Though that attempt was unsuccessful, one partisan chronicler later claimed di Gennaro's deputy had been imprisoned for life as a result, and the archbishop himself excused only after lengthy imprisonment. Though this account was discredited in the twentieth century, Vatican documents confirm that two years after the bishop of Bova's accusations, Rome did exempt him from di Gennaro's ecclesiastical jurisdiction for five years "because of civil and criminal litigation involving the interests of the bishopric of Bova."

Then, in 1666–67, six years before the fire, the syndics of Reggio, with Francesco Barone among them, filed suit in Naples and Rome against Archbishop di Gennaro for several high-handed actions against local clergy, the cathedral chapter, and members of the laity. He had, for example, commanded abbot Massimiano Turbulo to remove his cherished silver-embroidered *mozzetta* (a short, elbow-length cape reserved exclusively for popes and fashion-minded cardinals) whenever the archbishop was also in attendance at cathedral services. He had disdained Turbulo's earlier special privilege, granted him by the Sacred Congregation of Rites in Rome, to don this particular garment. The suffragen bishop of neighboring Oppido would also petition the Congregation of Rites about di Gennaro's participation in possible violations of the dress code involving the *mozzetta*. In response to the resulting visitation in 1666–67, di Gennaro claimed to have been "slandered for my zeal in bringing those subject to me back to perfection in God's service." He also offered to pay part of the visitor's travel and housing expenses.[24]

The accusation of misappropriation of funds from the convent of San Niccolò, and the nuns' starvation that allegedly resulted, might have figured in the suit filed six years before the fire. But starvation was much more widespread in those years. In 1671–72 famine around Calabria was so severe that Reggio's neighbors in Messina sought to fend off their own starvation by waylaying shipments of grain bound for Reggio. As a result of the famine, more than 4,000 inhabitants of the environs reportedly perished. Although one contemporary chronicler remembered di Gennaro for "showing greatest charity toward the poor, reaching to thousands of scudi, which he handed out to the poor with his own hands"[25] during the famine, ironically, the nuns and their aristocratic supporters laid their own suffering at the archbishop's feet.

Matteo di Gennaro's interrogation of the nuns of San Niccolò incarcerated at Santa Maria della Vittoria reveals that the sisters' long-standing accusations continued to smart. He repeatedly interrupted his interrogation about the fire to ask, "Since you first entered this convent, have you ever lacked any sort of nourishment that was customarily provided?" In response, his carefully chosen witnesses claimed they had wanted for nothing, a phrase di Gennaro carefully underlined in the transcript before he sent it to Rome.

After his initial witnesses had testified, the archbishop also began to ask, "Have the Strozzi convent's earnings ever been used for gifts to anybody, either as sweets or other things?" An obliging witness responded, "My Lord, when you returned to Reggio you promptly passed an edict for the Strozzi convent, forbidding the nuns to give gifts to anybody, not even edibles." The prioress, for her part, also let slip the convent custom of cooking up "mostaccioli and lasagna to give away to outsiders." The implication, of course, is clear. The nuns' own gift giving must account for any drastic shortages at San Niccolò. According to the recorded testimony, rather than causing starvation, di Gennaro had done his best to eradicate its cause: the nuns' own profligacy.[26]

In the course of his questioning, the archbishop also tried to justify his ban on the nuns' contact with outsiders, while also hoping, perhaps, to suggest wider implications. "Did members of the laity frequent the convent while you and the nuns were there before the fire?" The prioress responded that "only Candeloro Battaglia visited without having any kinship ties, and he had contacts with Sister Giovanna Monsolino." Battaglia's name also came up in one convent servant's response to the same question. "I know that Sister Giovanna Mansolino, subprioress, Sister Felicità Rota, Sister Maria Oliva, and Sister Teresa Morabita had dealings with Candeloro Battaglia, who would come to the convent and speak with them at the grates. And one time I saw him eating some little treats they'd given him at the grates."

Di Gennaro pounced on the name of this Candeloro Battaglia. His accusations rival the inflammatory charges in his adversaries' letters. "In my absence for so many years, they got into contact and had dealings with Candeloro Battaglia, a man of the worst character, and a murderer. He, one imagines, was the origin of such an evil stratagem." The local laity seems not to have shared di Gennaro's dim view of Candeloro Battaglia. He was, after all, related to a current syndic of Reggio. They customarily addressed him with the then comparatively rare title "Dottore," and over time they also elected him twice to high office, as a syndic of the city.[27]

By late May the Sacred Congregation confronted a voluminous file, weighed down not only with Archbishop Matteo di Gennaro's damning accusations, but also with the local nobility's comparably damning denunciations against him. Such cases of allegations and counterclaims were the Sacred Congregation's worst administrative nightmare. In implementing the decrees of the Council of Trent, the seventeenth-century Catholic bureaucracy was less monolithic than sometimes imagined. The Sacred Congregation's decrees in most instances were not national or global. For the most part, rulings had to be tailored to different times, places, and situations. The cardinals relied on local bishops to provide a clear analysis of local circumstances before they ruled. Hence the Congregation's most common initial response was, "Write the bishop for information and his opinion."

In this case the counterattack by Reggio's aristocracy may have intensified initial concerns in the Sacred Congregation that the archbishop's own carefully orchestrated interrogation of the nuns allowed the accused no voice at all. Apart from the two oldest nuns in the community, di Gennaro had limited his questioning almost exclusively to a cohort of sisters who were most distantly related to the founder and who had also fled the fire as a group. These women also readily offered each others' names as potential witnesses. Such circumstances strongly suggested exactly the sort of factionalism that the nobles of Reggio alleged in their letters.

Was the archbishop also afraid to risk affording Giovanna Monsolino and her gang of three their day in court over this current offense? His ears had already been scalded when they testified against him before the apostolic delegate in the earlier suit. If he gave the accused an opening, his vicar-general would be required to record their unflattering testimony, and di Gennaro could not have deleted it from the transcript headed for Rome. The wiser course, from his perspective, was to permit no opportunity for their voices to be heard.

Potentially just as disconcerting for the cardinals in Rome, what were they to make of the archbishop's own judgment? Of course, by the early 1670s he already had a certain notoriety within the cardinalate. One might expect outrageous accusations from nuns' family members. But the cardinals had also read di Gennaro's own extraordinary suggestion that a prominent nobleman had incited the nuns to burn down their own convent.

In any case, how the Sacred Congregation ultimately responded in this matter had little to do with judgments of "truth," virtually nothing to do with religion, and a great deal to do with politics. The cardinals chose to proceed as they often did in complex situations—they procrastinated.[28] Perhaps most telling, they seem never to have responded directly to Archbishop di Gennaro again. After bringing the matter to the table in early June, they postponed it until midmonth. Then the Sacred Congregation sidestepped di Gennaro altogether by appointing a special *cardinale ponente*—a very revealing decision. Such an appointment happened only when no prelate directly involved in a case seemed appropriately impartial. The cardinale ponente would examine all the evidence and render judgment to the Congregation. But in this case the cardinale ponente also delayed and delayed—so long, in fact, that he died in September without reaching a decision.

In the waning weeks of 1673, the nuns of San Niccolò, still imprisoned at Santa Maria della Vittoria, petitioned for a replacement cardinale ponente. The matter was then referred to a cardinal who had received his red hat only the week of the previous ponente's demise. In the hubbub of assuming his new powers, this man had too many distractions to pay attention to some nuns down in far-off Calabria. So in late December, the Sacred Congregation had to name a third cardinale ponente.

Word filtered back to the imprisoned Giovanna and Anna Monsolino. Then, for the first time since the fire, we actually hear a word from the accused. Unfortunately, they only sent a brief note to the Sacred Congregation. They had languished in prison for eight months, awaiting some sort of resolution, simply because "some of the nuns blamed them for the fire out of hatred and spite." "Recognizing their own innocence . . . since by now the truth of the matter has clearly come to light," they beseeched the Congregation to request new information or to enjoin di Gennaro or the cardinale ponente, "since the truth has become clear, to render judgment in accordance with justice."[29]

That is all we hear from them. Determinedly they proclaimed their innocence with no hint of remorse or self-justification. We cannot know what they would have made of civic leaders' hints that "their desperate hopelessness caused them to lose heart in a similarly desperate act." Nor can we estimate how much blame civic leaders and family were actually ready to share for that desperation. But the sisters' desperation certainly must have been extraordinary for them to have committed that desperate act.

Giovanna and Anna Monsolino's removal from the world in their teens was never tempered by the strategies or enticements that commonly eased the transition between the world and the cloister in better-established monastic communities. There had been no childhood visits to doting cloistered aunties. They had not abandoned the world and family before forming strong attachments there or before they recognized alternative possibilities for their lives. The Monsolino sisters did not seek—or find—solace in a religious calling. They had lived with the same dozen faces (and perhaps petty personalities) for over twenty years. Silkworm season may have offered the rare distraction from the boredom and loneliness of day-to-day convent life.

For more than a decade of their lives behind the grille, a series of natural disasters played havoc with existence for all of Reggio Calabria: the plague in 1658; the quakes in 1649, 1659, and 1660; a second outbreak of plague in 1668; topped off by Etna's devastating eruption in 1669. The volcano was sixty miles away and on the other side of the strait, but ash clouds affected the mulberry groves, and therefore local sericulture. After short visits in earlier decades, famine settled in to stay in 1672 and did not depart until the 1690s.

For Giovanna and Anna, di Gennaro's arrival in Reggio constituted the final calamity. Accusations of his financial malfeasance aside, the archbishop's apparent approach to convent government further weakened the fabric of San Niccolò's fragile society. Until he banned them (if the allegations are true), family visits effectively counteracted the endemic tedium and isolation of convent life. Good, wise father confessors often had a gentle hand in encouraging community among sisters of the cloth. Ill-chosen confessors could readily prompt favoritism and factionalism inside convent walls. Allegedly di Gennaro sent a plague of the latter to San Niccolò.

During the years when the wider community had attempted unsuccessfully to oppose di Gennaro in Naples and Rome, the nuns of San Niccolò continued to suffer the consequences. What were their options? Earlier in the century, a fiercely independent and intellectual Venetian nun, Arcangela Tarabotti—who without a religious vocation had been forced into a convent—had vented her frustrations with the pen in the treatise *L'inferno monacale* (*The Monastic Inferno*). Confronting a grimmer reality in Reggio than Tarabotti did in Venice and without her substantial literary gifts, Giovanna and Anna

Monsolino enacted an "inferno monacale" of their own, recalling the mouth of Dante's hell.[30]

Finally, cardinale ponente number three rendered an opinion. On January 26, 1674, the Sacred Congregation accepted it (though the cryptic minutes in the Congregation register do not say what that opinion was). But given the leaden feet of his earthly representatives at the Vatican, God seems possibly to have lost patience. Earlier that very week, on January 21, Archbishop Matteo di Gennaro passed to the better life. With due solemnity, he was interred in the lavish marble tomb that had been awaiting him for a decade, appropriately inscribed, "Lest sudden death pluck him unprepared, just as he long ago prepared himself for his tomb, so now he makes ready that tomb for himself. Neither indifferent nor fearful of destiny, as is only right, he erects it while he lives, not to memorialize his name, but his burial. In the year of our salvation 1663." The tomb survives to this day on the south side of the modern cathedral, one of its two most imposing ancient monuments. "Abundant tears of the poor" marked his passing, one chronicler recalled. Whether during the Neapolitan plague of 1658 or the local famine of 1672, di Gennaro's reputation seems to have excelled among those who were neediest and most readily grateful rather than among his peers.[31]

In no time the chapter of Reggio cathedral fulfilled its obligation to elect a vicar capitular to run things until Rome could appoint a new archbishop. The cleric the chapter elected to fill di Gennaro's somewhat scuffed shoes was his old adversary (over fashion, at least) Massimiano Turbulo, who presumably donned his cherished *mozzetta* again in triumph.

With Matteo di Gennaro in a better place, Rome concentrated on reestablishing friendlier relations with the laity of Reggio. Whatever the actual circumstances of the fire—and presumably few set much store by the Monsolino sisters' protestations of innocence—nothing could be gained by carrying on with the futile attempts to crack down on the women of San Niccolò. That would surely drive a wider wedge between the Curia and Reggio's independent-minded first families.

Most likely, the Roman outsiders' final assessment ran something like: The late archbishop had always acted stiffly and uncharitably toward his enemies. He was also prone to singular accusations against them. At the same time, while one expects peasants regularly to burn down their barns, chicken houses, and outhouses by trying to raise silkworms in them, gentry really ought to have more sense than to fill their attics with dried branches and cane, then light stoves around the room. Nonetheless, the cardinals in Rome may have thought, it was Calabria, after all!

In March 1674 the Congregation commanded Vicar Capitular Turbulo to release the nuns still under lock and key at Santa Maria della Vittoria. He was also instructed to provide the cardinals with an update on the convent's rebuilding. Turbulo freed the nuns and assured Rome that by next August he hoped San Niccolò would be complete again. After Turbulo sent them a gentle reminder in August, the Sacred Congregation ordered him to grant the nuns formal absolution and left him to pick out an appropriate penance for them.

Fate seemed finally to smile a bit on the sisters of San Niccolò di Strozzi. But not, it seems, on the rival house of Santa Maria della Vittoria. Mother Maria Padiglia wrote to the Sacred Congregation herself in late summer of 1674 that her Benedictines had been putting up with these recalcitrant Dominicans for fifteen months. In the meantime, the vicar capitular certainly seemed to have been dragging his feet. "In fact, they have not even begun to take the necessary steps for the rebuilding." No doubt the best that cardinals in Rome might hope for between the sisters of San Niccolò and their reluctant hostesses was an uneasy peace. And as it turned out, the unsettled condition would continue much longer.[32]

Eighteen months more passed. This time the new abbess of San Niccolò wrote, for the old abbess for life, Mother Maria Maddalena Monsolino, had joined Monsignor di Gennaro in that better place. Now the petitioner was none other than the nun arsonist Giovanna Monsolino, on whom the role of abbess had devolved at her aunt's death. The sisters of San Niccolò were still abiding at Santa Maria della Vittoria because funds for the rebuilding had run out. To finance the rest of the job, the Sacred Congregation granted permission to sell off some convent property.

Almost three years to the day after the fire, Reggio's new archbishop wrote to the Sacred Congregation with good news for all involved. Despite uncertainties provoked by continued hostilities between Spain and France during the year since he took office, the archbishop had expedited the convent's completion, since "scant peace can be maintained between them [the nuns, not Spain and France] with almost daily unrest." The nuns' return to San Niccolò was imminent, he reported.

When the nuns reentered the restored cloister at San Niccolò di Strozzi a few weeks later, they were led yet again by a member of the Padiglia family, "endowed with exemplary devoutness and administrative talent," in charge for as long as the archbishop required. It is likely that the archbishop deemed prioress pro tem Giovanna Monsolino inappropriate for the permanent job, given her past leadership style. So the Monsolino sisters and their various cousins settled back into their accustomed surroundings on strada Maestra. Outside the cloister, Reggio carried on, but literally as an armed camp, because it had become the center of Spanish operations as the conflict with France over Messina continued disorder in the region until 1678. Within the walls of San Niccolò, something similar may have prevailed, or at best the nuns may have brought home the uneasy peace that reigned at Santa Maria della Vittoria. After all, Giovanna and Anna Monsolino, as well as their two co-conspirators, now had no choice but to readjust to life in close quarters with the rival sisters who had spilled everything to Archbishop di Gennaro.[33]

But in 1680, whatever rivalries persisted, the whole community of San Niccolò closed ranks against a common enemy, as evinced by yet another letter from the prioress to the Sacred Congregation.

> This convent was founded with the express prohibition not, in any circumstances, to admit girls on payment of a dowry, but only to admit the founder's kin. We now hear that many other sorts of girls demand admittance here. Because the convent is constricted and incapable of accommodating them—and because it violates the founder's prohibition—it would provoke the greatest inconvenience here. Moreover, there are in this city two other convents that accept the commoner sorts of girls, with dowries. We therefore humbly beseech Your Excellencies to order Monsignor the Archbishop not to make changes of any sort against our founding statutes.

FIGURE 3.4 "Vue de la Ville de Regio . . . detruite par le terrible tremblement de terre . . . 1783." Photograph: M.-C. Thompson, the Jan Kozak Collection, PEER, University of California, Berkeley. This roughly contemporary engraving attempts to depict the cataclysm as it was happening, without faithfully reproducing exact details of Reggio's cityscape.

If it had been revealed to them, the nuns of San Niccolò would have been infuriated to learn that their late adversary, Archbishop di Gennaro, had tossed around the same idea in 1673: "It would offer great relief if the founder's wishes were set aside, permitting other girls, from other families, to become nuns, on payment of a dowry. This would augment convent earnings, and perhaps establish greater piety." Certainly Diego Strozzi—not to mention many other Catholic benefactors—would have been surprised to learn how carelessly Rome might dispense with requirements of their bequests to the church, for all the best reasons. In 1680, however, the Sacred Congregation chose to preserve the status quo.[34]

After 1680 the flood of paperwork, having dwindled to a trickle since 1676, dries up. Throughout most of the next century, the convent endured as an exclusive residence for genteel women. By the 1750s its numbers had swelled to twenty-nine sisters, pupils, and servants. But the earthquake of 1783, which left most of Reggio in rubble, changed things almost overnight.

Nature succeeded where the Monsolino sisters had failed a century earlier. Their convents partially in ruins, the nuns of Reggio were sent away by the archbishopric—in some cases under duress—to live with their families, whose homes were often in no better shape than the convents. A dozen years later, the divine irony cranked up another notch. In 1796 authorities dictated that the remaining nuns of San Niccolò, their once-restored home in strada Maestra now beyond repair, should be taken in again by Santa Maria della Vittoria. In that way their old Benedictine rivals would reap the benefit of Strozzi's endowment.

Any Dominicans who refused the Benedictine rule received a pitiful allowance to keep them with their families. Although some sisters stayed home, a few entered Santa Maria della Vittoria, only to depart quickly when they discovered its pitiable state, fully twelve years after the quake.

Unlike its buildings on strada Maestra, Diego Strozzi's century-old endowment for San Niccolò remained largely intact and yielded a windfall for the Dominicans' old rivals. As the century closed, die-hard local aristocrats clamored for San Niccolò's restoration as an exclusive haven for their daughters. In fact, no fewer than eighty-one members of the Calabrian gentry signed a petition to that effect in 1799.

The old San Niccolò had been knocked down, of course. But the Benedictines of Santa Maria della Vittoria had only just moved from their dilapidated buildings into newly refurbished quarters, which civil and church authorities simply confiscated from the Friars Minor Conventual of San Francesco di Assisi and handed over to them. The church hierarchy also chose that moment to pass along the Benedictine's broken down, hand-me-down cloister, in turn, to the Strozzesche, who managed to scrape together funds from the sale of the former site of San Niccolò for some sort of rebuilding.

In consequence, a few nuns formerly of San Niccolò di Strozzi found their way, one more time, to old Santa Maria della Vittoria, which would serve as their last refuge. Longtime aristocratic enthusiasms, no matter how firmly held, would ultimately prove no match for the vicissitudes of early ottocento Calabria. By 1806, in fact, the numbers at this latter-day Santa Maria become San Niccolò had dwindled to thirteen: five nuns, five students, and three servants. They vanish completely from the historical record during the social depredations at the end of the decade.

We do know that one last aging Strozzesca, a Sister Colomba Dainotto, chose instead to live out her days not at the resuscitated San Niccolò but amid the consolations, however limited, of her own family.[35] For better or worse, her like-minded predecessors from 1673, Giovanna and Anna Monsolino and their fellow arsonists, might have understood her motives. Apparently, 130 years made less difference in the lives of churchwomen than those of us who have never lived inside a cloister might suppose.

4

PERILOUS PATRONAGE: GENEROSITY AND JEALOUSY

Santa Maria Nuova (Bologna, 1646–80)

In artistic matters, Bologna's Dominican convent of Santa Maria Nuova was largely eclipsed by such equally select convents as Sant'-Agnese, Santa Cristina, or Santi Naborre e Felice. On Joan Blaeu's detailed bird's-eye view of the city, *Theatrum civitatum et admirandorum Italiae* (1663), no fewer than nineteen other convents were carefully identified for potential visitors. But Blaeu overlooked Santa Maria Nuova (though its buildings are clearly visible).

When Carlo Cesare Malvasia compiled his seventeenth-century guide to Bologna's artistic treasures, *Le pitture di Bologna*, he tarried in Santa Maria Nuova's external church only long enough to list three or four paintings (all lost) by artists only art historians are likely to recognize. Alessandro Tiarini's *Ecce Homo* rated a star in the guidebook, but Malvasia warned it would soon be replaced by a new work. Subsequent editions of *Le pitture* disparage the replacement. Two of the church's side altars apparently contained nothing at all. Perhaps Malvasia was in a rush to get to the convent of the Convertite around the corner, with Ludovico Carracci's sublime *Madonna dei Bargellini*. Santa Maria Nuova's artworks simply couldn't measure up. The most familiar "artistic" distinction attributed to the nuns of Santa Maria Nuova may well have been the confection of thin, flat marzipan candies that could be mistaken for Bologna sausage.[1]

One of the dozen more venerable female monasteries in Bologna, Santa Maria Nuova liked to trace its origins back to AD 992—the date Malvasia cites—though the earliest surviving documents in the convent archive date from 1279.[2] Until Napoleon's suppression of convents in 1799, Santa Maria Nuova stood in the borgo delle Lame, along via Riva di Reno (at modern number 72, now the Cineteca di Bologna), between via delle Lame and via Azzo Gardino. Eventually its church would face the Canale di Reno, from which water was diverted for the large field and ample, pleasant gardens within the convent walls. Nothing of the old convent remains today. Taken over by tobacco processors in the nineteenth century, the buildings were gravely damaged by Allied bombing late in World War II and subsequently demolished.

In 1574, when the Bolognese church hierarchy began its attempts to bring female monasteries into line with reforms of the Council of Trent, Santa Maria Nuova housed 87 professed nuns, 17 above the number church authorities prescribed for it at that time. It had burgeoned to 135 women (96 professed, 25 converse, and 14 students) by 1639, when our story begins in earnest. Obviously the archbishop's membership quota had little effect during that half century. Even forty years later, when our story ends, their number had diminished only to 91 (56 professed, 19 converse, 11 students, and 5 other residents who had not taken vows).[3]

Throughout most of its history, Santa Maria Nuova enjoyed little more distinction for music than for the visual arts. Various chronicles that describe festivals and services in Bolognese palaces, churches, and monasteries during the sixteenth and seventeenth centuries hardly ever mention Santa Maria Nuova, apart from infrequent visits there by the *Madonna di San Luca*. This painting of the Blessed Virgin, attributed to the gospel-writing artist Saint Luke, regularly toured the city every spring (she still does, in fact), inevitably calling in at several convents, which did their best to entertain her with music and ceremony.

Music must not have received much encouragement at Santa Maria Nuova. A brief discourse on the subject, included in a "selection of the most important memoranda for nuns, whether prioresses or abbesses" from the archive, seems to have been taken seriously.

Of religious women, Jesus Christ does not require sweetness of voice, but purity of heart. And whoever might be curious to know the evils done to religion by music may consult the *Religious Looking*

FIGURE 4.1 BCB, MS 3574, a seventeenth-century Dominican nun from Santa Maria Nuova, holding marzipan imitations of Bologna sausage. Reproduced with permission of the Biblioteca Comunale dell'Archiginnasio, Bologna.

Glass of Giovanni Pietro Barco: "Whoever sings more to please the public than God sings with Herodias in the palace of Herod. Beguiled by melodious voices, he caused the head of Christ's harbinger [John the Baptist] to be set out amid the delicacies of the banquet."[4]

Yet after a long artistically fallow period, heightened musical activity begins at Santa Maria Nuova in the mid-1640s, continuing through the 1650s and into the 1660s. In 1663 it culminates with the appearance of one of the most elaborate collections of music ever dedicated to a Bolognese nun. Giulio Cesare Arresti's *Messe a tre voci, con sinfonie, e ripieni à placito, accompagnato da motetti, e concerti* honors "the most illustrious lady, the most respected lady and patron, Her Ladyship, Giulia Vittoria Malvezzi." These three masses, six motets, and two sequences for three voices and basso continuo accompaniment stand out from other collections of Bolognese convent music. Remarkably, they include unusually elaborate instrumental *sinfonie* and *concerti*, plus optional violin parts to double the soprano voices.

The musical flowering at Santa Maria Nuova turns out to have its equivalent in other arts as well. The convent's patronage of architecture, for instance, achieves its high point in 1660 with the completion of the much-heralded total reconstruction of the monastery's external church. Thanks to the patronage of another Malvezzi, Donna Maria Vinciguerra, aunt of the younger musical dedicatee, both the sisters and the townspeople could enjoy an impressive new house of worship. This midcentury renaissance—the convent's artistic heyday—would not have happened without the direct participation, influence, and persistence of women from two generations of the Malvezzi family. The productions that survived them (at least for a time, if not down to the present) illustrate the workings of patronage by a single powerful aristocratic family within one convent's walls. At the same time, they reveal how such beneficence could prove a mixed blessing.

For over sixty years, Donna Maria Vinciguerra Malvezzi and her sister Donna Maria Vittoria Felice remained a force at Santa Maria Nuova. The Malvezzi were one of the city's most illustrious families, and their influence came with them to the convent. The women's father, Giacomo Malvezzi (1574–1620), knight of San Biaggio and

Santiago, had served Pope Clement VIII in the takeover of Ferrara in 1597. Subsequently he acted as papal representative to the courts of France, Spain, and Vienna, where he covered himself with glory. Noble and decorated as he was, their father was almost eclipsed by the nuns' illustrious mother, Vittoria, daughter of Antonio, count of Collalto and San Salvatore and brother to Rambaldo di Collalto, knight of the Order of the Golden Fleece, who had been victorious in the imperial takeover of Mantua in 1601.[5] And nobody at Santa Maria Nuova would ever be allowed to forget the Malvezzi nuns' high station.

The family's seventeenth-century connections with Santa Maria Nuova began inauspiciously, to say the least. Maria Vinciguerra's sister, Anna Maria, might have joined her sisters at Santa Maria Nuova too. But when she had been taken to visit the convent at age three, a careless nun had dropped her out of an upstairs window. Her parents therefore decided to enroll her elsewhere, among the Discalced Carmelites of San Gabriele, across town.[6]

Donna Maria Vinciguerra, the donor and prime mover in the lavish rebuilding and decoration of the convent church, is more difficult to identify than her sisters among Giacomo and Vittoria Collalto Malvezzi's offspring. Her name in religion does not appear in the exhaustive genealogy of the Malvezzi family, for example. But probably she is identical with Maria Carola Malvezzi, born to them in 1610 and therefore about the right age. In contrast, we know considerably more about her sister, Donna Maria Vittoria Felice Malvezzi, born in 1605, who professed at Santa Maria Nuova in 1621 shortly after their father's death.

For nuns, the choice of a religious name represented a modest opportunity for a bit of creativity. Newly professed nuns commonly "remade" the name of a deceased mother or aunt as part of their name in religion, combined with the inevitable "Maria." Maria Vittoria Felice's selection obviously honored her mother the countess, still very much alive. Since "Vittoria Felice" also implies "happy victory," perhaps she was also trying to acknowledge the Mantuan successes of her illustrious uncle, to whom she remained close, as we shall see.

Maria Vinciguerra's choice is much more unusual, perhaps even startling for a nun. "Mary, Victorious in Battle" might encompass some play on "Madonna della Vittoria." Since the Madonna of the

Victory was credited with a number of Catholic military successes over the centuries, perhaps Maria Vinciguerra intended another reference to Uncle Rambaldo's victory at Mantua. On the other hand, given her own rather bellicose behavior in subsequent decades, one has to wonder whether she identified herself in her religious name.

Soon after her profession, Donna Vittoria Felice came down with a mysterious malady, apparently of a psychological nature. So severe was her condition, so sinister the nature of the illness, that her recently widowed mother, the countess, built a residence near the monastery from which she looked after her daughter. Beginning in 1625, the Sacred Congregation of Bishops and Regulars received a string of complaints from the nuns about Vittoria Felice's declining health and state of mind. "With her usual fits of illness, she has now reached such a severe state that between day and night she is always out of her head for some nineteen hours. If something isn't done about it, by sending her to recuperate at her mother's home, the nuns fear for her life."

The Sacred Congregation's initial cautious response—that Vittoria Felice should stay inside the convent under the care of special servants—proved ineffective and unacceptable. Within three months, the Congregation yielded to the nuns' insistence. Vittoria Felice could be moved to her mother's residence for up to a year. Yet she still failed to improve. So her uncle Rambaldo Collalto went right to the top. Pope Urban VIII granted Vittoria Felice permission to recuperate at her mother's country residence in Udine, northeast of Venice. This license, initially for a month's sojourn, ultimately extended for two years.

The results were salutary. In June 1628, remarkably restored to health, Donna Vittoria Felice Malvezzi could reenter Santa Maria Nuova. Her mother did not abandon her at the convent doorway, however. She followed her inside and took up official residence there herself. The countess resided at Santa Maria Nuova for another thirty-four years, with special papal permission to take three vacations from clausura annually. When she periodically reentered the cloister, she "was accompanied quite often by the most eminent Lord Cardinal Barberini and courted by all the nobility of Bologna," as the nuns proudly recalled.[7]

Santa Maria Nuova's artistic heyday really got rolling when Donna

Vittoria Felice assumed the position of sacristan. In collaboration with Maria Vinciguerra, she undertook an unprecedented program of musical and artistic adornment for the convent chapel. In 1646 she commissioned an ornate series of embroidered hangings and cloth decorations. This artistic medium had long represented an important aspect of patrician female culture, of course. Needlework offered women distraction and relaxation; at the same time, they could exhibit their taste, wealth, and status. Such refined women's "work" often provided an acceptable means for transferring nobility's preference for lavish display from the secular world to the theoretically less ostentatious cloistered environment.

Needlework also was much more likely to win male religious superiors' praise than other forms of female accomplishment carried over from the world. While nuns might, in effect, embroider their way indirectly into public view, needlework was an approved medium for noblewomen's artistic virtuosity. Though shown publicly to great advantage and admiration, the work of nuns' hands demonstrated female accomplishment humbly, carried out within a sphere even more reclusive than women's quarters within the city's palaces. Most important, by contrast with dangerous forms of self-display such as the printed word or, more dramatically, music, fine needlework was always mute. While the sisters within the cloister might know whose work it was, to the public it usually remained anonymous and could be seen as the product of the entire community's virtuous industry. Unlike music, convent embroidery created no "stars" in the outside world.

The needlework and fabric work of various convents differed, depending primarily on the wealth and social status of the house. For less exalted institutions, it might offer a respectable source of additional income. In the 1580s, for example, nuns from Varese, near Milan, wanted to invite expert laywomen to teach them to weave and work silk as a way out of their house's poverty. Instead, the Sacred Congregation, "for the security of monastic enclosure and for the sake of monastic discipline," would only permit the acceptance of virginal, novice-age girls already expert at working silk. These young women could join the convent and then teach the nuns.

A century later, nuns at the country convent of San Carlo in Guastalla (sixty miles northwest of Bologna) followed the Congregation's approved strategy. They not only admitted young Anna Bolognini from Bologna, expert in the weaving of damask and other forms of silk, but persuaded her father to throw in looms and other silk-working paraphernalia. Within a year the novice, now Sister Maria Felice Bolognini, had adorned the chapel with numerous hangings and had begun to train the nuns for the cottage industry of making damask. Better still, the girl's brother, "a pupil of Guido Reni," agreed to paint a large altarpiece for the public church, gratis, and another for a small oratorio inside clausura.[8]

These nuns had driven an excellent bargain. This pupil of Reni certainly must be the artist's star pupil, Giovanni Battista Bolognini, whose works adorned many Bolognese churches and palaces by the 1660s and reputedly cost as much as a Guercino in their day.[9] In fact, Santa Maria Nuova acquired a Bolognini (*The Dying Saint Dominic with Saints*, including the Blessed Virgin and infant Jesus, Saint Eustace, and Mary Magdalene) for its own external church in 1662.[10] Giovanni Battista Bolognini and his works are still known today, while his talented sister Maria Felice, who brought about improvements at San Carlo, was soon forgotten—at least until now. Surely it is worth remarking upon a female offshoot of the more familiar male artistic family tree. In addition, she stands as an example of the talented and creative woman who constructed a productive life for herself within the restrictive bounds available to her, where she managed to exploit her personal talents.

In fact, Sister Maria Felice's talent and artistry expanded beyond a single branch of the family tree. Not through blood relations but through convent sisterhood, she passed on her skills to her religious family, and in doing so she changed it decisively for the better by enhancing both its artistic reputation and its finances. Also worth noting in connection with Maria Felice is the wisdom of the senior nuns of San Carlo, who recognized the potential for success of a strategy based on traditional women's work. They enlisted Sister Maria Felice to implement their vision and so established a firmer foundation for their community's long-term success. San Carlo offers a concrete demonstration of the often romanticized notion of the convent as a liberating space for female creativity.

At Santa Maria Nuova, the nuns would very likely have thought this sort of fabric work inappropriately close to wage earning. Any work they might do without demeaning themselves had to be defined more clearly in terms of a gift economy. Or, as in the case of Vittoria Felice Malvezzi's tapestries and other fabric ornaments, they paid professional embroiderers to do the work for them. Donna Vittoria Felice commissioned a male professional embroiderer in minor religious orders to undertake her project. The series of opulent wall hangings heavily worked in silver took him ten years to complete. Modern notions of comparative artistic worth would credit the donation of an altarpiece such as Giovanni Battista Bolognini's over Malvezzi's gift of needlework. In Vittoria Felice's day, however, opulent needlework frequently eclipsed a painting in value. Her stipulation of silver thread ensured that they would do so.[11]

Customarily, professional embroiderers first visited their patrons armed with engravings of patterns for them to consider. They would return repeatedly, sorting out how best to personalize standard designs, reworking details of pattern drawing, deciding which of twenty or so stitches best suited what portion of these designs, determining whether finishing materials, including gold and silver thread, met the patron's artistic goals. Monastic enclosure naturally complicated such collaboration between artisan and patron. Bolognese church authorities, with the backing of the Sacred Congregation, almost never looked kindly on requests for a professional embroiderer to visit a local convent. A single surviving license for an aging Bolognese embroiderer to provide a few lessons to a convent *educanda*, or schoolgirl, back in 1605 offers a rare exception to the hard-line policy. In 1646, however, the petitioner was a Malvezzi, who wanted to donate lavishly. Remarkably, her embroiderer gained special dispensation to meet with Donna Vittoria Felice repeatedly over many years.[12] Without a doubt, Malvezzi family prestige and influence opened doors—even convent doors.

During her time as sacristan, Donna Vittoria Felice also turned her attention to singular music. In collaboration with her sister, she initiated a string of elaborate services in 1646 of a sort previously unknown at Santa Maria Nuova. In fact, such elaborate chapel music seems to have been very unusual in all Bolognese convents at that period, given the archbishopric's abiding opposition to it. Back in the early 1620s, Cardinal Archbishop Ludovico Ludovisi had reinstituted stringent bans forbidding nuns to sing anything but plainchant, outlawing performances by lay musicians in convent chapels, and prohibiting lay or religious music teachers to instruct the nuns.[13] Only during the late 1630s, under Ludovisi's successor, do local chroniclers on rare occasions make note of convent performances of polyphony. It appears that the Malvezzi sisters' musical scheme was nicely timed with the arrival of a new archbishop in 1645. Archbishop Niccolò Albergati Ludovisi proved somewhat less restrictive generally in his approach to convents than his late cousin. But Malvezzi family influence may also have been at work: both the new archbishop and the Malvezzi sisters boasted kinship ties to Pope Gregory XV. Thirty-five years later, Maria Vinciguerra would invoke kinship with an earlier Pope Gregory to promote other artistic agendas, as we shall see.

Donna Maria Vinciguerra underwrote the first in this series of lavish liturgical performances at Santa Maria Nuova in 1646. On the feast of the Christianized former Roman general, Saint Eustace (September 20), to whom she was particularly devoted, Maria Vinciguerra paid an ensemble of outside musicians for a beautiful High Mass in the saint's honor. At its conclusion, the eminent and noble celebrant of the Mass—this was absolutely no occasion for the mere father confessor or some hand-to-mouth rent-a-priest to serve as celebrant—made a point of greeting the Malvezzi nuns at the convent doorway and did them other courtesies.

A convent chronicler later recorded that Donna Maria Vinciguerra underwrote a comparably elaborate Mass for Saint Eustace the following year. In the meantime, Vittoria Felice had presented two opulent musical rites of her own. Not to be outdone, during these eighteen months other nuns at Santa Maria Nuova sponsored two more sacred command performances, in friendly emulation of their aristocratic sisters. These half-dozen musical events stand out in an otherwise musically fallow period at the convents of Bologna, rivaled only by a spate of similar services at the convent of San Guglielmo during those same years. Archbishop Albergati Ludovisi eventually put a stop to them by revoking all licenses for music in nuns' external churches just a few weeks before resigning his position in 1651.[14]

Further, the Malvezzi clan was noted for enhancing Santa Maria Nuova's ritual life during these years in ways that brought money to the house's coffers. To encourage visits and donations from the faithful, another Malvezzi, Madre Caterina Verginia Malvezzi, supposedly acquired the body of Saint Eutichio the Martyr, "extracted from Rome's holy sites," and enshrined it in 1655 in Santa Maria Nuova's chapel. Henceforth the saint's feast was celebrated there every December 11. This claim in Antonio di Paolo Masini's *Bologna perlustrata* (1666), a guide to local churches and their feast days, would have surprised prelates at the church of San Lorenzo in Damaso in Rome had they learned of it. For Saint Eutichio had reposed for centuries beneath the high altar there. Santa Maria Nuova's own official history clarifies the mix-up: Madre Costanza Virgilia—not Caterina Verginia—had contributed a *relic*, not the saint's entire body. The important thing was that every December Bolognese indulgence seekers came dutifully to revere Saint Eutichio, whether in whole or in part. Santa Maria Nuova received the visitors' alms, and a Malvezzi got the credit.[15]

The upswing in artistic and musical activity at Santa Maria Nuova received another boost in the 1650s when a new generation of Malvezzi women, Giulia Vittoria and Maria Ermengilda, reached an appropriate age to join their aunts in the convent. The pedigree of this younger generation rivaled that of the senior Malvezzi sisters. Antonio Francesco Malvezzi, their father, served six years at the courts of Philip III and Philip IV of Spain and went on to be named knight of Santiago. In 1627 he also played the role in Bolognese government that was inevitable for scions of the Malvezzi family. Most likely Giulia Vittoria and Maria Ermengilda joined their paternal aunts at Santa Maria Nuova not long after his death in 1654.[16]

Of interest to our story, the first reference to these recent Malvezzi arrivals at the convent concerns music. In 1657 Bolognese prioresses complained directly to the Sacred Congregation (since their current archbishop was out of town) about the local vicar-general's decision to license "various teachers of languages, singing, and playing, of an age inappropriate for such places. These instructors are younger men, which provokes continual scandals for the nuns and the laity alike." The complainants also hinted darkly that the vicar-general might have been bribed to make these concessions. He responded defensively that, of twenty-eight convents in the diocese, only two— Sant'Omobono and Santa Maria Nuova—had received license to admit music teachers, and he suggested that his superior, the absentee archbishop, had granted them. One of the four girls taking lessons at Santa Maria Nuova was a Malvezzi—certainly the twelve-year-old Giulia Vittoria. The vicar-general further pointed out, rather archly, that "as for these teachers' habits, it should be amply evident that fathers of this quality would not assign their daughters to persons who were not above every suspicion."

Once again it is worth noting the singular nature of such licenses in Bologna, where archbishop after archbishop specifically forbade music masters in convents. Apparently the influence of an illustrious family had once again done the trick. It would have been difficult for the latest archbishop, Cardinal Girolamo Boncompagni, to say no not only to Giulia Vittoria Malvezzi's guardian, but also to her illustrious and charming doting grandmother, Countess Vittoria Collalto Malvezzi, still holding court at Santa Maria Nuova when she was not off on vacation. Besides, these Malvezzi women were also Archbishop Boncompagni's relatives, since, as we shall see, Pope Gregory XIII added luster to both family trees. When it came to the wishes of the Malvezzi sisters, the visiting embroiderer from the 1640s ultimately gave way, at least for a time, to the visiting music teacher of the 1650s.

It turns out that the complaint against the vicar-general did not exactly come from various prioresses in the city. As the vicar-general himself points out, "I discovered that some nuns at Santa Maria Nuova (from the former confessor's faction) had claimed there were disturbances and scandals for this particular reason. It is absolutely false. There was no other disruption beyond a little inconvenience to these nuns themselves, who could not be at the grates of the parlatorios when the pupils were receiving lessons."[17] This represents the first—but certainly not the last—evidence of intramural discontent provoked by the artistic and musical endeavors of the Malvezzi family at Santa Maria Nuova. It would also not be the last time an archbishop's absence would require the vicar-general to deal with some crisis. This time he opted to revoke such licenses in future, as he carefully noted to the Sacred Congregation.

Precisely during the period of this first recorded disturbance, the greatest Malvezzi artistic endeavor got under way when Donna Maria Vinciguerra came to serve her term as sacristan. The sacristan's primary responsibility was to oversee the adornment of the church, particularly the external church open to the public. Sacristans looked after altar furnishings, made sure liturgical vestments were ready when the priest arrived for Mass, and performed other such functions that exposed the best face of the convent to the outside world.

These puny notions of a sacristan's duties did not suit Maria Vinciguerra's grander ambitions, which could be satisfied only by pulling down the old church and putting up a new one. As the official convent history records, "Since childhood the Reverend Mother Maria Vinciguerra Malvezzi cherished the holy idea of building anew, and with modern architecture, the external church of Santa Maria Nuova." From the ground up. This would require permission of the Sacred Congregation, of course. Significantly, Maria Vinciguerra wrote to the cardinals in Rome herself, though they might have expected to hear from the prioress, writing on behalf of her community. In Malvezzi's opinion, the old church was run-down and constricted, having only three altars and being oriented in a particularly awkward direction. As the convent chronicle would later put it, "It therefore seemed unbecoming for divine service," at least as far as Maria Vinciguerra was concerned (the identical phrase appears in her petition to the Sacred Congregation).[18]

If we can trust Joan Blaeu's rendering of the unidentified edifice between via Riva di Reno and via Azzo Gardino on his bird's-eye view of the city, Maria Vinciguerra must have had her own notion of "constricted." For the old Santa Maria Nuova church buildings appear almost as substantial as the imposing Abbadia a few blocks away, and they look much grander than the convent of the Convertite just around the corner. But the old sanctuary was oriented roughly east–west, keeping the entrance discreetly on a side street, where it was unlikely to call public attention to the convent. Malvezzi's vision involved tearing down everything, including at least part of the lofty bell tower. The replacement edifice would be turned ninety degrees to put its entrance on the broad thoroughfare bordering the Canale di Reno. Instead of featuring an archaic long, narrow nave, the new external church would adopt the modern style and have a more open plan based on a square. On each side two shallow chapels would articulate the walls, and there would be an impressive high altar several steps up, on the north side of the building.

Most significant, the main southeast entrance would be pushed all

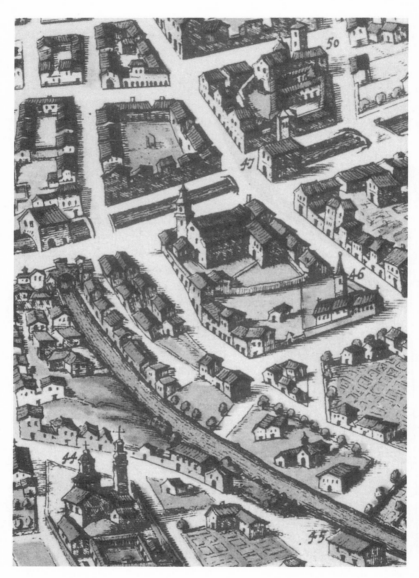

FIGURE 4.2 The old church at Santa Maria Nuova, oriented parallel to the canal and adjoining thoroughfare, from Joan Blaeu's *Theatrum civitatum et admirandorum Italiae* (1663). The Abbadia is number 50 and the Convertite is number 46; Santa Maria Nuova is unnumbered. Reproduced with permission of the Biblioteca Comunale dell'Archiginnasio, Bologna.

the way to the street by removing some old convent buildings. Now their front door would open onto the main thoroughfare and would line up with the bridge that crossed the canal in front of the new edifice. Its facade would not be hidden behind the typical Bolognese portico. Such porticos completely screened other convents such as San Vitale or San Leonardo. "I hear they're all but invisible," Maria Vinciguerra might well have remarked. On the other hand, Corpus Domini's looming facade, across town in via Tagliapietre (though positively medieval according to modern, mid-seventeenth-century tastes), loudly proclaimed that convent's presence to passersby, even forcing them to give way and take to the street. By following a similar model, Maria Vinciguerra's thoroughly contemporary conception for her new church would put Santa Maria Nuova on the map—literally!

It is interesting that eighty years later Cardinal Archbishop Lambertini would reach a similar conclusion about Bologna's cathedral of San Pietro. For centuries it had been eclipsed by the basilica of San Petronio only two blocks farther south in Piazza Maggiore. To give the cathedral a more public face, Lambertini tore down a fifteenth-century portico that obscured San Pietro and pushed the cathedral's new modern facade right out to the street, as Maria Vinciguerra Malvezzi had done at Santa Maria Nuova. In this instance, though, it didn't quite work. To this day, tourists walk right past the duomo's facade abutting via dell'Independenza as they aim their video and cell-phone cameras at Giambologna's Neptune fountain up ahead of them in Piazza Maggiore. Then they ask to be pointed toward "the duomo"—intending, of course, to have a look at San Petronio, not San Pietro.

But eighty years before Lambertini would vainly attempt to put a better front on San Pietro, Maria Vinciguerra obtained necessary permission from the Sacred Congregation and Bolognese archbishop Girolamo Boncompagni to begin rebuilding the convent church. Santa Maria Nuova's chronicle records that the archbishop was thoroughly delighted with the whole undertaking. "Often he visited personally to view the construction, loudly commending such a praiseworthy idea, and encouraged the progress with paternal persuasion." With financial assistance from her mother the countess (past eighty now, but still resident within the convent precincts), Maria Vinciguerra

FIGURE 4.3 Maria Vinciguerra Malvezzi's new church for Santa Maria Nuova, now facing the canal, on Gnudi's 1702 plan. Reproduced with permission of the Biblioteca Comunale dell'Archiginnasio, Bologna.

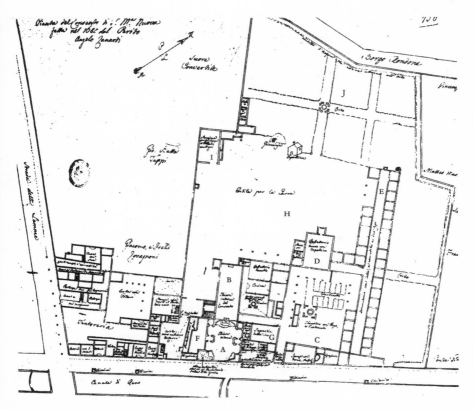

FIGURE 4.4 BCB, MS G170, cartel. 23–150. The convent of Santa Maria Nuova, ca. 1680. Reproduced with permission of the Biblioteca Comunale dell'Archiginnasio, Bologna. A, new external church; B, nuns' inner chapel; C, cloister; D, new refectory and small chapel; E, dormitory with individual cells; F, main parlatorios; G, sacristy; H, courtyard for supply wagons; I, woodshed and chicken house; J, fields and orchards.

paid the entire cost of construction. As an institution, Santa Maria Nuova need not spend a farthing on the project.[19]

But clearing the way for the new construction did not go quite as smoothly as the official convent history might suggest. Within months some disgruntled nuns quietly petitioned the Sacred Congregation to rescind permission for Maria Vinciguerra to rebuild the external church. They complained that her scheme would be "detrimental to many of them by rendering two of the best cells useless, as well as the sacristy, parlatorios, and rooms for fermentation [? *stanze de gassi*]. Besides stirring up dissension and trouble among the nuns, it is also against the most holy and right mind of His Holiness. He urges the cutting off of superfluous expenses, caused everywhere by convent sacristans."

Having thus implied that Maria Vinciguerra was part of a typical problem that commonly plagued convents, they went on to observations about such sacristans' character. "If one pauses to consider their methods for amassing so much money, one will clearly discover that these nuns must be lending money, selling resources and credits, maintaining outside friendships, and committing other improprieties that compromise their vows and their rules." Money, after all, is at the root of all evil, perhaps even when it is being spent in rebuilding God's house. At least, the offended nuns pointed out, the Malvezzi money could be better used to pay down Santa Maria Nuova's heavy indebtedness.[20]

Of course Maria Vinciguerra, with Archbishop Boncompagni's backing, carried the day. Rebuilt from the ground up, the new edifice was enlarged as much as the site allowed, and it extended all the way to the public street. As the archbishop put it, "It is far better to dedicate the old loggia that was in front of the old church to God's service. It had previously served merely for diversions among the laity." As the offended sisters accurately maintained, the parlatorios, the sacristy, and those two prime cells all had to go, so they were shifted to other locations.

For the two years of construction, the convent lived in turmoil, and not simply because it had been turned into a massive building site. The dissenters sent further petitions off to Rome. While these say no more about the chapel rebuilding specifically, they reveal continued intramural discontent. The final petition, dating from the closing stages of construction, suggests that convent life was swerving out of control. "The extremely serious unseemliness plaguing the convent of Santa Maria Nuova in Bologna has by now reached such a state that one fears total ruination and loss of public peace and regular observance if Your Eminences do not deal with the problems forcefully." The aggrieved sisters requested the intervention of a disinterested third party "who would be independent of the original diocesan superiors, to hear the oppression and travails they have suffered for years without managing to be heard by the one who ought to remedy these problems"—clearly a veiled reference to an unresponsive Archbishop Girolamo Boncompagni.[21]

Toward the end of 1660, Donna Maria Vinciguerra's great work was finished. Attended by four and possibly five Malvezzi nuns, plus the Countess Collalto Malvezzi, in the nuns' inner chapel and presumably a host of other family members in the new outer chapel, the inauguration of the external church highlighted the autumn social season. Following shortly thereafter, another high point for the local gentry was the profession ritual for the Malvezzi nieces Giulia Vittoria and Maria Ermengilda. Having completed their formal probationary year in the convent, the younger Malvezzi women took their final vows in October 1663.[22] Three of the names Donna Giulia Vittoria Maria Artemisia Malvezzi chose as her religious name match the secular and religious names of her aunt, Donna Maria Vittoria Felice (who had been baptized Giulia Maria Anastasia). This suggests that a special link probably existed between the two women.

Just a few months before the younger Malvezzi generation's profession, Giulio Cesare Arresti's Mass collection with its dedication to Giulia Vittoria had been published. The dedication is dated July 11. Because of its proximity to her profession, the publication of this musical volume strongly implies that it was prompted by that impending event. During the profession service, some of that very music may well have charmed the throng of Bolognese aristocrats who attended. In describing Giulia Vittoria as his "esteemed patron" (*patrona colendissima*), Arresti suggests that her "singular intelligence in music and playing" ("singolare intelligenza . . . nella Musica, e nel Suono") offered the primary motivation for the dedication. At the same time, the Malvezzi family's willingness to underwrite publication costs may well have provided a more pragmatic reason.[23]

Arresti seems to have tailored some motets in Malvezzi's collection—which includes two for Easter, two for Pentecost, and two for any feast—to the monastic environment. While one work from each pair is exuberant and rather universal in application, one of these three nevertheless plainly highlights convent music, and perhaps even Malvezzi's profession, in its phraseology: "Hasten ye people, assemble ye clans, for the singing, the applause, the sounds of celebration, the songs" ("Ad cantus ad plausus ad sonos ad melos, convocate gentes, accurite populi").

The other three more particular motets all speak confidently of nuns' relationship with their heavenly spouse: *Quid mihi est in caelo* (for Easter), *O bone Iesu* (for Pentecost), and *O quam suave eloquium tuum* (for any feast). Addressing Jesus as every nun's personal beloved, the extravagant, intimate language of these Jesus love songs echoes that of innumerable other nun motets: "Pierce my heart with the sweetest arrow of your love, so that I swoon for you, my sweetness!" ("Confige cor meum iaculo tui amoris suavissimo ut langueam prōte, dulcedo mea," from *Quid mihi est in caelo*). "Fan flames of love, O Jesus, sweetest hope of my sighing soul, and fill up my heart's secret parts!" ("Flammas amoris excita, O Iesu, mi dulcissime spes suspirantis animae et reple cordis intima," from *O bone Jesu*). These phrases illustrate the style at its most intense.

Other phrases such as "let my mouth be filled with your praises, O dear Jesus" and "may she sing a song of joy unto you, O sweetest Jesus" ("Repleatur os meum laude tue, O care Iesu" and "Cantet tibi canticum laetitae, suavissime Iesu," also from *O bone Iesu*) echo virtually identical phraseology from Jesus motets by Bologna's only published nun composer, Lucrezia Orsina Vizzana, serving as validations of her music. *O quam suave eloquium tuum* relies heavily and inevitably on borrowings and adaptations from that quintessential nuns' biblical text, the Song of Songs. The result is both romantic and, in many of its phrases, perhaps a further validation of convent music. The phrase "for your voice is sweet and your face is fair" ("vox enim tua dulcis et facies tua decora") runs through the repertory of nuns' music in support of their own singing.[24] The motet's rather contrived opening, "Oh how sweet are your words, my Jesus, which you made to sound in your ears" ("O quam suave eloquium tuum mi Iesu quod in aures tuas resonare fecisti"), implies that Jesus' own fiat prompts nuns' musical offerings based on his words, served up to please him (thanks, of course, to Malvezzi munificence in this case). Another possible affirmation of convent music can be teased out of a later combination of Song of Songs tags from this motet: "My soul melted because you said 'For your voice is sweet and your face is fair' " ("Anima mea liquefacta est ut locutus es vox enim tua dulcis et facies tua decora"). The singer's soul melts specifically because Christ affirms her music. Several motets, and *O quam suave eloquium tuum* in particular, thus seem chosen to connect Arresti's collection with the cloistered world and artistic interests of its dedicatee.

After the appearance of Arresti's collection, a mere half-dozen years passed before the two generations of Malvezzi nuns combined forces, with Donna Maria Vinciguerra in the vanguard, to press on into their next period of artistic productivity. Following Vittoria Felice's example from the 1640s and 1650s, Maria Vinciguerra set a new goal for the 1670s: the lavish adornment of her own new church with extravagant textiles and needlework. Though she commanded others in the building of the church, this time Maria Vinciguerra would do the work herself. This was quite a departure from her cloistered competitors' usual generosity, which involved commissioning artistic good works, not executing them. Her latest ambitious plan characteristically surpassed the dabbling of genteel ladies. Both the Malvezzi sisters and the nieces would all need to participate. It would also require dipping once again into the deep pockets of Maria Vinciguerra's habit, of course. But it would also display the Malvezzi sisters' personally exalted tastes and talents appropriately, not to mention that it would enhance Maria Vinciguerra's previous architectural donation.

Perhaps Donna Vittoria Felice, after a decade's observation and supervision in the 1640s, now guided even Maria Vinciguerra in the work. The women began with a length of crimson damask. Next they tackled another in the style perfected in the previous century by French Huguenot embroiderers, with flowers, birds, and foliage in silk floss of various vibrant colors. Then a third piece they edged with French-style gold fringe. In all, the enterprise stretched on for eight years and kept all four pairs of refined Malvezzi hands at nearly constant work. Even having done it all themselves, the Malvezzi nuns ultimately claimed to have spent more than two thousand scudi on materials. Wall hangings of the sort already mentioned gave way to pallia, tunicles, and chasubles for officiants to wear at Mass in their chapel, many set off by various altar vessels of silver.

All the Malvezzi adornments were carefully cataloged in the convent's official description of chapel furnishings. It lists the pallia, the chasubles, the tunicles, the cope—all confected of iridescent red ermisino silk, heavily embroidered in gold. After it mentions the pair

FIGURE 4.5 Silk chasuble embroidered with silk floss and metal threads; Italian, 1650–1700. Victoria and Albert Museum, London (T.295–1972). Photograph: © V&A Images. The Malvezzi sisters' chapel needlework and the paliola embroidered by the uppity Terentia Pulica dated from the same period and may have aspired to this complexity.

of silver candlesticks and the beautifully embroidered hangings of crimson damask, everything courtesy of the four Malvezzi relations' munificence, the convent catalog ends rather abruptly, "and the two silver cushions from Reverend Mother Maria Anna Ratta."[25] This gift sounds singularly meager when juxtaposed with the extravagant description of the Malvezzi clan's largesse—and that may have been exactly the chronicler's intention.

We know little of this other would-be benefactor, Donna Maria Anna Ratta. She had been born about 1650 to another of Bologna's first families. Though a bit less socially preeminent, perhaps, than the Malvezzi family, the Ratta clan was renowned for lavish charity to convents. At the end of the preceding century, Maria Anna's ancestor Dionigio Ratta had already surpassed even Maria Vinciguerra by building not one, but *two* new convent chapels, for San Pietro Martire and for San Giovanni Battista, each with a masterwork by Ludovico Carracci over its high altar.

In 1664 Donna Maria Anna had professed at Santa Maria Nuova, not long after the younger Malvezzi generation. She may never have been a very pretty sight. Shortly after her profession, she developed a chronic running sore that extended downward from her right eye. Apparently the infection grew so severe that her superiors assigned a servant to attend to her special needs.[26]

In the late 1670s, as the Malvezzi sisters were putting the finishing touches on their chapel decorations, Donna Maria Anna took a turn as sacristan. As the end of her much less showy term approached in 1679, Maria Anna resolved to present the chapel with a *paliola* (probably a pallium or liturgical covering), decorated in silk French embroidery. In early May of that year, on the octave of the convent's annual feast day, she displayed her gift on the railing before the Blessed Sacrament in the nuns' inner chapel. This show took her fellow nuns quite by surprise—Donna Maria Vinciguerra most of all. For her, this donation came as no pleasant surprise. As Sister Maria Anna Ratta later recalled:

> Sister Vinciguerra Malvezzi found my gift intolerable, for no other reason than her assumption that it incorporated a design similar to a decoration she had donated to the church when she was sacristan—something that is far from the truth. With extreme impropri-

ety toward the Sacrament, to the shame of the nuns present, and with manifest damage to the sacristy, she angrily removed it from the railing. She ripped it off, tore it apart, and finally burned it. She did all this despite Sister Maria Anna's pleas, amid the violence, for her to stop the removal and destruction.[27]

With this double display—Maria Anna's "passive" donation of the paliola and Maria Vinciguerra's more belligerent display of pique over it—there began another convent battle, with ripples extending from the cloister throughout Bologna and all the way to Rome. In the archbishop's absence, the vicar-general was forced to take matters into his own hands on May 16:

> We command, Reverend Sister Maria Vinciguerra Malvezzi, that in holy obedience you must restore, or do your best to have restored and replaced, the vestment that you violently removed from the internal church, to the Reverend Mothers' shame, and with scant reverence and respect for the Most Holy Sacrament. Should you decline to restore that paliola, you are required to make another like it within a month, entirely at your own expense, on pain, should you disobey, of deprivation of active and passive voice, access to the grates, ruote, and door of the convent, and of other penalties to be determined by His Eminence, the lord cardinal archbishop.

But Maria Vinciguerra showed little inclination to comply with the orders of her superior (in matters ecclesiastical, if not genealogical). Instead, she simply handed over to the abbess twelve scudi, together with some green lining and gold lace salvaged from the ravaged original. Then she apparently suggested that the abbess see to the work. Clearly Maria Vinciguerra felt herself above such decrees, "vaunting to the nuns some family relation with the lord cardinal archbishop through common descent from a niece of Pope Gregory XIII," as Maria Anna Ratta puts it.[28]

In any case, the church hierarchy proved notably slow to compel Maria Vinciguerra to comply with the vicar-general's orders—or at least to try to persuade her it might be prudent to do so. When the Sacred Congregation called him to task about the ongoing disobedience at Santa Maria Nuova, the archbishop claimed to have been away at the abbey of Vidor, near Treviso, when the matter first flared up. Though he had returned three weeks after the Sacred Congregation put the matter in his hands, he promptly retreated for another extended period of recuperation from his latest opportune but unspecified ailment.

In his defense, he pointed out that when he first returned from Vidor abbey, the affair had already spread beyond the convent and into the city. Men of the Ratta and Malvezzi families had become involved. Angry exchanges had occurred between them, and rumor said some had headed for the countryside with arms, presumably to settle the matter on the field of honor. For the good of the larger community, the archbishop declined to act precipitously lest he provoke further crises or confrontations by forcing Donna Maria Vinciguerra to comply before some agreement had been reached among all parties.

In the meantime, a stream of petitions from Sister Maria Anna and Sister Maria Vinciguerra—as well as replies from the Sacred Congregation to the Bolognese archbishop—passed back and forth between Bologna and Rome. Yet this latest scandal seems to have been brewing for a long time, as another negative reaction to Malvezzi patronage. Two years after the Malvezzi clan had begun its various chapel hangings, a kitchen conversa, Terentia Pulica (or Pulega or Pulga), had decided to make the paliola that would become the object of Maria Vinciguerra's wrath in 1679. She had finished it in 1675. Since Pulica's handiwork also employed French embroidery, the Malvezzi sisters believed she had expropriated their own design and intended to upstage them before their own needlework could be made fully presentable. So the Malvezzi faction complained to the vicar-general. Maria Vinciguerra claimed that she and her relatives had acted "to remove the potential for scandal inherent in this servant's competitive act, perhaps fomented by others." The implication of this closing phrase suggests that the Ratta crisis may have arisen in old factionalism still hanging on from earlier opposition to Maria Vinciguerra's big projects.

For his part, the archbishop had tried in vain to convince Malvezzi back in 1675 that "the convent servant couldn't in any way eclipse with this paltry gift the many charitable works that the Malvezzi family had done—and continue to do—for the good of their convent." When that ploy failed, he insisted that the servant hand the vestment over to church authorities, which she did. But during another of Boncompagni's frequent and prolonged absences, his vicar-general unwittingly returned the offending needlework to its maker. After several attempts to give the beautiful but dangerous item to various professed nuns who wisely did not take the bait, the kitchen maid finally cajoled Sister Maria Anna Ratta into accepting it as a gift and displaying it in chapel in May 1679, setting off the fireworks.[29]

In the aftermath of her chapel meltdown, Donna Maria Vinciguerra did her best to clarify what she believed should have been patently clear. "Without any opposition, and in the presence of only four nuns," she had taken it upon herself to remove the offending vestment. After all, her relative the archbishop, in whose hands the matter officially rested, had left the field. She had taken it undamaged to her cell, where she removed the lace and lining and "dispersed" the rest "in order thus to abolish the material causes of the scandals." She marveled at "the unbecoming willfulness of a *convent servant*, demonstrated toward *a lady of such distinguished lineage*, devoted to divine service, in her declining years, the benefactress of the monastery, where there are four nuns from the same family."[30]

Donna Maria Vinciguerra surely expected the archbishop, the cardinals in Rome, and others of her rank to understand fully. Giovanni Battista Ciotti's late sixteenth-century *First Part of Flowers and Designs of Various Sorts for Modern Needlework* had appealed to social climbers with extravagant claims about needlework as a way for lesser women to excel, even perhaps above their station.

> For many maidens but of base degree,
> By their fine knowledge in the curious thing:
> With Noble Ladies oft companions be,
> Sometimes they teach the daughter of a King:
> Thus by their knowledge, fame, and good report
> They are esteem'd among the noblest sort.

If she knew of it, Maria Vinciguerra would certainly have recognized this bald sales pitch for what it was. Her response to Terentia Pulica's impertinence had spoken loudly for all people of quality, who, as one acerbic seventeenth-century critic of the foibles of the

Bolognese aristocracy put it, "adopt with their inferiors a less civil manner." Maria Vinciguerra's reaction to the conversa's perceived disrespect illustrated in the extreme that local nobility were quick to become "severe with their inferiors if they do not give way to them at once." Her attitude also resonated with that of cloistered Venetian aristocrats, who regularly complained about converse who acted "as if they were like us."[31]

Impatient with Boncompagni's dilatoriness, Maria Anna Ratta complained to the Sacred Congregation that she could not get his ear. In her mind, the cardinals should stick with the original severe judgment, "since it is improper for such a misdeed to set a bad example for the other nuns. Especially since Malvezzi is accustomed to using such duress and excessiveness with other sisters." Apparently, Maria Vinciguerra's methods had made her a convent bully. When Boncompagni still failed to act, Anna Ratta requested that a cardinale ponente be appointed to rule in the matter, since she could get nowhere with her Bolognese superior. A few weeks later the cardinale ponente advised the Sacred Congregation that the vicar-general's original decree should be enforced.[32]

Obviously Boncompagni procrastinated still further to avoid eliciting the ire of his kin, the powerful Malvezzi family. Virtually trapped by the cardinale ponente's determination, the archbishop tried additional diversionary tactics. He sent a long, detailed summary of the entire affair back to Rome so that the Sacred Congregation itself might judge and advise him how to act. He dumped the hot potato back in their laps. Without a doubt, Boncompagni's summary betrays an unsurprising bias toward Maria Vinciguerra and her deep pockets. Boncompagni points out, for example, that she "never declined to repair the damage, but would have liked to re-create it as part of other, more costly, works to benefit the sacristy. She shows some disinclination to re-create the vestment exactly as before." In other words, Malvezzi hoped simply to absorb it within her own artistic efforts.

Boncompagni acknowledges that "it seems to Malvezzi as though she should enjoy special merit at the monastery for having rebuilt the church from its very foundations at her own considerable expense, and for having adorned it so nobly and expensively herself. And it seems curious to her that a simple convent servant would have desired, in a certain way, to compete with her." He also remarks, without passing judgment, that after the first flap in 1675 about the paliola subsided, Maria Anna Ratta had accepted it from the uppity conversa and put it on view without first inquiring about the propriety of such a move. Moreover, she did so even though she, and everybody else, knew all about the controversy.[33]

Unfortunately for him, Boncompagni was not to get off lightly. In January 1680 the Sacred Congregation insisted once again that he decide the matter. The cardinals also suggested, somewhat backhandedly, that Boncompagni might need to enlist backup from the Bolognese papal legate to make sure the Malvezzi and Ratta families did not undertake further misadventure. Still the archbishop delayed, and still Sister Maria Anna got no satisfaction. In April she wrote to Rome yet again. Three times the Sacred Congregation had told the vicar-general to require Maria Vinciguerra to replace the vestment. Still nothing. Another month passed. She wrote once more. Could they appoint another cardinale ponente? Yes. And he too firmly ordered Boncompagni to execute the original decree, by now almost a year old.

A week later, on May 18, 1680, Boncompagni finally promised the Sacred Congregation that within days and "with divine aid" he hoped to send word that the entire affair was settled. Apparently he succeeded, because the records of the Sacred Congregation on this matter end there.

It is interesting that the elaborate manuscript history of Santa Maria Nuova from its foundation to 1680, which the convent had copied as the affair played itself out and dedicated to the archbishop, catalogs in detail every act of patronage by the four Malvezzi nuns as well as every other scrap of aristocratic needlework commissioned abovestairs "by various Lady nuns, zealous in honoring God and their church." But the gifts of Maria Vinciguerra's rival Terentia Pulica, remarkably extensive as they were for someone below-stairs in the kitchen—four silver vases, a chalice, various pieces of linen, and silver crowns for images of the Madonna (according to documents in the Sacred Congregation's files)—all go unmentioned. There is also no mention of any re-created vestment with gold lace and French embroidery. For her part, Maria Anna Ratta, whose chapel gifts included the two elaborate cushions of red satin, garnished all around with silver appliqué, is consigned, invariably, to the bottom of the list. Following the extensive descriptions of Malvezzi generosity, she receives the nondescript note "and the two silver cushions from Reverend Mother Maria Anna Ratta."[34]

Perhaps Donna Maria Vinciguerra got her way in this affair and lived up to her name. Yet though her heavy-handed tactics may have won the patronage wars, they apparently failed to win the hearts of her *consorelle*. Apart from such effusive and pro forma praise of her artistic patronage as appears in the convent's official history dedicated to her relative the archbishop, her fellow nuns had surprisingly little to say about her. More tellingly, she seems never to have advanced any higher in the convent hierarchy than the midlevel job of sacristan, in distinct contrast to her sister and one niece. Vittoria Felice was elected prioress three times and served no less than twenty-four years as bursar. Giulia Vittoria served ten years as subprioress and two terms as prioress. Maria Vinciguerra, it seems, was left to her needlework.

Over another forty years, the Malvezzi four slowly faded as a prime force at Santa Maria Nuova. Having survived grave illness back in the 1620s, Vittoria Felice lived to the grand old age of ninety before death came calling in 1696. Donna Maria Ermengilda, the last of them to pass away, made it to 1720. Of the four, Vittoria Felice (who had gone on extended sick leave to Udine), Giulia Vittoria (the musical sister), and Maria Ermengilda (apparently the sole notably pious one among the four) all receive substantial memorials and "positive reviews" in the convent necrology. Donna Maria Vinciguerra had been the first to exit the stage back in 1684, only a few years after her chapel tantrum. While she may have greatly enriched the musical and artistic life of the house, rebuilt the chapel from the ground up, and furnished it with opulent gifts, she seemed always to leave turmoil in her wake. Despite her "victories" in life, in death Maria Vinciguerra would be remembered in Santa Maria Nuova's necrology only with the date of her death.[35]

5

SLIPPING THROUGH THE CRACKS:
A CONVENT'S POROUS WALLS

Santa Maria degli Angeli (Pavia, 1651–75)

On a bleak January day in 1675, the bishop of Pavia glanced back at the convent of Santa Maria degli Angeli receding behind him, then began mentally to compose a letter to the Sacred Congregation of Bishops and Regulars. Because of its dwindling numbers, poverty, location, and "other reasons," the Sacred Congregation had commanded his predecessor to stop admitting postulants at Santa Maria degli Angeli "in order to facilitate the convent's eventual suppression." Time for that eventuality had come.

The convent sits in a totally depopulated area, bounded on one side by the city wall, on the other by a military barracks, and shares two sides with the Third Order Franciscan Friars [of San Gervasio]. The walls separating their dormitories are so thin and fragile that they can clearly hear each other's conversations. The convent consists of little houses, by now so timeworn and dilapidated that they threaten to cave in. The church is a sort of little chapel, so ugly, devoid of ornament, and lacking in necessary furnishings that it would be unseemly to hold services there. Only six nuns and five converse are left. The prioress is past eighty, paralyzed, and totally incapacitated. One nun is deaf, blind, and hasn't risen from her bed in years. Another is just as old. The younger three live as they please, unsupervised. Because they lack life's necessities, they constantly complain about wanting to quit the place. For these reasons there is no proper observance, no common life, no service in chapel. Every day I dread to hear of some disturbance among the younger ones, or of some building collapse, which cannot be set right because of the convent's poverty.[1]

Various causes might be proposed for the slow decline and fall of Pavia's only Ancient Observance Carmelite convent for women, which would vanish so completely that it appears as only a name on *Wikipedia*'s comprehensive list of the city's monastic houses.[2] Back in 1574, when an earlier bishop of Pavia had determined how many mouths his various convents' endowments could feed, Santa Maria degli Angeli had been at the absolute bottom of his list, capable of sustaining only five—including servants.[3] Carmelite superiors may therefore have thought it never really had a chance. Others may suggest that devastations and other effects of the Thirty Years' War and later French-Spanish hostilities eroded its puny foundation. Some point to unfortunate incidents during the 1660s. Those with clearer recall, or perhaps prone to fantasy, might decide that the decline began on a wet autumn day in 1651.

On Friday, September 29, 1651, the feast of Saint Michael the Archangel, any hint of festivity was dampened by a chilling rain that wouldn't quit.[4] Upstairs at Santa Maria degli Angeli, the old prioress had once again taken to her bed with a bout of quartan ague (a form of malaria), so she did not join the twenty or so others at lunch.

Things were no better in the damp, cramped quarters next door, where la Zoppa (the Cripple) supported her sixty-year-old husband by her work as a seamstress and by running errands for the convent. Here the couple was also fighting quartan ague, and it had kept her husband home from the fields for over two months. He could barely manage an occasional trip to the convent's parlatorio if someone offered him a tip for witnessing contracts there. Malaria had also laid low their neighbor from the hills outside town. The neighbor's wife Maria Montanara (Maria the Highlander) had risen from her sickbed that morning to lug loads down the muddy road to the home of a departing convent probationer.

There was little else to distract either family from enforced idleness as the fevers waxed and waned. Maria Montanara's youngest daughter, now returned from begging soup at the convent's lunch table, offered more irritation, perhaps, than diversion. Her thirteen-year-old, Zanina, who eked out a similar living at another convent just a block or two away, brightened her parents' day a little with one of her rare visits. Her mother complained that she "almost never comes home." So both the Montanara family and la Zoppa and her husband had virtually nothing to do but observe the comings and goings at the convent gate, which was visible from their beds when the doors were open, as they still were at this time of year. Today, especially, the carriage gateway at the convent was unusually busy, even apart from Maria Montanara's several trips. Porters loitered about, entering and exiting with loads of their own or standing around waiting to be told where to take the next load. Everyone was trying to stay dry.

"The prioress won't hear of the removal of convent property!" The bedridden crane their necks to see what the shouting is about. "Rest assured that your ladyship will have satisfaction—get down here—then you'll end up satisfied!" a man yells back smartly. At that, la Zoppa crawls out of bed and limps to the door for a better look, and she notices that Zanina too has emerged from next door. A brother to Giovanna Balcona, the probationer whose bundles Maria Montanara had carried away a short time earlier, is arguing with some nun about a cask sitting in the puddles between the inner and outer gates. Porters look on, smirking. After brief but heated discussion, a porter shoulders the keg and moves off. The nun in charge turns stiffly and retreats from the scene with as much dignity as she can muster. The gate stands open, quiet and unattended.[5]

A minute or two later, the bedridden audience sees a figure in the brown Carmelite habit appear at the outer gate. She pauses for just a moment, then steps gingerly out among the growing puddles. The probationer Giovanna Balcona follows almost immediately and catches the other woman by the sleeve. The pair speak vehemently to one another, but their voices are so soft that their neighbors hear none of the exchange. The older woman seems to hesitate, unsteadily. Then, taking each other by the hand, the two turn and walk off down the road, followed by Giovanna Balcona's brother. They head toward the Friars of San Gervasio, where la Zoppa loses sight of them.

Zanina, however, moves from the safety of her doorway out into

FIGURE 5.1 An Ancient Observance Carmelite choir nun, from Pierre Helyot, *Histoire des ordres religieux et militaires* (Paris: Louis, 1792).

the rain to keep the pair in view. She witnesses the brother reluctantly take off his cloak and wrap it around the nun, who must be soaked by now. He also places his cap on her head, where it sits incongruously atop her veil. The bedraggled trio trudges off, the two women still hand in hand. Finally Zanina loses sight of them too, as they turn into the San Gervasio cemetery.

Zanina hurries back inside to offer her father some water and tell him what he has missed. The nun must be Sister Angela Aurelia Mogna. La Zoppa agrees. She recognized her from a recent errand to buy her some butter. Zanina hastens through the abandoned convent gate to spread the word. There she encounters a nun sent to fetch the barber to come bleed another of the sisters. "Don't you know that Sister Angela Aurelia has run off, holding hands with la Balcona?" The nun turns and heads for the refectory to find the *portinara*, or gatekeeper. With many of the other nuns in tow, the portinara returns to discover the gate still standing open and unattended, with the key in the lock.

Now it is the portinara's turn to do an about-face and bustle off to find the prioress, upstairs in her bed. "Mother, Sister Angela Aurelia has left with Giovanna Balcona!" The dumbfounded prioress, still in her shift and starting to sob, pauses just long enough for a dose of medicine. Then she totters down the hall with the subprioress and another elder nun, headed for the missing sister's cell. They find it bare but for a stripped bedstead, two empty chests, and a few paintings on the wall.[6]

The frail prioress, already half dead and with another of her fevers quickly coming on, is really useless to anybody. So her subordinates put her back to bed. Somewhat belatedly, they now think to bolt the convent gate behind their eloped sister as they await the arrival of their brother superior from the Carmelite men's house, Santa Maria del Carmine, just a few blocks away.

Outside the rain continues. Farther south, halfway down to the river Ticino, the Benedictine nuns of San Gregorio are braving the downpour to bring a gift of quince apples and grapes in through their convent gate under their abbess's watchful eye. A carriage pulls up before the gate; the abbess sees a teenage girl jump out and head in her direction. Completely shrouded in black, a daunting figure follows the girl. As the abbess stands watching apprehensively, the

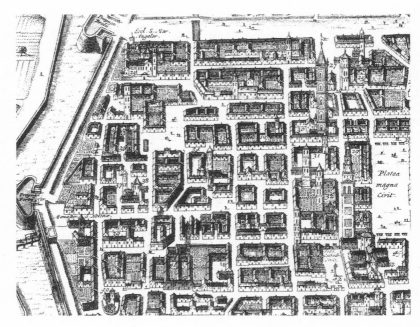

FIGURE 5.2 The upper west side of Pavia, from a map of ca. 1680. Santa Maria degli Angeli appears at the upper left ("Eccl. S. Mar. Angelor."); 35: Santi Gervasio e Protasio adjoins it; 38: San Gregorio, to which Angela Aurelia Mogna and Giovanna Balcona fled, is almost directly south; 30: Santa Maria del Carmine, the male Carmelite house, has the tallest spire; the duomo ("Eccl. Cathedr. Civit."), where Siro Magni served as canon, is near the lower right.

pair rushes the door. The abbess and a second nun throw themselves against it, and they might have managed to repel the trespassers except that the abbess falls down in a dead faint.

San Gregorio's defenders abandon their posts to find vinegar to hold under the abbess's nose. They sit her down beside a fire and quickly revive her. But by then the invaders are safely inside the walls and reverently on their knees beside the nuns gathered solicitously around their fallen leader. The older of the two intruders announces, "I am the sister of Signore Don Siro Mogni, canon of the cathedral. Disgusted with Santa Maria degli Angeli, I resolved to leave there, together with this young one. We have come to retire here, among you." The abbess promptly swoons again, lying "like a corpse, after the trials and terrors she suffered." Or so San Gregorio's male administrator informed the vicar-general of Pavia. And it wasn't even suppertime yet.[7]

By the time the vicar-general arrived at San Gregorio later that same afternoon, the abbess had recovered sufficiently to testify. Although she had as much to say about her physical condition as about her convent's recent invasion by the fugitive Carmelites, the story began to reveal itself. After the abbess finished, the fugitive nun and her young accomplice told their versions, but they had scarcely had time to get their stories straight. Whatever credibility they might have had at first, it would be severely undermined a few days later when la Zoppa, her husband, Zanina, and various nuns had their say. Probably the refugees' credibility was never much of an issue, for the Curia was disinclined to heed what they had to say in any case.

Both runaways maintained that they entered a waiting carriage at the convent gate. They made no mention of trudging off on foot. "Inspired by the Holy Spirit," they claimed to have driven immediately to San Gregorio. Apparently they hoped the ruse would shield Giovanna Balcona's family from implication in their escape and from the automatic excommunication that would follow such assistance. The facts would come out soon enough: the pair had stopped briefly at casa Balcona, where a borrowed carriage picked them up for the trip to San Gregorio. Later Giovanna Balcona would assert that her embarrassment at their undignified departure from the convent had prompted the first of a long series of lies. "I was so giddy headed—I'll tell the truth," she said. "I didn't speak truly earlier out of shame, saying to myself, 'What would they think if I said we left on foot?'"[8]

Some of the witnesses testified that the day before the two successfully fled, Giovanna had tried to orchestrate an even grander exit for herself, involving not only a carriage at the gate, but also half a dozen porters and a guard of twelve armed men. All in all, this ruse must have derived from a face-saving fantasy that she hoped would salve her wounded pride, for the truth is that the nuns had expelled her. Later Giovanna would contend that she believed such an army was necessary to protect her from the vengeful sisters.

Sister Angela Aurelia also tried to shield Giovanna Balcona from further implication in the nun's own flight than was already self-evident. After all, Giovanna had not fled the convent in the strictest sense but had been thrown out. "Recognizing the opportunity, since nobody was at the gate to stop me—because the nuns had all gone off to lunch, I exited the gate, got into the carriage with the girl, and we came here." At first Giovanna played along with her mistress's story almost word for word. But when called again for further testimony after a week of solitary fantasizing, the girl transformed the escape into high drama, worthy of a squadron of six porters and a dozen armed men.

> I didn't want to wait for the carriage my brother was bringing because I could hear all the nuns upstairs. They'd gone to my mistress's cell and were screaming "Get up here! Get up here to Sister Angela Aurelia's room! We want to finish her off and root out that kin of priests! We'll have none of them in the convent!" Hearing such a row, I put my arms around her neck and said, "Signora Maestra, you must try to save yourself! Trust me! I'll go myself to find your brother and tell him everything that's happened!"
>
> When I got to the gate, I discovered her there. I said, "Oh Signora Maestra, what are you doing! Go back inside!" She answered, "I don't choose to return to my death! Hush! Because you don't know everything. I know what I'm doing. I flee to escape this persecution and this hunger. Because I've nothing to eat here. Because this place has been turned into a public house. There's no monastic enclosure. I can stay here no longer, but must go to a cloister governed by priests." In that moment she fell to the ground. So I gave her my arm, and the two of us went forth all alone, with nobody around— not even a cat.[9]

In her turn, Sister Angela Aurelia explained that her flight and Giovanna Balcona's expulsion had resulted because she had admitted Balcona's two little nieces to the convent on her own initiative, without convent superiors' approval. After that act, years of intramural strife between her and other nuns—most notably Sister Anna Domitilla Langosca—erupted into threats and recriminations.

Anna Domitilla Langosca had perpetually complained that Mogna, Balcona, and their families tattled to religious authorities about convent improprieties. Sister Angela Aurelia claimed that some years before, during her time as prioress, her attempts at reform had in fact resulted in a pastoral visitation at Santa Maria degli Angeli that greatly embarrassed Langosca and her cohorts. As Sister Angela Aurelia told it, "Some confessed during their interrogation that they had prepared a toxin to poison me. So I renounced my office. Ever since then they've always despised me." Enmities and thoughts of violence had not diminished over the years. "La Langosca said to my face that I should be thrown down the stairs and broken in pieces," Mogna told her present interrogator in 1651.[10]

Giovanna Balcona's recounting of the other sisters' behavior toward her mistress was much more lurid. Sister Anna Domitilla Langosca not only had turned their male Carmelite superior against Giovanna's little nieces, but had "grabbed one by the arm and flung her out the gate." Langosca had wanted to go ahead and kick Giovanna out then too. "But I fled upstairs, and she said, 'Don't think you can get away, because we're bound and determined to throw you out!'"

Anna Domitilla Langosca and the senior nuns went to confront Mogna, lying sick in her cell. "Sister Domitilla, with her hands on her hips, said to her, 'If I don't get some respect, for the love of God, I'd like to strangle you.' And, miming with her hands, she said 'I've always wanted to throw you down the stairs, and I'll always want to, because you blab to the Curia about everything that goes on here in the convent.'"

Giovanna's retelling echoes Mogna. Langosca had "warned that she wanted to give my mistress a mouthful to poison her." Four or five years earlier, Langosca had tried to feed the ailing Angela Aurelia some ravioli. But another nun had seen the special seasonings Langosca was adding. She stopped Mogna from eating them "because she suspected they might be poisoned." According to Giovanna Balcona, Langosca's motive for urging her expulsion was so that the ailing Sister Angela Aurelia would be left defenseless, an easy prey.[11]

The vicar-general showed scant interest in the runaways' allegations of personal harassment and possibly attempted murder. His ears pricked up, however, when both suggested that the admission of Giovanna's nieces had only copied laxity in the admission of other girls to Santa Maria degli Angeli and the blind eyes turned to the young ones' comings and goings. The church hierarchy would have recognized that these unsanctioned admissions to the house were direct violations of monastic enclosure, not alleged and probably imagined personal affronts. When asked to name names, Angela Aurelia singled out a girl called Lucia and another nicknamed la Dornina. Both young women were known to have unsavory pasts.

Giovanna Balcona had more to add on this account. Apart from the same two "nice bits of stuff," as she called them, "who made a mess of their lives," Giovanna mentioned the niece of a priest from Voghera, who had stayed with the Carmelites for only a year, then went off to marry. Next there was a protégée of Langosca's, "her servant, more like her lady-in-waiting. She torments the nuns and talks back to them." This woman had come and gone from the cloister twice in four months. Then there was one other who had been in and out of the convent three or four times recently. "They each gave half a ducat to be handed over to the Carmelite father commissioner, and he gives them licenses. But because [the nuns] weren't quick enough with their half a ducat for my niece, he wanted her tossed out right away."

Giovanna had been informed about the lurid pasts of the two "nice bits of stuff" when she was visiting with Milanese gentlemen in the parlatorio. La Dornina, whom she already knew to be the daughter of a prostitute from Dorno, passed by the door. "Say, what sort of girls do you take in here? You must be the refuge for all the refuse!" The gentlemen explained that they had previously seen la Dornina in Milan, where she was being kept by a soldier.

Similarly, Lucia had previously been kept "closed up in a room for two months" by an army captain. "When he put her here, he said that she was his daughter and should stay for as long as he was on a war campaign. And the captain sent over an eel and a big dogfish for the convent, and a platter of dainty cheese for Prioress Tolentina. So they took her in."[12]

"SHE WAS MADLY IN LOVE, SO BADLY THAT SHE CARED NOTHING ABOUT HOLY OBEDIENCE"

Once the vicar-general dismisses Sister Angela Aurelia Mogna, we never hear from her again. Unlike others called more than once to testify, the fugitive nun would not be recalled. But even as she turned to leave the grates at San Gregorio, she stopped long enough to remark,

"So that none would think I left the convent to follow the girl, she can be sent away wherever you wish, for I shall willingly remain here."[13]

Of course, that plea probably held little hope of a favorable response. From the moment the fugitives set foot outside the cloister, they had set tongues wagging. The three neighbors who witnessed their flight all specifically mentioned that the two women had left hand in hand. That was the singular image that stuck in the head of la Zoppa's husband when he briefly caught sight of them from his bed. La Zoppa mentioned it twice, in describing both the pair's initial departure and her last view of them before they disappeared. The abbess also related that when Maria Montanara's daughter broke the news to the nuns, she had mentioned the detail that the fugitives had left holding hands.

Whatever the young lay messenger meant by this detail, her cloistered audience certainly knew what it implied. Since the early days of female monasticism, the church hierarchy had perceived particular danger in hand-holding within the convent. Some thousand years earlier, for example, the rule of Donatus of Besançon insisted that "it is forbidden to take the hand of another for affection, whether standing or walking or sitting together. She who does so will be corrected with twelve blows."[14]

Such an image painted itself ineradicably on the outside world's collective imagination at the time, and it resonates across the ages with fantasies that even to this day speculate about what nuns do together behind their wall. Perhaps the Carmelites' neighbors next door had even sung the irreverent sixteenth-century song "Monicella mi farei" ("I'd like to become a little nun"), one stanza of which simultaneously reflects and feeds fantasies of this sort among the laity:

Sopratutto vorria avere
'Na divota vaga e bella
Che mi dessi ogni piacere
Ed anch'io ne dessi ad ella.

[What would please me beyond measure?
One who's faithful, fair, and winsome,
Who would give me ev'ry pleasure,
As I'd give to her—and then some.][15]

On this subject, Erasmus of Rotterdam's 1523 colloquy *Virgo mi-sogamos* conveys similar attitudes that prevailed then among more educated and, one presumes, more elevated circles. He has Eubulus hint to Catherine, a would-be nun, that in cloistered communities "there are more who copy Sappho's behavior than share her talent." The naive, uncomprehending Catherine returns shortly thereafter from some brief, hands-on experience with monasticism, her illusions shattered. But primly and at the same time pruriently, Erasmus's heroine leaves readers to imagine for themselves what might have driven her from the convent.[16]

Unlike the laity—educated or otherwise—the church hierarchy was less likely to snicker and much more likely to fret about relationships, real or imagined, that began with hand-holding and must certainly devolve into shared convent beds, as well as about the closed doors or darkened rooms that might encourage them. The outcome of a pastoral visitation to Bolognese convents in the 1590s was typical of churchmen's attitudes. In this case, nuns were threatened with six months' incarceration, deprivation of their veils, and no access to the parlatorio if they "should dare or presume in future to sleep together in the same bed or in the same room." Forty years later, a similar Bolognese convent visitation demonstrates how ticklish the church hierarchy could be about the slightest whiff of presumed impropriety. A Sister Lesbia Ildebranda got her name changed on the spot to Sister Maria Teresa by an embarrassed and particularly fastidious clerical inspector to whom she had just been introduced.

Male superiors were always especially sensitive about probationers and novices such as Giovanna Balcona. Initiates were expected to live and sleep completely separate from professed nuns. During a pastoral visitation in 1665 to the convent-orphanage of San Domenico in Conversano (at the top of the heel of Italy's boot), the local bishop made an alarming discovery. For want of a separate dormitory, young virgin girls were sleeping "in disorderly fashion" amid the grown-up nuns, "and at least two of them in one bed." The bishop therefore ordered the nuns to build a separate dormitory for the girls within six months; otherwise he would send them all home. On this occasion, such measures probably seemed especially justified to the churchman, since most of the professed nuns at San Domenico were *convertite*—reformed prostitutes.

Apart from issues of inappropriate intimacy, probationers and novices were also instructed to live apart from the professed for monastic security. In 1658, for instance, the nuns of San Michele in Pescia (thirty-seven miles from Florence) complained that for lack of space they had to sleep, work, and eat in their new arrivals' company. This situation caused them considerable embarrassment if the girls later left to get married, after having discovered all the convent's secrets. In the case we are concerned with, the relationship between Sister Angela Aurelia Mogna and Giovanna Balcona perfectly embodied that problem.[17]

In her testimony, the portinara, who had been first to hear about the pair's flight, suggested that Angela Aurelia suffered from "melancholy humors." She was also the first to drop the fact that the couple slept together. When asked what she meant by melancholy humors, the portinara responded, "I heard that she was madly in love with la Giovanna—so badly that because of her [infatuation] she cared nothing about holy obedience or observance."

A preliminary summary forwarded from Pavia to Rome took this line, ignoring Sister Angela's concern for misperceptions about why she had left Santa Maria degli Angeli. "Witnesses agree as to the cause: she was madly in love with la Balcona, whom she kept to sleep with her as well," a view the nuns, from the prioress on down, enthusiastically promoted. According to the prioress, "La Mogna left the convent to follow Giovanna Balcona, whom she was dead crazy in love with. Every time we other nuns talked about expelling Giovanna from the convent, she always said she wanted to leave with her—as, in fact, it's clear that she did leave with her, as all the nuns heard her say she would."[18]

Other convent insiders built on the fugitive pair's relationship. The prioress cited an earlier illustration of Angela Aurelia Mogna's long-standing desire to flee, inflamed by similar romantic aberrations. At the time of the French incursions into the duchy of Milan during the 1640s, three nun refugees from Portecorone, twenty-four miles away, temporarily lodged at Santa Maria degli Angeli. As the visitors prepared to depart, Sister Angela Aurelia spoke insistently about leaving with them. At the last moment, the prioress surreptitiously tied her habit to the chain on the gate. When Mogna tried to dart out after the departing carriage, her habit nearly throttled her, giving the other nuns time to hold her back.

A second portinara subsequently linked this incident to Angela Aurelia's "melancholy humors." Because Mogna had become infatuated with one visiting nun, she was desperate to leave with them. As the carriage rolled away and the nuns held onto her, she cried out, weeping, "Poor me! What will become of me without my dear heart?"

One nun described Mogna as overcome with rage when told that Giovanna Balcona's nieces were rejected: "'In spite of the father commissioner and all the nuns, I want those girls here in the convent. And I hold you all to account. Don't be trying to break my head—I want things my way!' . . . They were yelling, and so was she, and Balcona too, so that it seemed as if the convent would topple."

According to another, "La Mogna started screaming so much that the nuns declared not only would they send the little ones away, but Giovanna had to go too. And la Mogna said, 'The little girls are one thing, but Giovanna is another—she's not leaving! You've tried many times to get rid of her. You never succeeded then, and you'll not succeed now. If you send her away, I'll do things that will make you all gasp. I'll uproot this convent!'"[19]

The vicar-general waited until late in his investigation to interrogate the more junior witnesses, those closest to ground zero because they spent most of their time in Sister Angela Aurelia's cell. Members of this group of present or past novices in training were called her "disciples." One former disciple testified that Mogna "was so in love that during the entire seven years when Balcona was here in the convent, Sister Angela Aurelia always wanted her to sleep with her. And when Sister Angela Aurelia was deathly sick about a month ago, she still kept insisting that la Balcona sleep with her. And when I exhorted her that she should sleep alone because of the illness, she answered, 'Absolutely not! Alive, or dead, I want la Balcona with me!' And each called the other Mommy."

On this point, Giovanna Balcona seems not to have dissembled. "Where did you stay while you were in the convent?" her inquisitor asked.

"I was always in my maestra's cell."

"With whom did you sleep?"

"I always slept with her."

"Where did you sleep when your maestra was sick?"

"I always slept with her, and if I took in some illness thereby, it's at my own peril. Only during two months, when she was so very sick, did I sleep on top of a chest instead. And I always took care of her myself, and lost those nights, when all the other nuns abandoned her. Because they said her sufferings came from the wages of sin."[20]

The fugitive pair's relationship largely contrasts with many sixteenth- and seventeenth-century stereotypes of such entanglements. Outsiders' often prurient notions favored the scenario of the lecherous, hairy-chinned older nun who leads astray the naive and tractable newcomer. As the witty, chaste figure of Helena puts it in Aphra Behn's play *The Rover* (1677), which offers a contemporary English view of Catholic convents, "I should have stayed in the nunnery still, if I had liked my Lady Abbess as well as she liked me." Similarly, an older nun and her novice play equally enthusiastic parts as they romp through an eighteenth-century male fantasy in the *Memoirs of Jacques Casanova de Seingalt*.

In another case—this one real rather than fictional—the Italian nun Bartolomea Crivelli was repeatedly "taken by force" by Benedetta Carlini, abbess of the Theatine convent of Pescia. In the 1620s, Carlini was investigated and condemned for pretense of sanctity. During interrogation, the young, illiterate Sister Bartolomea appeared—or did her utmost to appear—naive, confused, and innocently led astray.

At Santa Maria degli Angeli, the community and our principals created a scenario closer to Denis Diderot's novel *La Religieuse* (written in 1760 but published only some thirty years later). There, an abbess's lust for a novice drives the older woman mad.[21] Giovanna Balcona, as re-created by the witnesses from Santa Maria degli Angeli, is the very opposite of the naive Sister Bartolomea from Pescia. She may be young and ill-educated, but Giovanna is dishonest and scheming, not passive and compliant. The witnesses leave little doubt that she deluded the unstable, melancholy, middle-aged Sister Angela Aurelia, who was already prone to unhealthy attachments (as her interest in the visiting nun from Pontecorone demonstrated). All of the most unseemly circumstances resulted "from the persuasion of Giovanna Balcona, who was always going to la Mogna, promoting wicked ends, and saying evil things about the other nuns."

Balcona's deeds were as bad as her words. A portinara claimed that their Carmelite male superior had wanted several times to expel the girl "because she stole whatever she could lay her hands on." Several sisters referred to copper, pewter, and majolica items she had hidden inside feather beds and amid linens, all removed at the time of the Saint Michael's Day breakout. The same portinara even claimed extravagantly that Giovanna had so worn down the sisters with her ceaseless bad behavior that three senior nuns finally died of the abuse.

In time Giovanna Balcona also emerges as the chief executor of the escape plan and the spiriting away of extraordinary amounts of convent property, not to mention the less successful attempt to enlist a small army to carry it all off. Several nuns testified that in the days immediately before the elopement, Balcona induced Mogna to write letters to her brother, Monsignor Siro Mogni at the cathedral, condemning convent abuses. The resulting confrontations between the prioress, Mogna, and Balcona, vehement accusations by the prioress, and equally vehement denials from Mogna came to a climax when the nuns locked Monsignor Siro's servant girl between the inner and outer gates while they tried to figure out how to lay hands on the letter they imagined she was carrying from Mogna to her brother. Shouted down by Sister Angela Aurelia and Giovanna Balcona, they finally let the servant go, carrying who knew what with her.

Catterina Villana, one of Mogna's young disciples, testified that while the servant was waiting below Giovanna Balcona "said to me softly, 'Go downstairs to the parlatorio and say to Don Siro's servant that the nuns came to Sister Angela Aurelia's bedside because they wanted to strangle her. And speak ill of the nuns.'" Clearly, it had been much more the crafty Balcona than the unstable middle-aged woman who was in control of the situation.[22]

The investigation concluded with Giovanna Balcona's final testimony, which dragged on more than twice as long as anyone else's, from October 15 to October 17. Ten days earlier, she had been removed from San Gregorio and confined at the orphanage of San Patrizio, where she had plenty of time to work out her own defense. Even so, she spent much of the lengthy interrogation trying to climb out of holes she dug for herself. Each time, the vicar-general waited patiently to trap her by reading back other witnesses' contradictory testimony from his transcript. Though her quick-witted responses were sometimes plausible, her interrogator betrayed no inclination to believe her.

Like many a self-absorbed, superficially self-confident teenager, Giovanna kept herself in the spotlight. *She* had made her brother give his cloak and cap to the dripping Sister Angela Aurelia. *She* had told the carriage driver to go to San Gregorio, when her mistress lay "as one dead." *She* had told Don Siro's servant to hide the much disputed secret message in her shoe, not inside her blouse, before she was trapped between the convent gates. Giovanna even claimed that in the days before Saint Michael's Day, she had tried to arrange with the rector of San Patrizio for her admission to the orphanage, where authorities had only later decided to deposit the troublesome girl several days after the escape from Santa Maria degli Angeli.

Voluntarily, at the very end of her testimony, she included one revealing attempt to defend herself from charges of thievery: "Your Lordship, write that after the discovery that Sister Arcangela Margarita Alipranda had stolen money, the father commissioner ordered the prioress to restore my honor—I'd been accused of taking it. And when they discovered it was her, then he said they should restore my honor. Because if she'd taken the money, she would've also been the one who'd taken other things too."[23] Obviously the nuns had paid little attention to this particular command from their father commissioner.

In the end, the nuns and their Carmelite superiors, with a little help from the vicar-general of Pavia, turned the relationship between the ailing, melancholy, lovesick Sister Angela Aurelia and her scheming, undisciplined disciple into a casebook example of "particular friendship," the sort of affair that could wreak havoc on a convent. As the best-known Carmelite reformer and eventual saint, Teresa of Avila, had once observed in "The Way of Perfection,"

> It may seem that for us to have too much love for each other cannot be wrong. But I do not think anyone who had not been an eyewitness of it would believe how much evil can result from this. The devil sets many snares here. The harm these friendships do to community life is very serious. One result of it is that all the nuns do not love each other equally: some injury done to a friend is resented. These intimate friendships are seldom calculated to foster the love

of God. I am more inclined to believe that the devil initiates them to create factions within religious Orders.[24]

Sister Angela Aurelia Mogna's side of the story is curiously absent from the investigation. She and the lower-class, nosy next-door neighbors were the only witnesses never recalled during the vicar-general's investigation. For that reason, Mogna never had the chance to trip herself up in rebuttals as her disciple often did. Witnesses frequently cited her brother, Monsignor Siro Mogni, who was actually quoted in testimony even though he was never summoned before the vicar-general. Nor was his servant called to testify, though she had been briefly trapped between the convent gates with Mogna's message in her shoe. But in perhaps the strangest omission from the investigation, Angela Aurelia's archenemy, Sister Anna Domitilla Langosca, was never asked to respond to allegations of attempted assault, battery, poisoning, and strangulation.

Instead of unraveling every exposed thread of the tale, the Curia of Pavia apparently covered the matter sufficiently for its purposes without such extraneous details. In Rome, far from the scene of the crime, the bishop of Pavia remarked in a letter of November 10, 1651, "This case is turning into a Hydra. In order to notify the Sacred Congregation as soon as possible about such an important matter, my vicar-general has sent me for now the enclosed pages, which he believes prove sufficiently the substance of the matter." Certainly Giovanna Balcona—and perhaps Sister Angela Aurelia, too—would have been nonplussed to read what the bishop chose to emphasize as this substance: "The abasement of the rule of enclosure in that convent, not only by introducing students without Your Most Reverend Excellencies' license, but also other persons to run various errands, and still others simply at their pleasure, without the ordinary's license, or even written license of the convent's superior. . . . In that city and diocese that disorder is hardly uncommon in all convents governed by Regulars—I acknowledge this to cleanse my conscience."[25]

Through this focus, the bishop of Pavia picked up a stick often used to flog religious orders, whether Dominican, Benedictine, or Carmelite, who were often at odds with local bishops about decorous government of convents exempt from direct diocesan control.

Thus the plight of the fugitive pair was eclipsed by the larger issue. In his letter to the Sacred Congregation, the bishop made no mention of the women's relationship, much less of their nocturnal sleeping habits, though the accompanying summary did acknowledge the fugitive nun's infatuation with her disciple. This attitude was basically in line with the church hierarchy's general view at the time. They might inveigh against shared beds, but in the absence of more concrete and egregious evidence of what may have gone on in them (as in the case of Benedetta Carlini), they often took little or very measured action based on such allegations.

It would be more than three months before the Sacred Congregation responded, in late February 1652. The two fugitives should be absolved of excommunication, and unspecified but appropriate penances should be imposed on them. Giovanna Balcona was to be sent home, never again to set foot inside any cloister. Sister Angela Aurelia Mogna would return to Santa Maria degli Angeli, where she should be imprisoned, deprived of the veil, denied active and passive voice (the power to vote in convent elections or to be elected to office), and permitted no access to the parlatorio. The sentence from the Sacred Congregation is vague about how long any of these terms should last. More significantly given the bishop's argument, Santa Maria degli Angeli was forbidden to admit any girls without the Sacred Congregation's specific permission. The bishop was instructed to punish transgressors to the full extent of the law.[26]

Giovanna Balcona leaves San Patrizio and disappears. Sister Angela Aurelia also disappears shortly thereafter, though she seems to have lingered at San Gregorio a while longer. In April 1652 the nuns at Santa Maria degli Angeli complained to the Sacred Congregation that their wayward sister had not been returned to them and requested that the dilatory bishop of Pavia be ordered to do his job.

Upon her return to Santa Maria degli Angeli, it is hard to say exactly what awaited Sister Angela Aurelia. Despite their usually casual attitude toward their own rule, one can well imagine that the sisters might in this case even have sought out Saint Teresa's Constitutions for reformed Discalced Carmelites for guidance and culled them carefully for the most appropriate penalties they could discover—particularly if Mogna's fierce opponent Sister Anna Domitilla Langosca had anything to say about it. The paradigmatic reformist saint's Constitutions, in any event, reasonably suggest what Sister Angela Aurelia might have anticipated. Saint Teresa stipulated, for instance, that the convent prison "must be set apart. No sister in prison must be spoken to by any nun, save by those who act as her wardens." What other terms might constitute an "appropriately salutary penance"? For "sowing discord," Saint Teresa required that the offender "prostrate herself and bare her shoulders to receive the sentence she deserved. In the refectory she shall sit in the middle of the room, on the bare floor, and take bread and water." For "giving anyone letters without leave from the mother prioress," the offender should "at the canonical hours and at grace after meat, lie prostrate before the church door in view of the sisters as they pass." As necessary for their access to chapel or egress from refectory, the other nuns could simply step over her.

If a nun had slandered other sisters, Teresa was very specific. "At dinner, without her mantle but wearing a scapular on which have been sewn two tongue-shaped strips of red and white cloth, let her sit on the floor, in the center of the refectory, and take bread and water, as a symbol of punishment for her great sin of the tongue. And let her be taken thence to the prison."[27]

We know that Sister Angela Aurelia had been ailing for half a dozen years at least. She had been so near death just a few weeks earlier that the ever-practical Carmelite male superior had carefully inventoried all her belongings in anticipation of the inevitable, which did not happen just then. By the time the vicar-general returned to San Gregorio to continue his inquiry on October 3, a week after her escape, he found Sister Angela so gravely ill that she could not leave her prison bed when he summoned her to the grates. So however soft or harsh her eventual penance back at Santa Maria degli Angeli, the lovelorn, lonely woman may not have endured it for long.

"A WOMAN ALWAYS RENOWNED FOR GOODNESS, GREAT WISDOM, AND ELOQUENCE"

Very soon Santa Maria degli Angeli, the diocesan Curia, and Pavia would have worse things to worry about. Thousands of Franco-Savoyard troops besieged the city in 1655, while roving armies pillaged the countryside. When the Spanish army of Lombardy finally broke the siege after almost two months, famine and pestilence did not end.

Records of Santa Maria degli Angeli next resurface in January 1657. During its intervening travails, the community had shrunk from twenty-four to only thirteen. Without the girls removed in 1652 and with the Sacred Congregation's moratorium on admissions, no younger women took profession as the older generation slowly died off. By 1657 living conditions at the convent had become so constrained that when a nun named Sister Anna Domitilla Chini wrote to the Sacred Congregation, she claimed that "they can maintain neither regular monastic observance nor observance of their rule, and do not live according to it."

Like Angela Aurelia Mogna before her, this Chini, a professed nun since 1647, wanted to flee, but she hoped to do so through official channels. She requested permission to reclaim her dowry, still safely on deposit in Milan, leave Santa Maria degli Angeli, and transfer to the Franciscan convent of Sant'Agata. There, she asserted rather piously, "they live with greater discipline, by their rule, since their circumstances are better, and there are enough nuns." Both convents voted in favor of Chini's proposal, she claimed, so it seemed (at least to her) to be a win-win situation. But the Sacred Congregation must have thought otherwise. The cardinals read the petition but declined to respond at all. Perhaps Chini's apparent lack of selfless concern for her consorelle at Santa Maria degli Angeli, or simply her temerity, left them speechless.[28]

Apparently Chini grew tired of waiting for word from Rome and decided not to abandon her fellow Carmelites after all. When news from the convent next reaches Rome in 1658 and 1659, the sisters of Santa Maria degli Angeli, seconded by none other than the Duchess of Mantua, petitioned to elect Chini prioress. The sticky issue prompting the nuns' petition to the Sacred Congregation was that before her profession in 1647 Chini had been married from 1633 until her husband's death in 1643. They explained, "The convent is in such a miserable state of poverty that all the nuns refuse the burden of becoming prioress. On the other hand, Sister Anna Domitilla Chini displays such exemplary lifestyle, ample income, and extraordinary energy that they would happily appoint her if her prior marriage did not render her ineligible." So they hoped for an exception to the rule—"otherwise they cannot solve their dire financial and administrative predicaments."

In his supporting statement, the vicar-general pointed out that the nuns' constitution did not really exclude widows from high office. He was also quick to assure the cardinals in Rome that Sister Chini "has an exemplary lifestyle and manners, and is diligent in chapel." More especially, "She has more than sufficient income, not only for her own support, but also to relieve the convent's extreme poverty, and she is most capable of addressing and stabilizing its affairs." In light of such compelling evidence, the Sacred Congregation was pleased to concur. For a short while at least, Santa Maria degli Angeli's future finally looked a little less dire.[29]

Alas, not for long. Nearly a decade later, Santa Maria degli Angeli resurfaces, and we learn that life in the convent has taken another turn for the worse. Its community has shrunk to only ten sisters. Once again Sister Anna Domitilla Chini is looking to leave. The enterprising, energetic, and pious sometime prioress reports to Rome in 1667 that she has lately promoted among some of Pavia's well-heeled faithful the notion of erecting a second Carmelite convent—not of the Ancient Observance, but a *reformed* house of Discalced Carmelites that would bear the name of the order's founder, Saint Teresa. Sister Chini has been collaborating with the bishop, whom the Sacred Congregation has already ordered to discover how best to fulfill this devout desire. Sister Anna Domitilla intends to move into Saint Teresa upon its completion. "But because word has gotten out that she will leave her present convent and be transferred to the new one, the nuns have come to despise her. They torment her so that her life is now in danger." In the meantime, Chini hopes to transfer to a less hazardous institution until Santa Teresa can be made ready for occupancy.

This time the bishop himself responded to the Sacred Congregation's request for information. Indeed, the inhabitants of Santa Maria degli Angeli were furious because a rival reformed Carmelite convent would certainly damage their cause (and perhaps their reputation), not to mention that Chini's transfer would lose them her sizable personal income. "Two (a choir nun and a conversa) overheard other nuns say that they all needed to unite and finish off this woman, to resolve every problem. And the choir nun added that she'd heard among the nuns that it would be a good idea to poison her." The Congregation ordered the bishop to intercede personally in restoring peace at Santa Maria degli Angeli. If his actions proved ineffectual, Chini would have to be moved as she requested.[30]

Ultimately, Chini's grand plan for Santa Teresa was doomed, and no such house was ever built. Meanwhile the bishop of Pavia had to figure out what to do with this woman who had become so unpopular at her home. He presented Chini to the venerable Benedictine model of convent piety, the Monastery of San Martino del Leano, as "a woman always renowned for goodness, a woman of great wisdom and eloquence, whose words have won the souls of many gentlemen, governing officials, and great ladies, with whom she has promoted her present convent's interests," as the nuns reported.

The prioress, the subprioress, and at least half the sisters of San Martino very much liked what they heard concerning the woman who might come to live among them. Thus the bishop had good reason for optimism when Sister Anna Domitilla Chini was formally proposed for acceptance by the forty-one professed nuns on August 13. After the vote, however, the black balls numbered eighteen. Without support from two-thirds of the community, Chini could not join them. The bishop was so astonished that he descended on San Martino three or four times during the ensuing week, and various local, refined ladies followed him, all lobbying on behalf of Sister Anna Domitilla. On August 23 the assembled nuns balloted a second time. When finished with this count, the abbess declared twenty-seven in favor and fourteen against—a marked improvement over the first ballot (though at least fifteen subsequently swore they had blackballed Chini). Unfortunately for Chini and the bishop, even this figure was still not a clear two-thirds majority, but it came tantalizingly close—or alarmingly so, depending on whether the perspective was inside or outside the convent wall.

With both sides proclaiming victory and the bishop still backing Chini, those piously opposed decide it is time to write to Rome. Yes, Sister Chini has money and certainly talks a good game. Yet her personal history raises serious objections. Before becoming a nun at Santa Maria degli Angeli, she had been married, as was well known to the Sacred Congregation. Between her husband's death and her entry into Santa Maria degli Angeli, however, Chini was taken by Marchese Langosco (also Casalasco), who brought her here and kept her as his concubine for many years in Pavia, where he was killed, as it came out, in a place he should never have gone, even in his thoughts. Then she reformed, apparently. Although this city maintains a convent for reformed prostitutes, for reasons nobody knows, she was accepted at Santa Maria degli Angeli. She was even made prioress there, with the blessing of the Sacred Congregation. It had only been informed, however, that Chini had been married and widowed. There was no mention of the other blot on her reputation. But this circumstance was—and is—so manifestly known throughout Pavia that even now this nun is called only "Langosca" and not "Chini."[31]

Given the perennial avalanche of paperwork the Sacred Congregation confronted year after year and given the normally brief life expectancy of many who were elected to the Sacred College of Cardinals, we should not expect "la Langosca" to have rung any bells in the Congregation's collective memory. Indeed, readers of this narrative may have lost "la Langosca" in the confusing stream of unfamiliar Italian names. But surely her name had been on some sisters' lips at Santa Maria degli Angeli back in 1651.

If Giovanna Balcona had managed to survive into her thirties and was still living in Pavia, she must have laughed out loud as this delicious scandal about her former home made its way around the city. Giovanna would never have forgotten her old enemy Sister Anna Domitilla Langosca trying to hide behind her old married name, Chini. Giovanna would also have recognized that the archdiocesan Curia of Pavia really could not claim ignorance and innocence in the affair. After all, Giovanna herself had alluded to Langosca's shady past in her sworn testimony before the diocesan vicar-general twenty years before: "Paola Antonia da Voghera, servant or lady-in-waiting to Sister Domitilla, *whom she brought along with her from the convent of the Magdalene*, entered the convent without a license."[32] Il Monastero della Maddalena was, of course, an institution for reformed prostitutes. That Giovanna made nothing more of this presumably potent tidbit of convent gossip strongly suggests that it was common knowledge. So in 1668 even the Curia could hardly dispute San Martino's assertion that "this circumstance was—and is—so manifestly known throughout Pavia that even now this nun is called only 'Langosca' and not 'Chini.'"

A good number of citizens in Pavia lined up behind San Martino's perhaps more pious, but no more "forgiving" sisters, who exclaimed bluntly, "We don't know wherein lies this Langosca's vaunted wisdom, since she didn't know how to manage her own self wisely, which scandalized an entire city." Various letters landed on the Sacred Congregation's desk. They came from nuns' sisters, nuns' cousins, and nuns' friends in high places. Some discreetly expressed concern that the objectors dared not write openly because of recent episcopal attempts at coercion. Others articulated local concern that the bishop himself was lobbying for the Congregation's dispensation to transfer Chini, a.k.a. Langosca. After all, the Langosca family numbered itself among the noble lines in the region, and the late marquis's largesse may have accounted for the well-lined pockets of Sister Anna Domitilla's habit. Even though somewhat sullied, perhaps the old luster of the Langosca name, together with Anna Domitilla Langosca's winning words, might have blinded the bishop to the sorry blot of concubinage, but it was bound to stain San Martino's unblemished reputation for virginal purity.

One writer pointed to obvious alternatives: the morally appropriate institutions for Langosca. The Sacred Congregation could, and should, send her (back) either to the Convertite or to the Casa del Soccorso. Probably the most compelling argument, however, took the form of a warning from a few of the less timid nuns of San Martino: "One must recognize that if Chini were ever to enter our convent, she would immediately learn about those against her. Without doubt, then, continual rifts and discord would ensue. A danger would forever linger that the devil might suggest to someone within these walls the remedies of poison, which she already claims to fear where she is now."[33]

Perhaps one of these threats found its mark. In any case, out of these lesser ironies a larger one emerges, for Sister Anna Domitilla Chini Langosca vanishes, just as her forgotten foe, Angela Aurelia Mogna, had vanished before her. And she leaves behind a host of ambiguities that ironically recall those that shrouded the disappearance of Angela Aurelia back in 1651. Both claimed their attempted departures were inspired by a sanctifying spirit of monastic reform.

As prioress, had the energetic, single-minded Anna Domitilla perhaps sincerely attempted a return to the spirit and letter of her convent's rule, as Angela Aurelia had attempted decades before? Whatever may have motivated intramural responses to both their actions, for each of them the consequences could potentially have been fatal. Was Angela Aurelia's flight truly inspired by the Holy Spirit, as she claimed (and might even have believed), or by a decidedly earthly, even infernal love, as her consorelle unanimously insisted? Had Chini Langosca, the former concubine turned Carmelite, undergone a sincere spiritual conversion, if not in the 1640s and 1650s (as her rivals' earlier characterizations of her certainly suggest), perhaps in the 1660s, when an apparently exemplary lifestyle won her the esteem of many outside, if not within, convent walls? Or was she simply loath to waste away (and waste her money) in the spiritual and temporal wasteland that Santa Maria degli Angeli had become? Perhaps the only certainty is that in the end both Angela Aurelia and Anna Domitilla passed into an inauspicious future, one that probably—or at least ultimately—involved their Maker.

"WITH THAT, THE MATTER WILL BE CLOSED"

For Santa Maria degli Angeli as a whole, a similarly dire future awaited. Long an embarrassment to the diocesan Curia and to its male Carmelite superiors, whose own reputations must have suffered from the latest debacle, its numbers now drastically reduced, virtually insolvent financially, and with its only moneyed member scurrying to abandon ship, the convent became an obvious target for Rome's monastic housecleaning of the day. In 1649 Innocent X created the Congregation on the State of Regular Clergy to ferret out and suppress monastic houses that were too small and too poor to be viable. On the whole this was a sensible and humane strategy, rather than allowing tiny religious communities to struggle and gradually wither. The shoe fit Santa Maria degli Angeli perfectly.[34]

Nonetheless, Rome chose to hold off a little longer. Forbidding the admission of any new sisters, the Sacred Congregation left the remaining ten sisters—even now twice the quota set a century earlier—to confront on their own their few remaining options. No such option was positive, but the end was clearly inevitable.

Which brings us back to the bishop's final visit in the bleak early days of 1675 and rounds out this tale. The description of Santa Maria degli Angeli's desperate circumstances was sent off to Rome. On February 2, 1675, the Sacred Congregation ruled that Santa Maria degli Angeli should be suppressed. The remaining six nuns and few converse who had managed to endure since the latest scandals of 1668 would be transferred, preferably to a convent of the same order. Anna Domitilla Chini Langosca's dream of a convent of Santa Teresa had ended abruptly, and the nearest Carmelite female house (either Ancient Observance or Discalced) was more than thirty miles away. That being the case, the few survivors from Santa Maria degli Angeli may have confronted life under a different monastic rule at a house closer to home.

When the bishop reported the completion of his mission in early summer, he simply indicated the nuns' removal "to another convent." Presumably they all stayed together, though that may have been a mixed blessing, judging by the group's history. In this communiqué, the bishop requested permission to dispose of convent property immediately, since the transplanted sisters still needed dowries and furnishings. Santa Maria degli Angeli's contents were largely worthless or in such bad condition as to be useless in the nuns' new surroundings. Sold as junk or salvage together with the dilapidated buildings, the convent's property might bring, all told, eight hundred Roman scudi.

Since it would be indecent—indeed, dangerous—to celebrate Mass in the virtually ruined chapel, it should be deconsecrated. But there remained the matter of generations of nuns reposing peacefully beneath the chapel floor, quietly oblivious, we assume, to decades of turmoil that had gone on above them. The bishop recommended that their bones be dug up and reburied in some cemetery or other. "And with that," the vicar general concluded, "the matter will be closed."[35]

And so it was not long thereafter that Sister Angela Aurelia Mogna, with little fuss and less dignity, but this time with full approval of her superiors both in Rome and in Pavia, at last may have found her way out of Santa Maria degli Angeli.

6

NIGHTS AT THE OPERA: THE TRAVELS AND TRAVAILS OF CHRISTINA CAVAZZA

Santa Cristina della Fondazza (Bologna, 1708–35)

BOLOGNA:
"A CRIME MOTIVATED SIMPLY BY IDLE CURIOSITY"

Settecento Bologna prided itself on a rich cultural life, second only to Rome among cities of the Papal States. Goings-on in the city kept self-appointed chroniclers busy describing dramatic, musical, and religious spectacles as well as the aristocratic altercations in matters of honor that frequently seemed to erupt at these occasions. Among the city's spectacles, operatic performances had a history almost as old as opera itself. By the 1630s they centered in the Teatro Formagliari in via Castiglione. After 1653 Teatro Formagliari developed a serious rivalry with Teatro Malvezzi, built not far from Bologna's present-day Teatro Comunale. Over time, Teatro Malvezzi's elegant interior, which the Galli-Bibiena family enlarged and redecorated in the late 1690s, became the favorite musical haunt of the city's first families.

The dawn of the settecento, however, found Bolognese music drama in the doldrums. Clement XI's five-year ban on carnival festivities, which he hoped would buy God's deliverance from the repeated earthquakes that struck Rome in the winter of 1703, would keep the stages of Teatro Formagliari and Teatro Malvezzi dark until 1708. Devotees of dramatic vocal music had to content themselves with private performances in noble houses, if they were lucky enough to be invited. Or they might attend sacred dramas—whose numbers swelled from five to ten in 1703 and to twenty-one in 1704—produced by churches such as San Domenico and confraternities such as Santa Maria della Vita. Having banned carnival fun, at least the pope helped underwrite edifying sacred productions in Rome. Presumably Bolognese performers were left to fend for themselves.[1]

Naturally then, a rush of excitement accompanied the end of the ban, when the cardinal legate reinstated carnival in Bologna on New Year's Day 1708. Until Ash Wednesday the whole city was transformed or, as some say, turned upside down. The public could go about masked and in disguise—except for prostitutes, who were specifically forbidden to do so. Ordinary behavior was swallowed up in a jumbled succession of spectacles, formal and informal, rehearsed and spontaneous. There were masked parades, tournaments, and relatively organized tourneys that involved chasing pigs and bulls. And of course the inevitable fights and brawls. Very likely the townsfolk developed a baroque equivalent of today's "boobs for beads" or other public displays of lewdness. In streets, porticos, plazas, and palaces, carnival reigned. Though festivities were not to occur on holy ground, archdiocesan enforcers mostly fought a losing battle to prevent maskers' indecencies in churches and cemeteries.[2]

As in many places that celebrate carnival, Bolognese maskers regularly created this topsy-turvy world each year as they had done for centuries. During carnival patricians became peasants, fresh-faced maidens became toothless hags, men became women, and women became men. And of course the laity could try to masquerade as any of an endless variety of clergy. Bolognese maskers made an art of such diversions. As far back as the quattrocento, Bologna's mask makers had rivaled those of Ferrara and Modena. Galeazzo Maria Sforza, fifteenth-century Duke of Milan, specifically sought the Bolognese mask because it was not simply smeared with plaster outside and pitch and sulfur inside. Bologna's masks could be had in linen layered with pitch, then waxed within and without. Some of them were so artfully made that they could be mistaken for flesh.

Organized parades of maskers customarily formed around Porta San Mammolo, south of downtown, snaked their way toward the city center, then continued eastward along via Santo Stefano. In ambitious years they might adopt a theme. An enduring favorite was

Ghibelline King Enzio of Sardinia's entry into Bologna in chains. Defeated by the Bolognese Guelphs in 1249, Rè Enzo had lived out his last twenty-three years imprisoned in the city.

For Bolognese "running of the bulls," sometimes even the animals wore costumes. In 1537 a crowd of wild, irreverent *mattaccini* (carnival buffoons whose Venetian counterparts were notorious for flinging eggs filled with perfume) battled a "bull"—a mule disguised in a cowhide—until the bleachers in Piazza Maggiore collapsed, breaking numerous arms, legs, and heads. Two years later maskers disguised as more mattaccini and Jews challenged a straw-filled carnival figure to a horse race down via Santo Stefano. Back in Piazza Maggiore in 1692, twelve blindfolded "Germans" did their best to bludgeon two pigs to death as the crowd roared in delight.

The city offered more refined carnival entertainments, of course. Chiefly for patrician pseudopeasants and lady milkmaids pro tem, these happened mostly in the palaces of the rich. Shortly before the papal ban, in January 1699, no fewer than six such masked balls offered amusement to Bologna's genteel families in a single carnival season. There were not only the inevitable dances, but also other diversions: a hothouse filled with grapefruit trees, entirely illuminated, at Palazzo Alamandini; a lavish banquet setting of delicacies on silver gilt at Palazzo Aldrovandi; dazzling illumination of the courtyard and ballroom at Palazzo Caprara (without benefit of electricity, it goes without saying); and, inevitably, jam, candies, grapefruit, chocolate, and liqueurs to refresh the ladies and other maskers. In 1693 Bologna's papal legate and vice legate reputedly had spent no less than two thousand scudi for a single such evening's delights.

Among the uniquely Bolognese carnival entertainments were demonstrations of anatomical dissection performed in Bologna's elegant anatomy theater of polished wood and marquetry, an architectural marvel that draws tourists to this day. As the anatomist, with appropriately theatrical flourishes, dissected the star of the show (who, thanks to January temperatures, took longer to offend refined noses than he would in another season), maskers looked on in queasy fascination from surrounding amphitheater seats. In a nearby chapel, priests said Mass for the soul of the dismembered, at the officiating anatomist's expense.[3]

When the archbishop's beadles weren't guarding churches and

cemeteries against masked revelers' naughtiness, they did their best to shield convents from the distractions of such carnival excess. Boy bishops or lords of misrule, who had become traditional figures in male clerical environments during the freer festive seasons, were too dangerous for women religious, whom the ecclesiastical patriarchy presumably judged too prone to forget their proper place once sobriety returned. Yet the regular republication of archiepiscopal bans on masking in and around the convents of Bologna gives the impression that cloister walls were rarely tall enough and seldom solid enough to keep out all carnival enthusiasm. In 1676 the astonished Bolognese archbishop even received a "nonsensical request" from lay maskers—either extraordinarily naive or extraordinarily cheeky—who actually requested archiepiscopal license to play, sing, and dance at convent doorways.

Ever since Cardinal Archbishop Gabriele Paleotti's late sixteenth-century attempts to enforce the dictates of the Council of Trent, righteous reformers repeatedly complained that whole convents would forget about God for the two months of carnival. The women danced, sang songs, presented plays and pageants, even played cards and threw dice. The efficient nuns of San Guglielmo elected one sister as "vicar of carnival" to supervise their intramural festivities. Some nuns went so far as to trade in their habits for lay clothing—and not just female clothing, either! Extravagant lapses of monastic decorum during carnival were regularly reported by both amused diarists and outraged clerics. During a carnival ball in the parlatorio at Santi Naborre e Felice in the 1560s, the abbess assigned a dozen young nuns, dressed as brides, to specific "husbands" when certain lay gentlemen arrived in the parlatorio. Then the couples danced "together" for the evening. Even with a grate interposed between them, the dancers performed quite successfully, since some cinquecento dances required little or no physical contact.

In 1708, the Clementine ban had scarcely ended when the enthusiastic but misguided father confessor to the nuns of San Guglielmo got an extraordinary idea. He removed the Blessed Sacrament and the tabernacle that, inconveniently for his purposes, blocked the large grated window over the high altar in the convent's external church. He had a bench constructed before the window so that it could accommodate an enthusiastic crowd of maskers who arrived to view a spiritual carnival play performed by the nuns in their inner chapel beyond the grate.[4]

Every winter the Sacred Congregation anticipated a few indignant communications about convent carnival excesses ranging across Italy from Milan to Messina. Mostly humdrum tales of dancing, presenting plays, or exchanging monastic habits for lay clothing cropped up predictably. (The greatest outrage was typically spent on men's or actresses' attire and its improper use.) Occasionally something a little more imaginative would eclipse the commonplace. In 1673, for example, officials in Volterra (fifty miles west of Florence) reported that a pair of monks had thrown snowballs ("as the laity here customarily does during carnival") at nuns who seemed to have intentionally stationed themselves at doors and windows as targets. In 1630, irate nuns' relatives from Amelia (north of Rome) complained that a local father confessor enacted a "running of the bulls," though in this case the animals were calves confined within the convent parlatorio.[5]

After the lifting of the papal ban, Bologna's reopened opera houses offered more refined attractions for the populace's attention. A diary from the papal legation noted performances beginning in the public theater as early as January 5, 1708. The season proper began at Teatro Formagliari on January 16 with *Le rise di Democrito*. By the early 1700s this was an old chestnut, first heard in Vienna back in 1670, with music by Antonio Draghi, regally assisted with the composition by his employer Emperor Leopold I. The performance at Teatro Formagliari would revive the Viennese revival of 1700, this time with music by Bologna's own erstwhile child prodigy now made good, Francesco Antonio Pistocchi, brilliant singer, renowned singing teacher, and *principe* of the Accademia Filarmonica di Bologna. Intermezzi offered additional diversion between the acts. *Le rise* held Teatro Formagliari's stage throughout the carnival season.

Opera audiences had to wait until early summer for the reopening of the rival theater. In early May Teatro Malvezzi heralded its own season. *Il fratricida innocente: Drama eroico per musica* promised local maestro Giacomo Perti's brand new music for Apostolo Zeno's libretto *Vencesclao*. The libretto had premiered in Venice five years earlier and would become a staple of opera houses from London to Barcelona over the next fifty years. At Teatro Malvezzi, Zeno's drama would alternate with the lighter *Lo scherno degli Dei: Pastorale per musica*, a group effort by several composers, enlivened by intermezzi titled *Melissa*.

Singers, several making Bolognese debuts, would include stars regularly heard from Venice to Naples, some of them on loan from the courts of Tuscany and Mantua. Of equal importance, the house had commissioned new sets from the illustrious Ferdinando Galli-Bibiena. Posters slapped up around the city exhorted anyone wanting reserved seats to pay the impresario directly, before May 12 at the very latest. The season opened on May 19 "with all the magnificence in scenery, costumes, and musicians one could desire." It was attended by such worthies as the Bolognese papal legate and Gian Gastone de' Medici, Grand Duke of Tuscany, who had come to observe with pride the performances of singers from his musical stable.[6]

While informal carnival entertainments might occasionally find their way to the cloister, productions at Teatro Formagliari and Teatro Malvezzi were quite another matter, unimaginably beyond any sister's reach. Music enthusiasts within the cloister could experience only pale reflections of what went on at the theaters, as relayed by aristocratic relatives who visited them in convent parlatorios. The most avid audiences for such secondhand accounts were very likely singing nuns who enjoyed artistic reputations of their own beyond convent walls. In fact these very same convent divas might have discreetly helped fill the musical void during Clement XI's ban by offering select audiences edifying and respectable opportunities to experience female soprano singing. But Archbishop Giacomo Boncompagni had nipped that prospect in the bud by forbidding all convent music except plainchant back in February 1702, even before Clement XI's earthquake-assuaging ban.

Convent singers, visiting with relatives at the grates of the parlatorios, must have listened with particular fascination and a little longing to descriptions of the long-anticipated musical spectacles. If a sister was lucky, an especially audacious relative might have slipped her the pocket-sized printed libretto sold at the theaters, though the nun would pay a price if discovered accepting or reading such a text. Of course nuns who were singers may have hoped for more detail about the performances and rather less about the audience, chocolates, oranges, and liqueurs that were the focus of these occasions for much of society.

For the Curia, any such incursion of the outside world demonstrated yet again the evils of convent parlatorios and other chinks in clausura—doors, gates, grates, ruote. After five years of relative calm regarding carnival, in 1708 they were once again distracting the sisters from their true calling. Even if the problem did not involve the more scandalous carnival maskers' infractions, this sort of idle talk brought worldly vanities where they least belonged. More devout sisters could scarcely escape distraction. For those nuns who were more fanciful, imaginative, or independent-minded, distraction could certainly lead to temptation, the church hierarchy warned. No wonder, then, that one zealous convent reformer dubbed parlatorios and convent grates *finestre della morte*—windows onto death.

Clement XI had even feared that convent misbehavior at such weak points in the cloister's defenses might provoke further quakes, so he ordered church authorities throughout the Papal States to tighten security at confessional, communion, and parlatorio grates and to guard their keys closely. The nun's vicar of Bologna responded somewhat smugly in February 1708, "True, some men visit the gates. It's easy to post an edict, difficult to compel obedience. But one can reimpose it with greater severity. Whoever wants to talk secretly goes to the grates, and those who frequent the gate are nobility wanting a look at daughters and sisters. They're quick about it, though, because in this city we don't have that practice of laypeople hanging around the nuns, as in Ferrara and all the other surrounding territories."[7]

Just a few months later, in the early morning hours of June 27, 1708, the portinara at Santa Cristina della Fondazza was completing her rounds of exactly such gates, grates, and doorways that looked from the cloister out to the world.[8] The portinara's responsibility was to see to it that all convent openings were always secured. She played a role equivalent to that of a modern-day security guard. At Santa Cristina two sisters shared the office, alternating weeks on duty to lessen the boredom. Typically that morning, she was largely just going through the motions still half asleep, but she came fully awake when she discovered that the chain meant to secure the carriage gate was

FIGURE 6.1 A Camaldolese choir nun, from Pierre Helyot, *Histoire des ordres religieux et militaires* (Paris: Louis, 1792).

unlocked. She was certain—or so she claimed to the convent bursar just a little later—that it had been firmly attached the night before.

The portinara and the bursar were both old enough to remember a morning fourteen years earlier when the nuns awoke to discover that thieves had managed to get inside overnight.[9] This time a quick check of the sacristy and the altars revealed that the house's treasures were all in their proper places. Just to be safe, though, the bursar ordered a few nuns to begin taking turns the next night to stand watch from the safety of the *camerino della messa*, which offered views of both the public church interior and the courtyard inside the carriage gateway.

Three nights passed without incident. By then, novelty and anxious anticipation had already given way to the boredom customary among night watchers. But two hours after sunset on the fourth night, the posted sentry was startled from her doze to hear the gate quietly open. Peering out the window she glimpsed what looked like a figure in black disappearing through the gap. Off she went to rouse the bursar. On inspection, the door proved to be open. Now seriously alarmed, the bursar enlisted a squadron of four other sisters to serve as that night's extra sentries. Unsure what might confront them and remembering well the nocturnal thieves of the 1690s, the bursar also rousted out the aging convent maintenance man for some masculine, if no more "virile," backup.

Well past midnight the anxious lookouts thought they heard a soft grating. The door opened slightly inward. Dark as it was, they could make out a darker figure slipping inside. As the figure turned to re-secure the gate, a hesitant "Who's there?" disturbed the stillness. The figure stiffened for only a moment before it seemed almost to wilt. Now the maintenance man's masculine courage was required as he advanced gingerly across the no-man's-land of the shadowy courtyard toward the figure, its menace quickly dissipating. The five others waited just inside the boundary of clausura. In timorous fascination they saw the mysterious figure advance into the dim light from the camerino della messa. Rather spare, it appeared to be a male religious. Why was an abbot sneaking into the convent courtyard in the middle of the night? Then, incredibly, the mysterious cleric mumbled a name they knew in a voice they recognized. Goodness! Was this Donna Maria Christina? The figure entered the light. Sure enough—

this lanky abbot had the face of Donna Maria Christina Cavazza, one of the professed nuns of Santa Cristina.

In an instant, fearful anticipation turned to dumbfounded consternation. Why was Donna Christina dressed in an abbot's robes? What had she been up to outside the convent? Perhaps more important, what would her actions do to her—and to the convent as a whole? In the now vain hope of discretion, the bursar sent the workman back where he belonged. Then she dispatched one of the sentries to rouse the abbess. In the meantime, the mortified Cavazza was beside herself and desperately implored her captors for compassion. If they could forgive her and keep her discovery to themselves, she vowed to spend the rest of her life in repentance. The abbess's arrival put an authoritative end to such miserable and unrealistic pleading. Donna Christina was led off to limitless detention in her cell, while her fate rested in the hands of their religious superiors.

By morning the ridiculousness of Christina Cavazza's hope for sympathetic, sisterly discretion was patent. Long before lauds and first light, every nuns' rest must have been interrupted with the news that one of their number had slipped out of the convent disguised as an abbot—to attend the opera! Not once, but several times! Nor would the convent wall prove a barrier to such sensational gossip, thanks to the workman's inclusion in the proceedings. In the public's collective imagination, as subjects of gossip fugitive nuns were second only to lascivious ones. In short order, Archbishop Boncompagni dispatched his nuns' vicar to imprison the offender and expose every detail of the crime.

Just like the public of that day, our first thought probably runs like this: What sort of nun could have contemplated, much less committed, such an egregious violation of her vows as to leave the cloister without permission? To go to the opera! As has proved true for so many of our nun transgressors, we can discover little about Christina Cavazza before her notorious missteps in the summer of 1708.[10] Born in 1679, Maria Teresa Vincenza Catterina was the daughter of Giovanni Battista Cavazzi and Prudenza Andalò Branchetti. The Cavazzi were a respectable, upwardly mobile Bolognese family but had no real place among the local gentry at that time. They go unnoticed in Pompeo Scipione Dolfi's *Cronologia delle famiglie nobili di Bologna* (1670), which makes at least passing mention of the "Branchetti Andalò" family. So it may be that Christina's father married a step or two above his station.

If her story ran like that of other young women of the time, the future Donna Christina probably entered Santa Cristina around age fifteen, not long before she donned the novice's habit in 1694. As she formally entered the order, she assumed one of the longest religious names in her community: Donna Maria Christina Teresa Prudenza Deodata Cavazza. Her final vows followed a year later. In her widowed mother's will of April 1696, Donna Christina received what was legally due her from the family. In exchange for a silver fruit bowl, a crucifix, and a hundred lire, she was to light a candle before the crucifix in her mother's memory every Holy Week and on the feast of the Holy Cross. The following August, Cavazza began signing for her provisions, paid twice annually, like clockwork, by her brother Girolamo Cavazzi.

The Cavazzi family had no strong family connections at Santa Cristina of the sort that often eased girls' passage from the world to the cloister. The attraction, both for Maria Christina and for her fellow nuns, was the girl's musical talent. She was a singer with potential star quality, and Santa Cristina had a century-old reputation for excellence in music. In 1699 Maria Christina sang prominently and publicly during the Camaldolese ritual Consecration of Virgins. This ceremony capped an extended convent battle against Archbishop Boncompagni in Rome. Emerging victorious from that fight, the nuns retained the right to perform this ritual in their time-honored if controversial manner. Donna Christina (though technically speaking, she was five years too young to participate) and eleven of her consorelle marched publicly outside monastic enclosure and down the nave of their external church to be consecrated amid lavish music performed by the leading singers among them. Standing out in its boldness and opulence from Bologna's many religious, cultural, and social highlights of the 1690s, this Consecration of Virgins certainly had not endeared the nuns of Santa Cristina to Cardinal Boncompagni. The piqued archbishop had in fact spurned the nuns' lavish gifts acknowledging his grudging participation in the rite. He subsequently found his way to reinvigorate the war with them when he banned all elaborate convent singing in 1702.

Despite the archbishop's prohibition, Donna Christina boldly per-

FIGURE 6.2 Santa Cristina, after Filippo Gnudi, *Pianta iconografica* (1702). Reproduced with permission of the Biblioteca Comunale dell'Archiginnasio, Bologna. The wall surrounding the courtyard of the public church, since demolished, is clearly visible. Santa Maria del Piombo stands opposite the end of via del Piombo, running along the left side of the convent. Porta di strada Maggiore, through which Cavazza passed in 1735 on her way to via Fondazza and Santa Cristina, appears at lower left.

formed on the feast of Santa Cristina in May 1703. Although she did not sing before the convent's superiors, whom the nuns pointedly chose not to invite, such presumption never went unnoticed. Then, merely three weeks later, the local nuns' vicar was astonished to hear Cavazza once again, episcopal prohibition notwithstanding. On the feast of Santa Cristina in 1704, Christina Cavazza and two of her singing companions finally went too far. By boldly singing solos for vespers and Mass, they set off the next direct confrontation over music between Santa Cristina and Archbishop Boncompagni, who forbade the disobedient singers further access to the parlatorio, grates, and doorways for as long as he saw fit. After Rome's intercession, this episode ended in a draw and an uneasy peace. Her place near the center of these battles leaves little doubt about the strength of Christina Cavazza's musical enthusiasm and her independence of mind—or, as some would say, it showed her audacity or downright female foolhardiness.

In 1708 music turned out to be the woman's undoing. Although the full transcript of Christina Cavazza's interrogation and trial in 1708 has never come to light, its primary details were summarized in communications with Rome over the next two years, while the fugitive nun languished in her cell. I mentioned the hubbub that opera produced in Bologna that year. For Christina Cavazza, the fascination of the city's newly reopened opera houses proved irresistible. Secondhand reports in the parlatorio were completely inadequate. As the relatively relaxed atmosphere of carnival drew on, Donna Christina began to toy with the ordinarily unthinkable notion of taking in the opera at Teatro Formagliari in person. Once she hit on the idea of disguising herself in an abbot's robes, she had the means of turning her fantasy into reality. Since many others would wear masks and disguises for carnival, a nun dressed as an abbot could surely lose herself among the revelers.

As they reflected on the crime, one of the sisters claimed to remember that a black bundle destined for Christina Cavazza had passed through the convent ruota—or so she testified. That explained how the abbot's robes entered Santa Cristina. Clearly, Cavazza must have had an accomplice on the outside, and the mysterious black bundle proved it. Cavazza eventually revealed the name of Don Antonio Giacomelli, priest from the village of Piancaldolo, twenty-eight miles off in the Bolognese hinterlands. The archbishop immediately dispatched his constables to arrest him, but they arrived too late. Don Antonio had already gone to ground. Difficulties in snaring him further delayed an already protracted investigation.

Giacomelli had recently been named curate of Sassoleone, six miles from his hometown of Piancaldolo, but more important, he had also filled the chaplaincy of Santa Maria del Piombo, situated against Bologna's city wall—just behind the convent of Santa Cristina. All that separated the convent's back garden from Santa Maria del Piombo was a decrepit, crumbling wall, so dangerously overgrown with pomegranate trees, bushes, vines, and roses that the nuns constantly complained to the Compagnia del Piombo about keeping them pruned. In the seventeenth century there had even been a back gate to Santa Cristina almost opposite Santa Maria del Piombo; it is impossible to say whether this gate still existed in Christina Cavazza's day. But this porous boundary might well have been where the pair first met. At later meetings, either in the garden again or perhaps at the grilled communion window in the convent chapel or the nearby ruota of the sacristy, the two may have worked out Cavazza's audacious plan.[11]

In her abbot's robes and allegedly using a forged key, Donna Christina had first slipped away during carnival in late January. The greatest risk of exposure came as she crossed the convent courtyard and went out the carriage gate. Once the gate was locked for the night and compline finished, the sisters would go to bed. There was no nocturnal guard at the gate, and no dog to bark. But there was always the chance that one of the sisters might be about, or perhaps the convent workman next door would be up late. Yet once she cleared the gate Cavazza could relax—or at least try to. No one was likely to notice one more abbot among any other masked imitation priests on Bologna's streets.

Now outside the convent walls, Cavazza may have found her way the short distance along via del Piombo to Giacomelli's church right at the end of the street. From there, the two "clerics" would have headed west toward Teatro Formagliari, with Don Antonio in the lead. Again, there was little risk of discovery as they traversed the streets. Should Giacomelli encounter someone he knew, Donna Christina could keep quiet. Should she absolutely have to speak, some might raise an eyebrow at the priest enjoying female company, but it was carnival. If it came to it, the very gullible might even be convinced that Giacomelli's companion was a castrato in clerical garb. It is hard to imagine, however, that the masquerading nun ever relaxed while away from the security of the cloister. How would Christina Cavazza, who had not been outside the convent for fifteen years, respond to this abrupt reintroduction to the world—especially the world of carnival? It is almost easier to grasp the stunning audacity of the act than to imagine how she remained cool and collected during her escapades.

FIGURE 6.3 The restored church of Santa Cristina, 2008. Photo: Luca Salvucci. Christina Cavazza slipped out of the convent through the parlatorio, near the low wall at right, crossed the paved area, went through the convent gateway (now demolished), and probably walked down the street at left, via del Piombo, to meet her escort, Antonio Giacomelli.

The relief of her safe return must at first have been overwhelming. She not only had escaped detection but had navigated the challenges of an unfamiliar world at its most unpredictable. She also met the challenge of keeping quiet about her adventure. There is no evidence that she ever shared what she had experienced before her discovery, for none of her cloistered companions could imagine such lawlessness. Having once made it home safely, it is telling about Donna Christina's character that she was ready to risk a second escape within days. Before carnival ended she successfully violated clausura for an encore performance of *Le rise di Democrito*. Perhaps on a second excursion outside the cloister she was able to pay more attention to the music than to her pounding heart.

Only a few months later, even greater fanfare accompanied the re-opening of Teatro Malvezzi, and this occasion too proved irresistible. Cavazza's willingness to take added risks during a late June excursion definitely says something about her self-confidence. The extended twilight of summer meant that the darkness of Bologna's omnipres-ent porticos would be less impenetrable than during the middle of winter. More significant, blending into the crowds was far more dif-ficult when fewer people were in the streets. Without the pretense of carnival, Cavazza would need to impersonate a "real" abbot, not simply some reveler playing one. Despite the added risks and clear consequences of discovery, Cavazza hazarded being unmasked a third time to attend the waning days of the summer opera season.

Had she been just a little less comfortable because her two suc-cessful outings had gone unnoticed, had she been slightly less confi-dent in her ability to pull off the familiar gambit another time, had she been a little less dazzled by the whole experience, which probably had not paled by the third time, she might not have been distracted just for a moment on her third safe return. She cannot have failed to recognize the particular perils of the passage from via Fondazza, through the gate, across the courtyard, and into the parlatorio. She lapsed long enough at the end of her third excursion to leave the chain unlocked. A few days later, when she was ready to risk navigat-ing the no-man's-land between the parlatorio and via Fondazza for a fourth time and to join the audience at Teatro Malvezzi for a final performance of the season's second opera, she had no way of know-ing she had an audience of her own, on the lookout for unknown intruders.

As Donna Christina pined in her cell in October 1708, Antonio Giacomelli finally fell into the church's net in Florence, where he lan-guished for six months. Finally returned to Bologna for trial, he was locked up beneath the tower of the archbishopric. Ten days later the tower window was barricaded with stone for added security, leaving only a small hole for fresh air. After all, Giacomelli had already once eluded church constables.

One observer recorded, "They are carrying out the trial in great

FIGURE 6.4 The tower of the duomo in Bologna. Photograph: Luca Salvucci. This was probably the tower in which Cavazza's accomplice, Antonio Giacomelli, was imprisoned after his capture and return to Bologna.

secrecy."[12] The details of such a scandal were potentially so sensational that the Curia wanted absolutely no leaks. This secrecy might be why we know nothing definite about the extent of Giacomelli's crimes, if they exceeded playing escort to Christina Cavazza on her outings to the opera. Bologna would naturally assume that the couple enjoyed more delights than a few nights on the town. But the diarists who recorded the skimpy details of Giacomelli's crime, capture, and imprisonment found nothing more to embellish their records. One chronicler in fact even characterized the pair's relationship as "lecita e virtuosa" ("lawful and honest").[13] Perhaps there was nothing more sensational to find.

Those who would spin nun-priest fantasies in the world, whether today or in eighteenth-century Bologna, would be surprised and probably disappointed to learn that contacts between male and female celibates in post-Tridentine Italy usually centered on less salacious intimacies than those that might take place in bed. Often characterized by words such as *amicizia* (friendship, amity), *intrinsichezza* (intimacy, close inwardness), *domestichezza* (familiarity, acquaintance, conversation), these relationships commonly involved activities that seem positively "domestic" by most notions of shocking behavior. Cooking treats, mending clothes, sewing, washing, passing letters, exchanging gifts—these were the "crimes" the church often considered scandalous. Or, of course, there were the expected incidents of carnival silliness. All in all, when the post-Tridentine cloister wall became virtually impregnable, interpersonal preoccupations seem generally to have shifted from the more explicitly lascivious to what was more realistically practical. While some of these relationships might borrow elements of secular courtship or marriage, evidence suggests that in most cases the relationships were scarcely physical, much less overtly sexual.[14]

Cavazza always intended to return at the end of every night at the opera. This was no run for freedom, no outright rejection of cloistered life. Her objective was to experience something of the outside world, something in which she must have been deeply interested. In her relationship with Giacomelli she likely preserved the physical distance clausura had regularly imposed on such relationships for 150 years, a psychological clausura that she had internalized over her dozen years of convent life. In fact, her choice of disguise as a cleric of higher rank than Giacomelli might further indicate the distance between them. The possibility that the pair may never have so much as acknowledged the prospect of physical intimacy ought to elicit more interest than the possibility that they might have met the world's prurient expectations.

In October 1709 the Curia condemned Giacomelli to life imprisonment. Cavazza's sentence had to wait another year, until November 1710, when the Sacred Congregation condemned her to ten years' imprisonment within the convent, permanently stripped her of her monastic veil, deprived her in perpetuity of active and passive voice (the privilege to vote in convent elections or to be elected to office herself), and banned her completely from the parlatorio for a decade. That Cavazza's sentence was no harsher suggests that while she had obviously broken the rule of enclosure, her vow of chastity remained intact. In the Discalced Carmelite rule, for example, Teresa of Avila required life imprisonment, not merely ten years, for nuns who committed sins of the flesh.[15]

The week of Cavazza's verdict, the Congregation commanded Antonio Giacomelli's transfer to Rome, where he was to continue his life sentence at his own expense. When the priest pleaded insufficient funds, the Bolognese archbishop dispatched an official to interrogate Giacomelli's neighbors in Piancaldolo. The Giacomelli family had plenty of money to pay his keep, the attaché reported. But by the time this investigation was done in May 1712, it looked like a waste of time. Don Antonio Giacomelli, his health failing, died in his Roman prison a few months later.

Donna Christina Cavazza seemed to be slipping dangerously toward the same fate. In communications with the Sacred Congregation, it was chiefly Archbishop Boncompagni who painted a dire picture of her disintegration. She could not escape the censuring looks of the other nuns, particularly the five from that early July night. In her mind, the bursar need not have kept so quiet after discovering the gate unlocked. The nun who had seen her leaving could have stopped her at that moment. All five sentries could have shown a little mercy on her return. Instead they had exposed her, and in such a way that the news spread all over Bologna.

The convent doctor testified that Cavazza's physical health had deteriorated, and the archbishop further suggested that her declining mental state made her a threat to herself and to others. "The devil torments her perpetually with intense temptations to anger, hatred, and revenge. If she sees any of her five betrayers she is tempted to kill them. If she encounters them face to face she becomes so enraged that she hurls herself at them, hoping to do them in." According to Boncompagni, the only thing keeping Cavazza from killing herself was the hope of transfer elsewhere.

Within months of her discovery, authorities had begun exploring the possibility of shipping Cavazza off to a Florentine convent. But the archbishop of Florence and his nuns wanted no part of her with her accompanying taint of scandal.[16] When the search for an alternative convent resumed, Boncompagni cautioned those involved to keep all overtures as circumspect as possible. If any institution got wind of Cavazza's recent actions in her prison or heard the language of her complaints against her sisters, she would be rejected out of hand. Cavazza's personal voice, largely drowned out in the sea of paperwork passing among prelates between 1711 and 1713, eventually surfaced with a definitive request:

> Donna Maria Christina Cavazza reverently ventures to point out that the pain of imprisonment she has endured these four years weighs heavier and heavier because of her palpable misfortune in seeing herself day in and day out the object of a damaging antipathy in this convent. Her eternal damnation seems inevitable if she cannot transfer, by the grace of your most benevolent favor, to another, more observant convent: Santa Maria Maddalena.

Boncompagni was quick to second Cavazza's request. Santa Cristina would get out from under the burden of Cavazza's disruptive presence but would also retain the lucrative advantage of her original dowry. Santa Maria Maddalena, with a yearly income barely a third of Santa Cristina's but with twice as many mouths to feed, would reap a financial windfall in Cavazza's required second dowry payment, at a time when the poorer convent had pawned most of its silver. Christina Cavazza, the archbishop suggested, would experience an element of salutary penance, for "it is certain that the nun will not enjoy all those comforts in diet and living that she presently enjoys at Santa Cristina."

Santa Maria Maddalena leaped at the proposal. The abbess reported that her consorelle had voted overwhelmingly (forty-five to two) in favor of Cavazza's acceptance. By then Boncompagni had already confirmed Santa Cristina's approval, and his own as well. The final, happy resolution awaited only the glacial pace of Vatican bureaucracy. More than a year passed before the Sacred Congregation handed down its ruling in September 1713. Donna Christina could transfer to Santa Maria Maddalena on condition that her family pay a new dowry, that she complete a new novitiate year there, and that all penalties imposed upon her in 1710 remain in force at her new home.[17]

These conditions were not exactly what Donna Christina had envisioned for this transfer. In turning her back on Santa Cristina, she imagined she would leave behind not only its antagonistic religious community, but the stringent penalties of her original sentence as well. On realizing that would not happen, she decided to stay put.

Then a singular transformation took place. The archbishop's earlier descriptions of Cavazza as a vengeful, deranged soul in peril gave way to a portrait of total resignation, humility, and spiritual peace. Christina Cavazza apparently turned into a model of convent piety. Moved by her miraculous transformation, the hard hearts of the nuns of Santa Cristina also softened with charity. They requested a moderation of her imprisonment, and Boncompagni concurred.[18]

Six years after her original confinement, the Sacred Congregation ruled that Cavazza might transfer from prison to a regular convent cell, but only to one in the highest reaches of the building (stair climbing must have seemed an appropriate penitential exercise). She was also allowed to resume chapel attendance. This was the first step in a carefully constructed spiritual and social rehabilitation. Early in 1716, the Sacred Congregation agreed to lighten Cavazza's sentence further. Before that year was out the entire convent, "ever more edified by her religious lifestyle, abiding humility, and moderation of spirit," petitioned for the restoration of Donna Christina's monastic veil. The Sacred Congregation promptly assented, in the spirit of the impending Christmas holiday.

After another six months, the nuns made a trickier request. They asked the Sacred Congregation to afford Cavazza every nun's regular access to the outside world, at those dangerous parlatorios and convent gateways. Boncompagni judged such a generous move to be premature, however, "because the nature of the nun's original offense was so astonishing and excessive that it still remains imprinted in the memory of other convents. For now, she could be permitted to go to the parlatorio a few times a year, but only to speak with her closest relatives." The archbishop's assertions rang true, for in August 1711 a nun at the convent of Santa Catterina, just up the street and around the corner from Santa Cristina, had tried to sneak out dressed as a peasant girl, with blond "hair" of straw, a homespun dress with blue sleeves, white socks, and buckled shoes. Her disguise fooled nobody, and she was apprehended almost immediately.[19] It is therefore not surprising that in August 1717 the Sacred Congregation agreed with Boncompagni that they should not set a bad example by being too lenient in Cavazza's case.

In April 1718 the nuns of Santa Cristina mounted one further assault on Cavazza's behalf. Now they claimed that Cavazza's notorious flight from the cloister really amounted to nothing more than "a crime motivated simply by idle curiosity." She has already suffered "eight long years" of punishment. She has "worked unstintingly for the good of this community, with her full capabilities, exemplary fervor, and true devotion to religion, to the complete edification of us all." The nuns therefore request full restoration of her monastic privileges and her total reintegration into their community. By now the community is aging and reduced in numbers, after all, and they will gain from Cavazza's assistance with convent offices.[20]

The independent-minded, adventurous young singer of 1708 and before, who had morphed into the vengeful, half-deranged potential suicide of 1713, by spring of 1718 had turned into a poster child for monastic propriety and spirituality. Such a transformation seems almost too good to be true. It is almost the stuff of sacred legend, of transformed and transformative saints' lives. On the other hand, when the disappointment of 1713 demonstrated there would be no easy return to normality, Christina Cavazza may have achieved new insight. Whether it came to her through the path of religious enlightenment that her fellow nuns described or by some more down-to-earth, practical route, Cavazza clearly saw the need for a life change and a new strategy for coping with her role in her world.

By late 1713, after she had rejected the chance to transfer, the sisters of Santa Cristina also recognized that the Cavazza problem was not going away. Christina Cavazza was no use to anyone as she was then. It was in the sisters' best interests too to work out some sort of accommodation with their community's most notorious member. By their own admission, they would soon need her help with convent offices. They would never elect her as abbess or bursar, of course, but perhaps to such humdrum jobs as overseer of the kitchen or keeper of the infirmary. Portinara was obviously not a good idea. Whether through religious sincerity or cynicism, tacitly or candidly, both sides chose the strategy most likely to succeed to their benefit.

After the battles of 1699 and 1704, the sisters of Santa Cristina had a clear sense of their adversary in the hard-line and basically unsympathetic Cardinal Archbishop Giacomo Boncompagni. The only plausible means of dealing with him was to display spirituality and subordination. Only submission could improve Cavazza's situation. Little by little, the strategy worked. Things went so well, in fact, that the nuns eventually suggested a bit too much too soon and prompted a negative reaction from Boncompagni in the summer of 1717. But by 1718 a happy resolution to everybody's problem seemed in sight. Then the Sacred Congregation requested Boncompagni's customary elucidation and final opinion on Cavazza's total reintegration into convent life.

But before he can respond, we next hear not from Boncompagni, but from Cavazza herself. Barely three weeks after the Sacred Congregation contacts the archbishop, a distraught Donna Christina laments "the deceit charged to me by the spiteful, who never tire of tormenting and damaging me, the most miserable creature alive." She entreats an unnamed patron to intercede with Boncompagni on her behalf.

After ten long years, just when I expected to receive a favorable decree, for which he had always led me to hope, not only in response to my own entreaties, but also to those of each and every member of our religious community, now the woeful news reaches me that the cardinal is set totally against me because of some sinister information, although false; moreover, with the understanding that I had made my last overtures to the Sacred Congregation without his collaboration.

It seems that the drawn-out, carefully orchestrated rehabilitation had collapsed at the eleventh hour. Perhaps the greater freedom afforded her by Vatican concessions after 1713 reanimated Cavazza's spirit to the point where her enthusiasm got the best of her. This frantic letter, which does not form part of the Cavazza files of the Sacred Congregation or the Bolognese archbishopric, suggests that she was indeed acting independently, despite her assertions to the contrary. Writing this letter was not the first time Cavazza contacted this unnamed patron, to whom she claims that "the long series of my well merited misfortunes is well known." She also suggests that Marquis Francesco Pepoli and Countess Ginevra Isolani Pepoli had been working on her behalf. Archbishop Boncompagni, who would have remembered Santa Cristina's discreet enlistment of cardinals, and even cardinals' mothers, in their fight against him back in 1699, may have found this level of independence unacceptable.[21]

The flood of paperwork collecting in the Vatican's Cavazza file dried up abruptly by mid-1718. Almost a year would pass before the Sacred Congregation next wrote to Archbishop Boncompagni. By then Cavazza's carefully constructed portrayal of spiritual patience and humility, hidden behind the intercessions of others, has collapsed. Now she returns to center stage in a guise reminiscent of the "madness" of 1712. Once again Cavazza is "the prime target and a convenient cautionary lesson for a convent that sees itself wronged." Once again "the threat of perdition is close at hand," the woman's soul "faces insurmountable obstacles," and her conscience "is visible on the brink of perdition."

Toward the end of 1718, now ten years after her original discovery and detention, Cavazza changed tactics. She renewed her request for transfer to Santa Maria Maddalena or some other convent in the city or the diocese.[22] If her rhetoric sounded familiar, it was because she had dusted off, updated, and recycled documents from her previous campaign to escape Santa Cristina during 1711–13. Of course, this tactic embodied exactly the sort of independent initiative that had alienated Boncompagni, and he appears to have removed himself from direct participation in further proceedings about Cavazza. Donna Christina now seems largely on her own, bombarding a reluctant Congregation with multiple petitions and duplicate copies of her arguments.

She was repeatedly ignored by the Sacred Congregation, "perhaps because she had not offered to continue the penance originally imposed upon her." So Donna Christina took pains to reassure the cardinals that she would willingly fulfill any penance. By the end of 1718 she also began to request transfer, if not to Santa Maria Maddalena, then "to the convent of Sant'Agostino in the territory of Lugo, in the diocese of Imola." It appears that by then the financially challenged nuns of Santa Maria Maddalena in Bologna may have had second thoughts about accepting the notorious fugitive from Santa Cristina for any amount of money. But because these new players in the drama, the nuns of Sant'Agostino, were off in the hinterlands, thirty-seven miles from Bologna, they were untouched by Cavazza and her reputation and perhaps less concerned that she would cause them trouble.

Getting wind that the prefect of the Sacred Congregation was prepared to raise the issue in Congregation, Christina Cavazza renewed her assault on the cardinals in Rome. This latest, hasty version of her case simply tacks on "or else in the one in Lugo, diocese of Imola" where the convent of Santa Maria Maddalena had appeared in previous petitions, which are otherwise recopied largely word for word. The proceedings also confirm that Girolamo Boncompagni had largely washed his hands of her, for no direct communication from the archbishop appears in the file from this time. Further, Donna Christina notes that the prefect of the Congregation would communicate Boncompagni's views viva voce.[23]

In April 1719 the Sacred Congregation requested a recommendation from the Bolognese archbishop. By the time he got around to responding four months later, the Congregation had also asked to hear from the bishop of Imola. After years of enduring the Vatican's usual leaden pace, Cavazza's head may have spun at the dizzying acceleration of events. On June 13 the abbess in Lugo affirmed that her nuns had voted to accept Donna Christina. On August 15 the abbess of Santa Cristina affirmed that her nuns had voted to be rid of her.

By then the Sacred Congregation had ruled as well. In late July the Congregation decreed that Donna Christina Cavazza might transfer to Lugo "provided that her initial dowry remain at her first convent, that a second dowry to be determined by His Eminence, the bishop of Imola, be paid to the second convent, and provided that she put off her old habit and don the habit of the convent of Sant'Agostino and complete a new probationary year there."

Early on August 27, under the watchful eye of the nuns' vicar of Bologna, Christina Cavazza, her face shrouded against the curious stares of nearby residents, passed through gates she had not crossed since the summer of 1708. After acknowledging the abbess and other nuns, gathered just inside the boundary of clausura, at the very spot where her crimes had been discovered, she was formally handed over to her late brother's widow and other relatives. Placed in a closed carriage, she was ordered to proceed to Lugo by the most direct route and without delay.

An hour after sunset that evening, the carriage arrived at Sant'Agostino. In the presence of the nuns' vicar of Lugo and the convent's
lay governors, Donna Christina was led into the parlatorio by her
sister-in-law and her niece. After formal presentation of relevant paperwork, she passed through a side door into the care of a new prioress and mistress of novices. The reported applause by the assembled
nuns of Sant'Agostino probably drowned out her relatives' discreet
sighs of relief, not to mention similar sentiments that echoed from
the halls of Santa Cristina to the archiepiscopal palace in Bologna and
the Sacred Congregation in Rome.[24]

LUGO: "THEY RECEIVED REVEREND DONNA MARIA CHRISTINA WITH PLEASURE"

In Bologna, Archbishop Boncompagni could focus his attentions
on periodic papal conclaves in Rome and on commissioning an
imposing monument to his ancestor, Pope Gregory XIII, for Saint
Peter's. On his appointment to additional high ecclesiastical office
in 1724, Boncompagni reestablished residence in Rome. After a few
years commuting between the two cities, untroubled by Christina
Cavazza, Boncompagni died in Rome in 1731. His final peregrination
brought him back to Bologna and the family chapel at the cathedral
of San Pietro.

Within weeks of Donna Christina's departure for Lugo, the ever
bustling social life of Bologna found new distraction in the local marriage of James Francis Edward Stuart, the "Old Pretender" to the
British throne. His regular visits to Villa Alamandini in the Bolognese
countryside during the 1720s provided an abiding source of fascination for the local aristocracy. In 1728 laity and religious alike also enjoyed weeks of distraction with the elevation to the cardinalate of
Prospero Lambertini, the popular local boy made good. His relatives kept musicians busy for weeks with services of thanksgiving at
various convents and churches. The congenial Cardinal Lambertini
would return to Bologna as archbishop after Boncompagni's death,
on a nine-year stopover before his election as Pope Benedict XIV
in 1740.

In Rome, the prefect of the Sacred Congregation of Bishops and

Regulars collected a sheaf of Cavazza documents, many dating back several years, tied them all up in a bale of other papers for 1718, and sent them off to the archive, where they were promptly forgotten as the post brought stacks and stacks of new petitions every week to occupy and vex the cardinals of the Sacred Congregation.

But the respite concerning Cavazza lasted only until 1734. In February of that year the secretary had to inform the bishop of Imola that Cardinal Leandro di Porzia, consultor of the Holy Office

> has referred to the Sacred Congregation the notorious case of the nun Donna Christina Cavazza. After her transfer from Santa Cristina in Bologna to Sant'Agostino in Lugo, despite the conditions imposed upon her [by the Sacred Congregation], she has assumed various offices in the second convent. Most notably, she has held the position of abbess twice—which she managed very badly. Recently she was reelected to the same office for a third time. The Congregation commands that—regarding Sister Christina Cavazza's recent reelection as abbess—you fulfill the original requirements imposed upon her on July 21, 1719, and that you proceed as you think most reasonable in the matter of Sister Cavazza's administrative malfeasance, making sure that all the present orders are carried out to the letter.[25]

When this news reached Archbishop Prospero Lambertini of Bologna, he may have smiled that Cavazza was out of his hair and entangled in the bishop of Imola's. But relief promptly turned to dismay in July when he received a letter from the fugitive nun herself. This plea was Christina Cavazza at her most eloquently rhetorical:

> Most Eminent and Most Reverend Prince
> The history of Donna Maria Christina Cavazza, nun of the convent of Santa Cristina, already well known to Your Eminence, could surely arouse in your magnanimous and most merciful breast every feeling of pity and sympathy at her most unhappy plight. She has resolved to return to her first religious calling—for she has in no wise professed in her present one—and thereby she will obey the voice of God, which, through such extraordinary and manifest events, calls her back to her original vocation. At your feet this humble and entreating daughter, repentant and obedient to her good father

and shepherd, with sighs and tears implores him as her strong and noble champion to bring about the return she longs for, thereby fulfilling the decrees of Holy Law and restoring her spiritual welfare on the right pathway to eternity. The only obstacle in her way is that Rome believes Your Eminence opposes her return and that you are more than a little reluctant to receive her as your loving daughter. Though she acknowledges her unworthiness of such a singular grace, that cannot prevent her, in reverent and respectful confidence, from prostrating herself before Your Eminence, imploring mercy, clemency, and protection from her true father, pastor, and prince, to whom his daughter and subject firmly offers herself as she kisses the Sacred Purple.

Lambertini's response, jotted on the back, stands in marked contrast: his terseness versus her effusiveness.

I am only too well informed about your various misadventures in years past, and also about your present state. Let me say plainly, in a few words, that this business cannot go forward unless you write to Rome, and unless Rome then asks me for my opinion. My response will never be favorable without the unanimous, or virtually unanimous, approval of the nuns of Santa Cristina. For it does not sit well with me to turn a whole convent of nuns on its head simply to oblige one solitary individual.[26]

What exactly had gone on, out in the countryside of Romagna, over the past fifteen years? We must rely primarily on Donna Christina's own memories. She had begun her new novitiate year at Lugo as required, even sitting with the novices in chapel and eating with them in the refectory. But she had not worn a novice's habit. The local nuns' vicar may have thought it inappropriate for a nun almost forty, with twenty-five years in religion, to dress like a monastic teenager. Perhaps he might even have thought Rome's stipulations took no account of circumstances and seemed unusually punitive (lest, by escaping Santa Cristina, Cavazza imagine she had "won"). So the morning after her arrival, the nuns' vicar had vested her with the full habit of a professed Lateran canoness—in private, with the convent doors shut. Sensible, if not quite the letter of the law that Rome had

FIGURE 6.5 Cardinal Archbishop Prospero Lambertini of Bologna, from an engraving ca. 1730. Reproduced with permission of the Biblioteca Comunale dell'Archiginnasio, Bologna (Raccolte 1 T. I, 12).

stipulated. After a year, the same nuns' vicar told Cavazza that since she had already professed back in the 1690s, she need not formally profess a second time. These country clergy, it seems, were not quite the sticklers for detail that their city cousins in Bologna or Rome were.

In the meantime, before her novitiate year was even finished, the nuns at Lugo had enthusiastically elected Cavazza to high office. They approached Bishop Ulisse Giuseppe Gozzadini just to be sure that Donna Christina's election would be valid. After all, she had arrived only a few months ago and was technically still a novice, even if she was already wearing the black veil and increasingly keeping company with the professed nuns. The bishop's favorable response certainly would not have passed muster in Rome or Bologna; yet in the hinterlands it seemed that nuns' wishes, quite extraordinarily, may have trumped Vatican pronouncements. Perhaps the bishop merely recognized that Cavazza's potential utility should not be wasted. In any case,

> Cardinal Gozzadini answered that they could go ahead and make me abbess if they wanted to. It would be on his conscience. So I was elected abbess there three times, each time for three years. I was also elected syndic twice, for three-year terms, elected each time— and every time by vote of the other nuns. I was elected abbess for the third time in February 1733, if I'm not mistaken, and would have continued in office until February of next year [(1736), had Rome not intervened].

Long before this latest acclaim by the sisters at Sant'Agostino, upon Cavazza's arrival there, "as she entered the convent, all the nuns, with the Most Reverend Mother Abbess, applauded. And they received and accepted the Reverend Donna Maria Christina with pleasure."[27] The welcoming sentiment must have been palpable for the notary to have remarked it and then affirmed and notarized his description back in 1719. And by all means, this was a singular reception for a former convent embarrassment, shunned both formally and informally and the object of scorn among her former sisters. Now Cavazza woke up to discover herself an object of interest. While Sant'Agostino may have ranked first among Lugo's few monastic houses for women, Lugo was not Bologna. In her new community, she became "Donna Maria Teresa Cavazza *da Bologna.*"

Unlike her original community at Santa Cristina, her newly adopted sisters, some seventy all told (almost three times the number at her old home), had never suffered collateral damage from Cavazza's scandal back in 1708. Most had never traveled outside Lugo, and since taking vows, none had so much as set foot onto strada Codalunga at the convent gate. Although Sant'Agostino's official archival record of her entry discreetly ignores any hint of her checkered past, her consorelle must have been fascinated, and more than a little curious, about Donna Maria Teresa da Bologna's rich life experiences of both adventure and misadventure. She had ridden through the countryside all the way from Bologna to Lugo. She had sung to dignitaries from Bologna and abroad, had entertained the likes of Cardinal Giacomo Boncompagni (who would not have been amused) and Cardinal Francesco Maria de' Medici (who, they said, listened incognito to the Consecration of Virgins back in 1699). She had experienced carnival firsthand in the streets, not the parlatorio. And of course she had been to the opera four times. The very same things that had made her a criminal may now have contributed to her role as something of a celebrity.

After ten years of enforced idleness and mandated intellectual stagnation, Cavazza's atrophied creativity and imagination were tested almost before she had time to recognize the transformation in her life. Called to high office within months after her arrival in Lugo (convent documents from October 1721 describe her as syndic, second in command to the abbess), Cavazza was soon at the center of major convent renovations. Thirty years before, on Palm Sunday 1688, an earthquake had destroyed the vault of the church of Sant'Agostino. In 1712, when the nuns requested permission to undertake a major building campaign, Bishop Gozzadini authorized the expenditure of no less than 3,200 scudi. So Cavazza's appearance on the scene in 1719 was well timed. She would direct the second phase of the project into the early 1730s. Although she gave some attention to new monastic buildings completed shortly before her arrival, adding a few comforts and artistic features, she concentrated chiefly on the church. She replaced the old sacristy. She recreated the church with three altars in modern, eighteenth-century style, which spread throughout Lugo's cityscape in coming decades.

On Cavazza's third election as prioress, circumstances took a decided turn for the worse. The apparently somewhat casual Bishop Gozzadini had died in 1728. His successor, Giuseppe Accoramboni, was seemingly cut from stiffer cloth. Transferred to the see of Imola six weeks after Gozzadini's death, Accoramboni retained all his positions as a Vatican apparatchik: *uditore santissimi,* consultor to the Sacred Congregation of Rites, consultor to the Roman and Universal Inquisition, examiner of bishops.

Early in 1733 the vicar of the Holy Office paid Cavazza a visit to inquire if she had ever completed her second novitiate and professed in the appropriate way. Obviously not. He therefore advised Cavazza to petition the Sacra Penitenziaria in Rome to cleanse her of any defect regarding her novitiate, profession, and eligibility for convent office. She dutifully (if rather naively) wrote to Pope Clement XII himself—a copy of her letter survives in the archiepiscopal archive in Bologna. But the request eventually worked its way through appropriate channels, and in June 1733 the Sacra Penitenziaria formally granted her request, permitting her to profess discreetly in the hands of her confessor. This was a pragmatic solution that would not have disrupted the ongoing life of the religious community.

But Cardinal Porzia of the Holy Office also happened to mention the matter to colleagues in the Sacred Congregation of Bishops and Regulars, who in February 1734 commanded the bishop of Imola to put things right. Cardinal Accoramboni pointed out that he could not confirm Cavazza's most recent reelection as abbess, since she had never completed her novitiate. He further claimed that the diocesan Curia could find no record of her dowry payment to Sant'Agostino. (They must not have looked very hard, since it survives to this day in the remnants of Sant'Agostino's archive.) The next day the convent confessor ordered Donna Christina—or Donna Maria Teresa—to assemble the nuns and resign the office of abbess. Cavazza replied, "I can easily do so, for I took on these offices out of holy obedience. Therefore, in holy obedience, I can just as easily vacate them. I don't believe, however, that I've ever done anything requiring my deprivation of this office. In fact I've done everything in my power for the good of my convent, in matters both spiritual and temporal."

As the nuns were assembling, the vicar-general himself turned up, demanding to know if Donna Maria Teresa had finished making her renunciation. She presented him with the Sacra Penitenziaria's recent decree and asked to fulfill its stipulations immediately by professing in the hands of the convent confessor. "All the nuns there present entreated him with the loudest cries, shouts, and pleading. They wouldn't hear of my being wronged in that way, especially since the matter could be resolved so straightforwardly, as the decree prescribed." After a perfunctory reading, he simply returned the document to Donna Christina, and in the presence of her fellow nuns, she resigned her office.

The busy nuns' vicar showed up again the next day. Cardinal Accoramboni would be very pleased, he told Cavazza, if she voluntarily renounced active and passive voice. Cavazza replied that she would renounce them in holy obedience if Accoramboni formally commanded her to do so. Next the vicar of the Holy Office and one of the lay governors of Sant'Agostino stopped by to reiterate the nuns' vicar's advice. Cavazza replied that they could deprive her of active and passive voice if they chose, but she was not going to renounce them herself. As she later recalled, "When they all saw that they couldn't achieve their ends by this means, they began to accuse me of having devastated the convent with debts. And I consistently replied that if they would collate the accounts to my face, they would discover that never had I spent a farthing frivolously, but only on what the convent needed. And if the convent is in debt, it is because of the nature of these times."[28]

An autograph accounting still surviving amid the scant remnants of Sant'Agostino's archive confirms her claim.[29] In it Cavazza minutely records her payments of almost a thousand scudi in 1721–22 for lumber, mortar, plaster, window glass, and other building essentials. Any aspersions on Christina Cavazza's administrative talents would probably have surprised citizens of Lugo. Local historian Girolamo Bonoli singled out her recent accomplishments in his weighty *Storia di Lugo,* published just the previous year, in 1732:

> The syndic [of Sant'Agostino] is Donna Maria Teresa Cavazzi da Bologna. Exercising great administrative responsibility in the past when she governed the convent as abbess for six years, she recreated the church in the modern style of our day, thanks to her own good taste, so that now it is one of the most beautiful and ornamental in Lugo. And since the old cramped and scarcely respectable sacristy was destroyed, she constructed a beautiful and spacious new one in its place.

Interesting in its coincidental juxtaposition, Bonoli's praise of Cavazza's successes contrasts with his subsequent brief description of abortive local attempts to establish another convent during the same period. That project, which the late Bishop Gozzadini declared "more idealistic than well founded," had to be abandoned when funds ran out halfway through.[30]

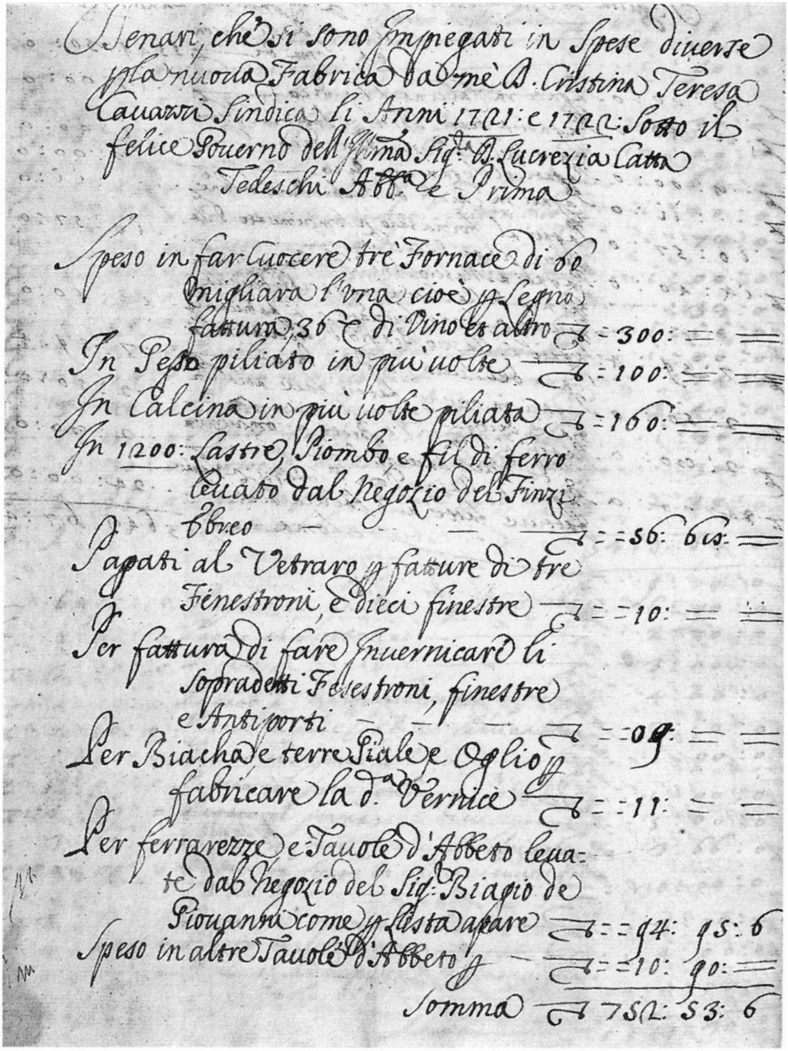

Denari, che si sono impiegati in Spese diverse
p. la nuova Fabrica da mè D. Cristina Teresa
Cavazza Sindica li Anni 1721: e 1722: Sotto il
felice Governo dell'Ill.ma Sig.ra D. Lucrezia Catt.a
Tedeschi Abb.a e Prima

Speso in far Cuocere tre Fornace di 60
migliara l'una cioè p. Legna
fattura, 36 ₤ di Vino et altro — ₤ = 300: = =
In Gesso piliato in più volte — ₤ = 100: = =
In Calcina in più volte piliata — ₤ = 160: = =
In 1200: Lastre, Piombo e fil di ferro
levato dal Negozio del Finzi
Ebreo — ₤ = = 56: 6 10: =
Pagati al Vetraro p. fatture di tre
Fenestroni, e dieci finestre — ₤ = = 10: = =
Per fattura di fare Inverniciare li
sopradetti Fenestroni, finestre
e Antiporti — ₤ = = 09: = =
Per Biacha e terre Giale e Oglio p.
fabricare la d.a Vernice — ₤ = = 11: = =
Per ferrarezze e Tavole d'Abbeto leva=
te dal Negozio del Sig. Biagio de
Piovanni come p. Lista apare — ₤ = = 94: 15: 6
Speso in altre Tavole d'Abbeto p. — ₤ = = 10: 90: =
Somma — ₤ 752: 53: 6

FIGURE 6.6 Christina Cavazza's autograph account of building expenses for the new church of Sant'Agostino in Lugo, whose construction she oversaw, ca. 1721–22. ASI, Demaniale 1./8590. Reproduced with permission of the Ministero per I Beni e le Attività Culturali, Archivio di Stato, Bologna

In earlier stages of the convent rebuilding, an unnamed abbess or her assistant had acknowledged that during construction many of the convent's usual payments might fall behind schedule, "but with a little economizing in coming years, they can be put right." She had concluded that "the expenses [of construction] may seem heavy with respect to the convent's finances, but it is a great relief and comfort to the poor sisters."[31] The ever obliging Bishop Gozzadini had gone along with the plan despite the financial risks involved. His successor, it seems, later chose to make Cavazza a convenient scapegoat for economic problems she may have partially inherited.

Having decided that the Sacred Congregation's command of February 1734 trumped the Sacra Penitenziaria's dictate of June 1733, Cardinal Accoramboni himself arrived at Sant'Agostino on May 12 to oversee the election of Cavazza's successor and to fulfill to the letter the terms of the Sacred Congregation's command. He reminded Donna Christina that she must complete her novitiate year and profess as stipulated when she had moved to Lugo fifteen years earlier. "In that case," she replied, "I am no longer moved, nor do I feel any vocation, to profess in this convent but instead wish to return to my original vows of the Camaldolese order." The cardinal bishop then proclaimed that she had no place among the professed nuns of Sant'Agostino and commanded the fifty-five-year-old former abbess to go down from her place in the chapel she had helped rebuild and find a place among the teenage novices. "And so in obedience I withdrew alone to remove my nun's habit and to put on a novice's clothing with my own hands. When I returned to His Eminence he made me show myself to everyone without the black veil, in a novice's rochet. Then I went to submit to the novice mistress. And from then until now I have always worn the habit of a novice."[32]

BOLOGNA: "SHE WILL OBEY THE VOICE OF GOD, WHICH CALLS HER BACK TO HER ORIGINAL VOCATION"

Donna Christina's comment that she wished to return to Santa Cristina almost certainly reached Archbishop Lambertini in Bologna long before her personal letter arrived in early July 1734. Expert concerning the ins and outs of Roman Catholic bureaucracy, Lambertini would recognize immediately that, unfortunately, the Curia had to be as punctilious about observing church law when it worked for Cavazza as it had been when it worked against her. The Sacred Congregation, seconded by Bishop Accoramboni, insisted that she had never fulfilled its stipulations for her transfer to Sant'Agostino. So technically there was no denying that she was still a professed nun at Santa Cristina.

The Council of Trent had decreed back in 1563, "The holy council anathemizes all persons who shall . . . in any way force any virgin or widow, or any other woman whatsoever, to enter a monastery against her will, or to take the habit of any religious order or to make her profession." Christina Cavazza could not be compelled to profess at Lugo if, as she asserted in her letter to him, she was "resolved to return to her first religious calling and thereby to obey the voice of God, which calls her back to her original vocation."[33]

Once again papers concerning Cavazza bounced back and forth between Bologna and Rome, while ricocheting off Imola as well. In September 1734 Lambertini heard from the cardinals of the Sacred Congregation, and they played the papal trump card to add clout to their unpalatable mandate:

Although she never actually satisfied the condition [of her transfer to Sant'Agostino in Lugo,] nevertheless—and nobody seems to know how it happened—Christina Cavazza was elected abbess no fewer than three times. Not a few disturbances were hatched as a result, so that now she insists on returning to her original convent. The nuns of Sant'Agostino happily consent to it and have supplicated His Holiness to this effect. His Holiness believes this mutual desire should be fulfilled. He has ordered the Sacred Congregation to write to you, so that you can persuade the nuns of Santa Cristina to take her back. We hope this can be accomplished all the more easily since the nuns at Lugo would let her bring her second dowry back with her. Santa Cristina would therefore reap a double windfall, because Cavazza is past sixty [sic]. If, however, you cannot get her accepted there under any circumstances, it would please His Holiness exceedingly if you would make every effort to place her in some other convent in your diocese. His Holiness cannot agree that she could profitably reside in the bishop of Imola's convent. We wait to hear in due course what it has pleased Your Eminence to arrange, so that we may inform His Holiness.

An atypically impatient Sacred Congregation contacted Lambertini again within a month, pointedly inquiring why it was taking him so long to settle this matter:

> The Sacred Congregation would like some response from you in the matter about which I wrote last month. It has ordered this communicated to Your Eminence, so that it might please you to fulfill the express desire of that same Sacred Congregation. Then that same Congregation can report expeditiously to His Holiness. So, while we continue waiting, I reverently kiss your hands.

Lambertini apparently had no success persuading Santa Cristina to take back their errant sister. Nobody—Christina Cavazza, Santa Cristina, Sant'Agostino, or the reverend cardinal in Lugo—could have been very happy with the Sacred Congregation's subsequent decree:

> The nun Christina Cavazza is to be kept at the convent of Sant'Agostino in Lugo—at the expense, however, of the convent of Santa Cristina in Bologna—until such time as some other convent can be found to accept her. And in the meantime, she is deprived of active and passive voice.[34]

Well into the new year, the Congregation continued to pester Cardinal Lambertini. Ultimately it would fall to Christina Cavazza herself to find a way out of this impasse, even though this one was only partially of her own making.

Not long after lunch on the first Sunday of November 1735, Francesco Veronesi, the aging sacristan of Santa Cristina's public church, set off up via Fondazza. He was headed for the church of Santa Catterina, around the corner in strada Maggiore, to find out if the instructors on Christian doctrine wanted the candles lit at Santa Cristina later that afternoon, when they were scheduled to appear. Halfway up the shaded west portico, he chuckled to see a curiously dressed trio, obviously not from these parts. In the lead walked a rather petite figure wearing some sort of skirt pulled up from behind over her shoulders and head and tied in place with a white kerchief. This one also wore a heavy black cloak that hid her face. A thickset woman limped after her, and she leaned heavily on the arm of an outlander, who was also burdened with a hamper. Francesco hurried on toward Santa Catterina without getting a good look at the fatter woman. Yet he noticed that she had on a moss green garment and was swathed in a heavy cloak that partially covered her pale and pudgy face.[35]

Returning from his errand, Francesco was hailed by curious bystanders outside Santa Cristina. They informed him that two strange women had just arrived at the convent and gone inside. "And from the different reports I heard," Francesco extrapolated, "I knew for certain that these were the same women I'd encountered earlier, in the street. Later I learned that the fat one was Donna Christina Cavazza, and the other, smaller one was another nun from Lugo in Romagna."

As Francesco wended his way up via Fondazza, the portinara's assistant at Santa Cristina was busy writing in the parlatorio while she kept a watchful eye on a nun who was chatting with a visitor. Suddenly they all heard a banging on the door. The assistant portinara opened it just wide enough to glimpse two strangers outside.

Without a word, they started pushing against the door. I pushed back with all my might to close it, because I didn't know who was behaving so violently, since the two were all covered up so I couldn't see their faces. But they pushed so hard, and I'm only one weak soul, and there were two of them, so that they forced the door open and pushed inside, even though I yelled loudly and called for help. And if I hadn't grabbed onto the door knocker I'd have certainly been knocked down. I ran to call the mother abbess. When I got back I heard more banging. I looked out through the peephole and saw it was a peasant woman, who said she wanted to give me a hamper. I asked who it was for, and she said the two ladies who'd just entered the convent. At that news, I pushed the hamper back outside.

Attracted by such commotion at the front of the house, a conversa left her kitchen chores and headed for the parlatorio. "I clearly recognized one of the women as Donna Christina Cavazza. For when Donna Maria Christina was removed from this convent and taken to Lugo, I was a professed sister [sic] here. So I knew her well, and I recognized her even though she'd gotten much fatter." The conversa ran off to find the portinara, who was inconsolable because this was all happening on her watch.[36]

The abbess immediately sent word to Archbishop Lambertini. Within days the vicar general appeared for the inevitable investigation. His notary described a heavyset woman of about fifty-five, dressed incongruously in the habit of a novice in the order of Lateran canonesses. Donna Christina seemed happy finally to have her say, which forms the primary basis for impressions in this story of what happened between 1719 and 1735. She placed in evidence the decree in her favor from the Sacra Penitenziaria, which Imolese churchmen chose to disregard altogether. And she presented her journey back to Bologna as an act of holy obedience.

As for your question on what authority I came to this convent, I have no license to show you. But I really must say that Lord Cardinal Accoramboni told me that His Holiness ordered that I return either to my first convent or to some other convent in the diocese of Bologna. Neither he nor the Sacred Congregation wanted me any longer in that convent in Lugo. And the cardinal also had a lot else to say, which he declared in the presence of all the nuns there.[37]

Before sunrise on that November Sunday, Christina Cavazza had slipped out of the carriage gateway at Sant'Agostino to retrace in reverse her thirty-seven-mile journey of 1719. This time no dignified matron relatives accompanied her in a carriage. Christina had to rely instead on a beggar woman whom she had enlisted the previous day to meet her outside the gate in strada Codalunga. Christina claimed not to know her accomplice's name, but she was subsequently identified as Domenica Colombina, nicknamed la Fuggatina. Domenica gave Christina a dark green garment to put on and a black silk cloak for her head. Then she shouldered Christina's hamper of belongings.

They had barely set out when they heard footsteps running after them—It was "Donna Valeria Rondinelli, a professed nun in the convent, my friend from the cell in which I slept. She was following me in her nun's habit, whose top layer was pulled over her head in singular fashion." Middle-aged Donna Valeria, clearly much attached to her well-traveled roommate from the big city, had been beside herself when a few nuns at Lugo turned against Cavazza during the new bishop's recent disruptions there. "I got so mad at them that I decided I'd rather die than stay at Sant'Agostino. One time my mind got so upset because of it that I wanted to drown myself. I would've done it, too, if they hadn't stopped me. I don't know what else to say about how they did it, except that afterward they bled me."

When Valeria realized that Christina was stealing away, she grabbed a hamper, pulled her top skirt up over the back of her head, and ran out after her. Donna Christina implored her to go back inside. "But I pleaded by the five wounds of Our Lord that she take me with her. Otherwise I'd just go drown myself in the river." Cavazza relented, and the fugitive pair set off, with la Fuggatina carrying Christina's hamper and directing them along strada Codalunga and out the city gate toward Imola.[38]

After walking the twelve miles to the gates of Imola, the portly Cavazza, now bone tired, had to stop. Sending Domenica Colombina off to find a carriage, she and Donna Valeria retired to the only haven they could entertain in this strange place: the tiny church of Santo Spirito near the city gate. They had just enough time to hear Mass before Domenica returned with a covered two-horse carriage. It was barely big enough to accommodate the two nuns and their hampers, much less la Fuggatina, but she managed to clamber up to the top of the load. By midafternoon the trio had covered the remaining twenty miles to Bologna, and they dismounted at Santa Maria Lacrimosa degli Alemanni just outside Porta di strada Maggiore. Donna Christina doled out a *mezza doppia* to the driver and a *doppia* to la Fuggatina, and the women continued from there on foot. The walk down nearby via Fondazza and past the chuckling Francesco Veronesi to the front gate of Santa Cristina was mercifully short. It left them enough strength to overpower the gatekeeper and force their way inside.

Apart from verifying details of the trip from Lugo, the fugitive nuns' entry into Santa Cristina, their dress, and their baggage, the nuns' vicar of Bologna worked hard to discover who might have aided Cavazza and Varinelli in their flight. He returned to Santa Cristina on

November 12 to interrogate the sacristan, the curious conversa, and the professed nuns most directly involved. Then he reappeared a few days later to examine Valeria Rondinelli again. She offered little new information and basically rambled on about her recent unhappiness at Lugo. "I've got nothing else to say except that I never want to go back to that convent in Lugo. And even if Donna Teresa were back there again I absolutely wouldn't want to be there—because they treated me very spitefully and made me very hateful. I would have been damned and I will be damned if I remain in that convent."[39]

The following day Christina Cavazza's reexamination proved scarcely more helpful. The nun's vicar accused her of lying to protect Valeria Rondinelli. He wanted to know who had really enlisted la Fuggatina. Christina responded with the time-honored evasion, "I cannot remember." Pressed harder, she stood her ground. "As for your assertion that the response 'I can't remember' is unacceptable and creates the presumption that I'm hiding some offense, I answer that I'd have no difficulty telling you if I could in fact remember. Because I don't deny, nor do I intend to deny, what I did."

"It isn't enough to confess your own crimes," the nuns' vicar replied, "without expanding upon accomplices, and aggravating circumstances, such as how it was worked out, and such things."

"It isn't true that I conspired with anyone in my escape from the convent at Lugo," she said, "and the facts remain as I stated them the first time."

The nuns' vicar was particularly incredulous about Cavazza's claim that the fugitive trio had gone directly to Imola and then, after Mass, directly to Bologna without some secret stop, for who knows what, along the way. He carefully added up distances, figured the hours realistically needed to traverse the thirty-seven miles or so from Lugo, and then compared his result with the nuns' stated hours of departure and arrival. But Christina remained intractable. "I hear your claim that what I say couldn't be true, that I'm telling lies. Well, I respond that I don't know what to say for myself, except that's how things were. If I had good legs like Donna Valeria, we probably could've gotten here more quickly."[40]

After more frustrated attempts to break Cavazza's resolve, the monsignor chose to "abandon the examination for now." He had Donna Christina sign her testimony and departed, perhaps intending to renew his assault later. He never got the chance. On the very day Christina Cavazza was facing him down, the Sacred Congregation wrote from Rome that the trial at Santa Cristina should be terminated immediately. Lambertini was to keep the fugitive nuns imprisoned while he tried his best to find another convent for Donna Christina. If he couldn't do so, he would have to settle her back at Santa Cristina without additional fuss. In the meantime, his fellow cardinals advised Accoramboni to look into the matter from his end, especially in regard to ferreting out possible accomplices.[41]

It did not take long to track down and imprison Domenica Colombina, la Fuggatina. A few nuns of Sant'Agostino were also censured for minor dereliction of duty, but the week before Christmas, Accoramboni received permission to absolve the negligent sisters. In the meantime, the unstable Valeria Rondinelli, who two weeks before had been so adamant about never returning to Lugo, had a change of heart. One gossiping chronicler noted that "after many disturbances she was forced to return to her convent." In late November her brother reported that she recognized her error and now wished to return home. The Sacred Congregation agreed. It was barely a month since her original flight. Now she too would have a few tales of the outside world to tell her cloistered sisters. In January 1736 Cardinal Accoramboni pointed out that only Domenica Colombina among his flock continued to be punished for an offense that was less hers than another's. "She is constantly pleading from jail to be absolved like the others, and she demonstrates total repentance for her offense." On receiving this recommendation, the Congregation promptly pardoned la Fuggatina too.

Accoramboni and his officious deputies would continue to vex the nuns of Sant'Agostino with their micromanaging, as they had done in the early 1730s, for a dozen more years. In the 1740s the exasperated nuns even petitioned the pope for an investigation into the matter by an apostolic visitor, someone "independent of the bishop of Imola," whose agent had "made himself perpetual financial overseer of the convent, with absolute authority."[42]

And Donna Christina Cavazza? Thirty years after her story began, after sheaves and sheaves of archival paperwork documented her various misadventures, she disappeared from the written record, behind the wall at Santa Cristina. The dearth of further paperwork may offer a clue to what took place. The Sacred Congregation knew full well that a woman religious of independent mind who lacked wealth or stellar family connections was no match for princelings of the church. Yet years of experience clearly demonstrated that time, effort, and vexation were the high cost of dealing with this particularly determined woman. Christina Cavazza's subsequent silence after her return to Santa Cristina suggests that the Curia may have decided that everyone had suffered enough and it was time for some quiet diplomacy. That they could leave to Lambertini.

Maybe it was Cardinal Lambertini's widely acknowledged wit and personal charm that finally cajoled Donna Christina and her cloistered consorelle into some sort of mutual accommodation. Many of those who had borne the brunt of the scandals had passed on. About half of the women who witnessed the original events of 1708 were no more, and a quarter of the sisters who had voted to release Cavazza in 1719 had gone to their reward. At the same time, two of the survivors were women who had been her usual singing partners and had been punished with her for singing without a license back in 1704. Like the sisters at Sant'Agostino, some more recent arrivals at Santa Cristina might have shown less indignation and more curiosity about this woman who was on her way to becoming something of a local legend. The only local chronicler to comment on the end to Cavazza's peregrinations claims, "Cavazza stayed there, though the sisters didn't want her. She did receive some penance, however." One can hope that this time it was light.[43]

Before long other monastic emergencies distracted Archbishop Lambertini and the city from the recent flurry of excitement in via Fondazza. That spring, amid lavish sacred ornaments and music, the cardinal officiated at the monastic profession of Marquis Spada's noble daughter at Santissima Trinità, two blocks away. As a workman ignited the barrage of fireworks, one broke loose and exploded in his face, striking him dead, while the cream of Bolognese society watched in horrified fascination.[44] Lambertini led the archdiocese for another four years and became one of its most popular archbishops of any era. He left Bologna in 1740 to trade in his miter for the papal tiara, after the longest papal conclave in modern history finally elected him as a dark horse, compromise candidate after some 260 ballots.

In via Fondazza, Santa Cristina at last settled back into the unremarkable everyday existence convents are supposed to manifest perennially. When Cardinal Lambertini undertook a pastoral visitation to all diocesan convents in 1736, Santa Cristina came through relatively unscathed. As a cost-cutting measure, he ordered the bursar to keep olive oil under lock and key, reserving it for the illumination of nuns' cells and not "as dressing for their favorite dishes." In a similar vein, he exhorted the mother abbess to reform the inordinate quantity of sweets currently being consumed.[45] We should resist interpreting this as evidence that corpulent Christina Cavazza may have settled a little too enthusiastically back into the convent's more opulent style of monasticism.

Cavazza's quieter life among the nuns of Santa Cristina continued for another fifteen years. One by one, she watched her fellows from the landmark 1699 Consecration of Virgins die off. By 1750 only she and four others of the original dozen remained. One member of the trio who had sung in defiance of Boncompagni's ban in 1704 died in 1748. The observer has to wonder how Donna Christina might have reacted to news in February 1745 that fire had destroyed the Teatro Malvezzi, site of her notorious indiscretions almost forty years earlier.

When Christina Cavazza passed to the better life during carnival season of 1751, the convent necrologist, who often tended to wax effusive in memorializing departed sisters, chose brevity, generosity, and discretion:

Donna Cristina Prudenza Deodata Cavazza—et canendi, et pulsandi artibus excellerit: ingressa est: d'an: 16. si vesti del 1695.: mori d'an: 56 e più p.i Kal Febr. d'appoplesia 1751.

[Donna Christina Prudenza Deodata Cavazza: She excelled in the arts of both singing and playing. She entered at age sixteen and took the veil in 1695. She died of apoplexy, after more than fifty-six years in religion, on the first of February 1751.][46]

7

EPILOGUE

It is not surprising that the heroines of the preceding tales are largely forgotten. In their day, church authorities would have preferred to suppress any remembrance of their acts, given the extraordinarily bad examples they had set. Semidea Poggi, one enthusiast for music and magic at San Lorenzo, nevertheless lingered in collective literary memory into the eighteenth century thanks to her poetry, and she has not been entirely forgotten even now. Christina Cavazza, whose many misadventures had been sketchily but often inaccurately recounted in a few Bolognese manuscript chronicles, resurfaced in print as late as 1906 when Italian playwright Alfredo Testoni alluded to her in his extremely successful "commedia storica," *Il cardinale Lambertini*. Testoni misdated her nights at the opera by a decade, misled by Bolognese historian Corrado Ricci. Ricci, who twice rehearsed Donna Christina's story, had made it even better by claiming *two* cloistered opera buffs had slipped away from Santa Cristina to enjoy Teatro Malvezzi's offerings. "Discovered, they fled to Romagna, whence they returned to their cells, pricked by remorse, only sixteen years later."[1]

The illustrious Malvezzi family and its palaces still leave their mark on Bologna, though Santa Maria Nuova, its elegant chapel, and the convent's preeminent Malvezzi benefactors have all vanished, replaced by the Cineteca di Bologna of today. Santa Maria degli Angeli in Pavia also disappeared long ago, of course. Not only San Niccolò di Strozzi, but all of historic Reggio Calabria except the Castello Aragonese vanished in the earthquakes of 1783 and 1908. Ironically, the sole surviving memorial linked to the tale of arson at San Niccolò is the tomb of the nuns' archenemy Archbishop di Gennaro, the oldest monument in Reggio's twentieth-century cathedral.[2]

Back in Bologna, the facade of San Lorenzo, restored in 1940, still conveys something of its quattrocento elegance, even if the edifice now tempts passersby with sewing notions, pastries, and gelato rather than musical delights. For decades the entire monastic complex of Santa Cristina languished in a precarious state of disrepair, its church locked and the convent turned into a barracks and finally abandoned. Now it has been gloriously restored in a form that recaptures artistic features Christina Cavazza and her consorelle would have known, frescoes that stayed hidden for generations behind subsequent rebuilding. Today music again resounds in the church, whose favorable acoustics make it a popular twenty-first-century concert venue.[3]

Though our heroines and most of their haunts have vanished, it seems that unruly female behavior continues to challenge the modern Catholic Church. As then, it provokes familiar responses from the church hierarchy, which in turn can inspire familiar reactions from some within the modern lay community. There is a notable difference—today's Catholic women who misbehave sufficiently to run afoul of their Catholic superiors usually follow strong if unorthodox religious vocations, in contrast to the unmanageable women in previous chapters, who were tied to their vows by custom and tradition much more than by spiritual desire. Strong sixteenth- and seventeenth-century female religious callings—as female mystics, would-be preachers, "living saints," and other vocations whose spiritual authority provoked opposition from the Catholic hierarchy— were extraordinary enough (certainly extraordinarily dangerous enough) to require careful, often evasive strategies and negotiation by their practitioners.[4] Yet the church hierarchy's reactions to such behavior, both in the early modern period and three hundred years later, seem remarkably in tune, though negative outcomes for the women involved today are arguably less grave—at least physically.

For examples one need look no further than my doorstep—by that I mean the steps of the Catholic archbishopric in St. Louis. In March 2008, then archbishop Raymond Burke excommunicated three religious women for singularly unruly behavior—getting themselves ordained as priests. The women were the latest to join a movement that has been gaining sufficient momentum, as well as sufficient support among the Catholic laity and even some clergy, to prompt the Vatican's Congregation for the Doctrine of the Faith (the Inquisition's new inoffensive title since Vatican II) to issue a blanket decree of excommunication in May 2008 against any woman who undergoes ordination and any bishop who performs the rite.

Not long before, in 2005, Archbishop Burke also excommunicated board members (male and female) of the city's century-old Polish parish, Saint Stanislaus Kostka, and canonically suppressed it for disobedience. The lay board, which has successfully governed the parish for a century with little involvement of the archdiocese, refused to relinquish control of the church and its endowment (which parishioners reportedly feared might be expropriated to settle civil suits resulting from *priests* behaving badly).[5]

To read Archbishop Burke's decrees in these cases is to step back into seventeenth-century Italy; their language and justifications in canon law (as well as some of their benignant, pastoral rhetoric) might well have been culled from Archbishop Paleotti of Bologna or Archbishop di Gennaro of Reggio centuries earlier. The logic reads impeccably to any who accept millennia of Roman Catholic canon law. After all, the twenty-first-century author of these decrees is a world expert on exactly this subject, and in late June 2008 he was transferred from St. Louis to Rome as prefect of the Supreme Tribunal of the Apostolic Segnatura, effectively becoming the Vatican's "chief justice" in matters of canon law.

Like Burke and much of the hierarchy in positions of power, of course, many faithful Catholics still hold firmly to the venerable perspective expressed in canon law. Indeed, they have discovered thoroughly modern ways to articulate their support for Rome's stance. Steadfast adherents of orthodoxy always find a voice, and presumably lots of willing "ears," all over the Worldwide Web (as do dissenters, for that matter). Further, it bears repeating that the more traditional Catholic religious orders for women are reputedly the ones least worried about withering communities in the new millennium.[6]

Even as these two twenty-first-century ecclesiastical dramas played themselves out in St. Louis, the archbishop also formally forbade the liberal inner-city Catholic parish of Saint Cronan's to host in its sanctuary a (female) Jewish rabbi whose Central Reform Congregation had earlier played host to the celebration of ordination for the excommunicated women priests. Resourceful Saint Cronan's parishioners then improvised a tent in the churchyard, and 150 of them huddled under it on a blustery December day to welcome the well-known local rabbi anyway. This act involves the same sort of creative literal reading of archiepiscopal directives that the nuns of San Lorenzo in Bologna and many of their sisters at other convents, not to mention many in the lay community, regularly employed in the sixteenth and seventeenth centuries to work within (and around) tough clerical prohibitions that they disagreed with.

Only a few months later Louise Lears, Sister of Charity, member of Saint Cronan's pastorate and an archdiocesan coordinator of religious education, received canonical admonition and was called before Archbishop Burke to answer accusations of multiple violations of canon law, chiefly in connection with the earlier outlawed ordinations. Finally, the day before Burke departed for Rome the next June, he made the admonition permanent when he imposed the penalty of interdict on Sister Louise, banning her from all pastoral and educational positions in the archdiocese.[7] Ironically, in short order thereafter the National Coalition of American Nuns announced that Sister Louise would receive its Margaret Ellen Traxler Award during the Coalition's fortieth anniversary celebration and conference in St. Louis in September 2009.

In the meantime, however, in December 2008 the Congregation for Institutes of Consecrated Life and the Societies of Apostolic Life at the Vatican had initiated a comprehensive apostolic visitation to "look into the quality of life" among women religious—but only those in the United States, and only those sisters active in the world, not within the cloister. Historically, such visitations have usually resulted from crises of the sort chronicled in previous chapters. In this case, however, Rome articulated no more specific cause for its investigation. In April 2009 the Vatican Congregation for the Doctrine of the Faith (formerly the Inquisition) announced another doctrinal investigation of the Leadership Conference of Women Religious, the largest such organization in the United States, reportedly representing 95 percent of the country's women in holy orders. This time less vague justifications were provided: abiding concerns about these women's approach to ecumenism, homosexuality, and Catholic ordination to the priesthood.[8]

Meanwhile, back at Saint Stanislaus Kostka in St. Louis, Christmas Mass, following hard on the board members' excommunications and the canonical suppression of the parish, welcomed an overflow crowd of some two thousand who reportedly packed the church. Many in that crowd apparently stayed on well past the Christmas holiday as part of the regular congregation (while some of the long-term parishioners left to reconcile with the archbishop). Apparently, informal lay networks among the faithful, of just the sort that supported hectored religious communities in seventeenth-century Bologna or Reggio Calabria, are still at work in comparable ways in twenty-first-century St. Louis, especially when they perceive inordinate archiepiscopal pressure to submit to "the will of the church."

That these two midwestern United States ecclesiastical crises dragged on so long illustrates how much harder it is to control insurgency in 2009 within the St. Louis Catholic community than it was in seventeenth-century Bologna, so close to the heart of the Papal States. (One suspects that religious insurgency in Reggio Calabria may never have been firmly under Vatican control.) After all, modern-day archiepiscopal pronouncements lack an intimidating executive arm to enforce them. No improvised prison like the one under the cathedral tower in Bologna threatens beneath the St. Louis archbishopric. No master inquisitor and no St. Louis Holy Office of the Inquisition can quite so decisively sort out the matter of the various local unruly women of 2008. Though the Holy Office's latter-day equivalent still issues directives from Rome, enforcing them is another matter. Long after Archbishop Burke's departure for Rome, these contentious matters continue to stew unresolved and without a clear path to an expeditious, ecclesiastically imposed solution.

Slightly less imperious curial approaches attempted elsewhere in the United States don't seem to have fared much better. After four long years of lay occupation, extensive negotiations, and considerable diocesan expense, the Boston archdiocese finally left the heat off at the doomed church of Saint Therese in Everett, four miles away, when the church boiler finally gave out in October 2008. A few months earlier, the Supreme Tribunal of the Apostolic Segnatura (which St. Louis's former archbishop had headed since late June of that year) rejected appeals from parishioners at Saint Therese and several other Boston area parishes to keep the churches open. Even without heat, twenty-four-hour vigils at Saint Therese continued through the winter cold, with regular checks on those keeping watch by solicitous police and the fire department; the local mayor continued to voice support for the parish's resolute occupiers, recalling more determinedly confrontational support by the syndics of Reggio Calabria for the nuns of San Niccolò back in the 1670s. In contrast, the New Orleans Catholic archdiocese applied a firmer hand when it successfully invoked civil rather than canon law in January 2009 to settle a similar conflict. There, city police used a battering ram to break into the barricaded Our Lady of Good Counsel, evicting and arresting trespassing faithful who had kept vigil there. For its part, the archdiocese then expressed its hope that "the Catholic community may now heal and move forward together."[9]

Official documents from these and similar proceedings presumably still eventually find their way to the Vatican Secret Archive, if not as hard copy dropped onto its miles of repository shelves, then as some modern-day space-saving digital equivalent. These days such documentation often lands far more quickly and publicly on the Web, of course, where nothing more than a Google search commonly unfolds a labyrinthine cyberjourney through largely useless sidetracks and worthless dead ends. Searching such "blogyrinths" is hardly less daunting than finding one's way through archives inside the walls of Vatican City. But a scholar returning after prolonged absence to the post-Y2K Secret Archive might be surprised—even disoriented at first—to discover how far that institution seems to be embracing the twenty-first century.

Even the idly curious can now get to know the place without leaving home, via virtual reality. A helpful Vatican Web site offers a detailed illustrated history of the institution and extensive examples · from important archive holdings, with commentary.[10] These include such controversial items as records from the Inquisition's proceedings against Galileo, which many outsiders (not just those in Hollywood) have long insisted the Curia was doing its best to keep hidden. Cybervisitors can even take a virtual tour of galleries, reading rooms, and storage areas (all of which seem disappointingly ordinary compared with the fabricated ASV in Dan Brown's overwrought *Angels and Demons* or as depicted in Hollywood's even more fantastical film version of the novel).

The serious researcher can now discover online, searchable, detailed information on archival holdings in six languages. This includes a downloadable index to collections and an extensive list of information, rules, regulations, and instructions—which now clearly proclaim the possibility of returning to work after lunch: "A written explanation must be submitted to the Prefect to request afternoon access (from 3:00 p.m. to 5:45 p.m.)." At the same time, few, I hope, would argue with one trenchant resistance to encroaching modernity added in July 2008: "The use of cell phones in the reading room and reference room is strictly prohibited."

Today a new face observes the reading room from within his frame high on the wall, but he might strike some below as looking a bit anxious amid all this modernity. Sleek Formica and Plexiglas have replaced most of the antique dark and heavy walnut. Contemporary streamlined, Italian-designed desk lights illuminate the tables now, and strategically placed electrical outlets accommodate researchers' inevitable laptops. The long-abiding rule requiring pencils only and absolutely proscribing both fountain pens and those newfangled ballpoints today seems quaint. The side reference room, where the few portable computers were banished in the early 1990s, and where any particularly slim, up-to-date model attracted as much attention as a flashy sports car on the street, houses an array of fancy computer terminals. As wallpaper, their screens show off attractive images from the collections when they are not displaying indexes, now available digitally.

Nevertheless, returning scholars must still submit their requests on paper call slips—those outmoded pencils are not quite obsolete yet. Then the investigator patiently awaits the arrival of manuscripts requested in writing. Even these days, scholars pass the time looking out for familiar faces. Far fewer musicologists seem to turn up, testimony to the changing tides and fashions in musical scholarship, which have retreated from medieval and Renaissance studies and "positivist" research in particular.[11] My former student who initiated me into rituals of the reading room in the late 1980s has not been back since the late 1990s. She now investigates Hollywood film music ("The Final Frontier: Composer James Horner and 'Apollo 13'"). In fact, several former early modern friends seem to have gone Hollywood. One went from studying Josquin des Prez to Beautiful Mon-

sters: Imagining the Classic in Musical Media; another made the transition from Antoine Busnoys to "Stemming the Rose, Queering the Song: *Brokeback Mountain*, Old Hollywood, and the Radical Politics of Rufus Wainwright." One former Vatican Archive regular apparently "went native": having learned a smattering of Navajo, he headed for the Four Corners region of the United States, where he was recently spotted doing the Navajo skip dance (rather badly) with an elderly Navajo matron on each arm during the Navajo song-and-dance competition at the Gallup Inter-Tribal Ceremonial.

"The count," now past eighty, finally growing gray and rather deaf, is otherwise still going strong and continues to publish the results of archival investigations about as consistently as he did twenty years ago. He turns up in the archive irregularly—less a concession to age, perhaps, than to the impossibility of getting coffee and a smoke, which he laments. Both the Vatican bar and the inviting courtyard went off limits in July 2007 when the Vatican Library across the courtyard closed for several years of comprehensive repairs and rebuilding.

The buste from the Bishops and Regulars finally arrive, and in no time at all they distract from this modernity and change. With comfortable, familiar regularity, they continue to yield up their intriguing tales.

> In 1628 righteously indignant nuns at the convent of San Giovanni in San Genesio (South Tyrol) demand that Don Fulvio Pacetti and Sister Maria Angelica should be fittingly punished "for flicking a handkerchief in the mother abbess's face and having spat in her face." The nuns declined to accept the irate siblings' sister. . . .

> Cattarina Bavona, student at the convent of Santissima Annunziata in Lecce (Apulia) in 1646, requests permission to dance the tarantella for two days inside the cloister—the treatment local doctors recommend as a cure for the potentially fatal "disease of the tarantula." Should her local bishop disapprove of her dancing in company with several similarly afflicted professed nuns, Cattarina proposes to dance apart, but within earshot of musicians specially brought in to accompany this form of convent music therapy. . . .

Relatives of the nuns of Santa Maria degli Angeli and San Giuseppe in Kotor (Montenegro), whose city is besieged by the Turks in 1651, proclaim their resolve to burn down the convents with the nuns inside before the city is overrun. They would "sooner cause their daughters and sisters to perish than allow them to fall under the power of barbarians." . . .

Renowned artist Pietro da Cortona has commissioned a new high altar carved in stone for the convent of San Girolamo di Cortona in 1660, and he promises to paint the altarpiece himself. The nuns therefore request permission to release the painter's aged cousin, Maria Martina Berrettini, from her onerous manual labors as a convent conversa. Naturally they do this out of gratitude for Maestro Pietro's generosity, but being practical women, also "in the hope that they may get still greater benefit out of him." . . .

Terrified sisters of Santa Maria Maddalena in Matelica (Marche) implore the Sacred Congregation in 1664 to deal with Sister Giovanna Vittoria Otthoni and her protégée Maria Francesca Cavalupi, who recently treated their many male admirers to a banquet in the parlatorio after the other nuns were asleep in their beds. As the pair flaunted themselves in male attire during an ensuing theatrical, an armed mob forced its way inside to murder some of the less savory audience members. The intended victims unsuccessfully sought sanctuary inside clausura, then hid all night in a wooden trough along the parlatorio. Yet the assassins continue to roam the neighborhood outside, so the Sacred Congregation must act quickly . . . but secretly. Should Sister Giovanna Vittoria discover they have written, the tattling nuns fear for their own lives. . . .

In 1703 the nuns of Santa Chiara in Acquapendente (Lazio) feel powerless in face of their mother abbess's immoderate affection for her little dog. When they objected to its birthing a litter of pups on the abbess's lap in chapel while the other nuns sang the office, their superior's outraged cries could be heard even outside the convent. More flagrantly yet, she now admits "a little male dog every day, who is using the little girl dog carnally, something unheard of here in living memory." They plead for the Sacred Congregation to command the animal's removal, "but to recite all the scandals it has provoked would make this discourse overlong." . . .

The befuddled vicar capitular of Torino (Piedmont) beseeches the Sacred Congregation's wise counsel in 1722 to solve a particularly ticklish problem. An unnamed nun at one of his convents (also unnamed) informs him that she woke up one morning to discover "male organs completely displacing, and visible, outside her female ones"—as she put it, a member "of the selfsame grossness, length, and girth, with the little bag and the two eggs—large, like a domestic nut."[12]

Bisogna pescare.
—Pietro Wenzel, second custodian, Vatican Secret Archive

NOTES

CHAPTER ONE

1. Craig A. Monson, "Elena Malvezzi's Keyboard Manuscript: A New 16th-Century Source," *Early Music History: Studies in Medieval and Early Modern Music* 9 (1989): 73–128. The complete ribald song text appears, together with a facsimile and texts for other naughty songs from the collection, on 104–7. The manuscript is cataloged at the Museo Bardini as MS 967.

2. Wenzel's succinct advice appears in Owen Chadwick, *Catholicism and History: The Opening of the Vatican Archives* (Cambridge: Cambridge University Press, 1978), 209. The 1927 exhortation appears in Maria Luisa Ambrosini with Mary Willis, *The Secret Archives of the Vatican* (Boston: Little, Brown, 1969), 303. Ambrosini's own remark appears on p. 19. For another, slightly more recent (but very similar) view of archival work at the Vatican, dating from after the opening of the Inquisition Archive, see Karen Liebreich, *Fallen Order: Intrigue, Heresy, and Scandal in the Rome of Galileo and Caravaggio* (New York: Grove Press, 2004), xxvi–xxxii.

3. British musicologist and Josquin scholar Jeremy Noble coined this apt description of old-style archival research back in the 1980s. See "Archival Research," in *Musicology in the 1980s: Methods, Goals, Opportunities*, ed. D. Kern Holoman and Claude V. Palisca (New York: Da Capo, 1982), 36.

4. ASV VR, sez. monache, 1650 (marzo–luglio), and ibid. (agosto–settembre).

5. The Latin is quoted in Graciela S. Daichman, "Misconduct in the Medieval Nunnery: Fact, Not Fiction," in *That Gentle Strength: Historical Perspectives on Women in Christianity*, ed. Lynda L. Coon, Katherine J. Haldane, and Elisabeth W. Sommer (Charlottesville: University of Virginia Press, 1990), 98.

6. On the seven cloistered Chigi sisters, see Colleen Reardon, *Holy Concord within Sacred Walls: Nuns and Music in Siena, 1575–1700* (Oxford: Oxford University Press, 2002), esp. 124.

7. Gabriella Zarri cites the Bolognese figure of about 14 percent in "I monasteri femminili a Bologna tra il xiii e il xvii secolo," *Deputazione di Storia Patria per le Province di Romagna: Atti e Memorie*, n.s., 24 (1973): esp. 144–45. Robert Kendrick mentions the astonishing percentage of Milanese upper-class daughters who

became nuns in "The Tradition of Milanese Convent Music and the Sacred Dialogues of Chiara Margarita Cozzolani," in *The Crannied Wall: Women, Religion and the Arts in Early Modern Europe*, ed. Craig A. Monson (Ann Arbor: University of Michigan Press, 1992), 211–12.

8. For the Bolognese critic Giovanni Boccadiferro's quotation, see BCB, MS B778, 175.

9. The original Italian appears in Gabriella Zarri, "Recinti sacri: Sito e forma dei monasteri femminili a Bologna tra '400 e '600," in *Luoghi sacri e spazi della santità*, ed. Sofia Boesch Gajano and Lucetta Scaraffia (Turin: Rosenberg e Sellier, 1990), 386, 393 n. 28. Detailed and engaging discussion of comparable aspects of Venetian convent life appears in Mary Laven, *Virgins of Venice: Broken Vows and Cloistered Lives in the Renaissance Convent* (New York: Viking, 2002).

10. The example of one such fugitive from a convent in Guercino (Alatri) is mentioned in ASV, VR, sez. monache, 1650 (marzo–luglio).

11. Charles Burney, *The Present State of Music in France and Italy*, facsimile of the 1773 London ed. (New York: Broude, 1969), 314.

12. Gottfried von Bülow, ed., *Diary of the Journey of Philip Julius, Duke of Stettin-Pomerania, through England in the Year 1602*, Transactions of the Royal Historical Society, n.s., 6 (London, 1892), 29. Burney's decidedly unenthusiastic assessment of nun singers at Sant'Agostino in Bologna, however, should temper an overly rosy impression of convent music: "What rendered this music still more tiresome, was the singing, which was rather below mediocrity." Burney, *Present State of Music*, 106–7 (Milan) and 220–21 (Bologna).

13. Margaret F. Rosenthal quotes Coryat in *The Honest Courtesan: Veronica Franco, Citizen and Writer in Sixteenth-Century Venice* (Chicago: University of Chicago Press, 1992), 73. For the poetry of another musically talented honest courtesan, see Gaspara Stampa's "Complete Poems: The 1554 Edition of the 'Rime,' a Bilingual Edition," ed. Troy Tower and Jane Tylus, trans. with intro. Jane Tylus, forthcoming in 2010 in the Other Voice in Early Modern Europe series from the University of Chicago Press.

14. Bolognese nuns' occupations are described and pictured in Mario Fanti, *Abiti e lavori delle monache di Bologna* (Bologna: Tamari, 1972).

15. As nuns and convents caught the attention of academic feminism and gender studies, many scholars began to interpret how individual nuns as well as monastic communities created successful and productive life strategies, from wide-ranging religious, historical, artistic, literary, and musical perspectives. Some that provide viewpoints that are particularly relevant, complementary, or alternative to those of following chapters include Gajano and Scaraffia, *Luoghi sacri*; Monson, *Crannied Wall*; E. Ann Matter and John Coakley, eds., *Creative Women in Medieval and Early Modern Italy: A Religious and Artistic Renaissance* (Philadelphia: University of Pennsylvania Press, 1994); Daniel Bornstein and Roberto Rusconi, eds., *Women and Religion in Medieval and Renaissance*

Italy (Chicago: University of Chicago Press, 1996); Gabriella Zarri, ed., *Il monachesimo femminile in Italia dall'alto medioevo al secolo xvii a confronto con l'oggi* (Verona: Segno, 1997); Lucetta Scaraffia and Gabriella Zarri, eds., *Women and Faith: Catholic Religious Life in Italy from Late Antiquity to the Present* (Cambridge, MA: Harvard University Press, 1999); Vera Fortunati, ed., *Vita artistica nel monastero femminile: Exempla* (Bologna: Compositori, 2002); Elissa B. Weaver, *Convent Theatre in Early Modern Italy: Spiritual Fun and Learning for Women* (Cambridge: Cambridge University Press, 2002); Renee P. Baernstein, *A Convent Tale: A Century of Sisterhood in Spanish Milan* (New York: Routledge, 2002); Laven, *Virgins of Venice*; Kate Lowe, *Nuns' Chronicles and Convent Culture in Renaissance and Counter-Reformation Italy* (Cambridge: Cambridge University Press, 2003); Helen Hills, *Invisible City: The Architecture of Devotion in Seventeenth-Century Neapolitan Convents* (Oxford: Oxford University Press, 2004); Gianna Pomata and Gabriella Zarri, eds., *I monasteri femminili come centri di cultura fra rinascimento e barocco* (Rome: Edizioni di Storia e Letteratura, 2005); Silvia Evangelisti, *Nuns: A History of Convent Life, 1450–1700* (Oxford: Oxford University Press, 2007).

16. On priestly collaboration in the writings of women religious, see, for example, Catherine M. Mooney, "Women's Visions, Men's Words: The Portrayal of Holy Women and Men in Fourteenth-Century Italian Hagiography" (PhD diss., Yale University, 1991); see also Catherine M. Mooney, ed., *Gendered Voices: Medieval Saints and Their Interpreters* (Philadelphia: University of Pennsylvania Press, 1999).

17. On the relations between ecclesiastical investigators' questions and responses to them, see Peter Burke, *The Historical Anthropology of Early Modern Italy* (Cambridge: Cambridge University Press, 1984), 40–47 ("The Bishop's Questions and the People's Religion").

18. Among many notable works of microhistory, Craig Harline, *The Burdens of Sister Margaret: Inside a Seventeenth-Century Convent*, abridged ed. (New Haven, CT: Yale University Press, 2000), Jonathan Spence, *The Memory Palace of Matteo Ricci* (New York: Viking Press, 1984), and Richard Wunderli, *Peasant Fires: The Drummer of Niklashausen* (Bloomington: Indiana University Press, 1992), also come immediately to mind. For a brief discussion of microhistory, see Giovanni Levi, "On Microhistory," in *New Perspectives on Historical Writing*, ed. Peter Burke (University Park: Pennsylvania State University Press, 1991), 93–113. For a history of the term, its reception, and its methods, see Carlo Ginzburg, "Microhistory: Two or Three Things That I Know about It," trans. John Tedeschi and Anne C. Tedeschi, *Critical Inquiry* 20 (1993): 10–35.

CHAPTER TWO

1. Eliseo Capis appears among Dominican theologians listed at the close of the Council of Trent. See D. Ignacio Lopez de Ayala, *El sacrosanto y ecuménico Concilio de Trento* (Barcelona: Imprenta y Librería de D. Antonio Sierra, 1848), 365.

His role as Venetian censor is documented in Richard J. Agee, "The Privilege and Venetian Music Printing in the Sixteenth Century" (PhD diss., Princeton University, 1982), 267–68. For his appointment as *reggente* of the Dominican *studium*, see John Tedeschi, *The Prosecution of Heresy: Collected Studies on the Inquisition in Early Modern Italy* (Binghamton, NY: Center for Medieval and Early Renaissance Studies, 1991), 62.

2. Antonio Battistella, *Il S. Officio e la riforma religiosa in Bologna* (Bologna: Zanichelli, [1905]), 105–6. Guido Dall'Olio, *Eretici e inquisitori nella Bologna del cinquecento* (Bologna: Istituto per la Storia di Bologna, 1999), 410–11. Maestro Eliseo had also deputized as master inquisitor in Bologna in August 1572.

3. It is safe to assume that San Lorenzo's organ followed in its facade the relatively standardized sixteenth-century Italian layout of pipe towers and flats as exemplified in Giovanni Cipri's surviving instrument for San Martino in Bologna (1556), illustrated in Peter Williams, *The European Organ, 1450–1850* (London: Batsford, 1966), 210. On the possible removal of San Lorenzo's altarpiece, see Carlo Cesare Malvasia, *Le pitture di Bologna, 1686*, ed. Andrea Emiliani (Bologna: Edizioni ALFA, 1969), [175]. The remnants of the convent facade were restored in 1940, and it is unclear how much of what we see today dates from before that restoration. See Corrado Ricci and Guido Zucchini, *Guida di Bologna: Nuova edizione illustrate* (1968; repr. Bologna: Edizioni ALFA, 1976), 37. An earlier drawing of the chapel floor plan (BCB, G761/bis, Cartel. 42/101) resembles the current shape of the exterior. The pre-restoration cornice, illustrated in Marco Pagan de Paganis, *Cornici di terracotta in Bologni* (Turin: Tip. Lit. Camilla e Bertolero, Editori, 1880), plate 6, is identical to the modern one. Original sources make no mention at all of Eliseo Capis's detour to the external church, though the details of the appearance of the convent, its chapel, and chapel furnishings are documented.

4. Gabriella Zarri, "I monasteri femminili a Bologna tra il xiii e il xvii secolo," *Deputazione di Storia Patria per le Province di Romagna: Atti e Memorie*, n.s., 24 (1973): 188–89. Malvasia briefly describes Santa Maria del Castello in *Pitture di Bologna*, 257.

5. All the documents relevant to San Lorenzo's musical reform survive in ASB, Demaniale 120/1460 (San Giovanni in Monte), "Miscellanea di notizie diverse del monastero."

6. See Craig A. Monson, "The Composer as Spy: The Ferraboscos, Gabriele Paleotti, and the Inquisition," *Music and Letters* 84 (2003): 1–18.

7. AAB, Misc. vecchie 808, fasc. 6.

8. Unless otherwise noted, details on Laura Bovia derive from Craig A. Monson, "Ancora uno sguardo sulle suore musiciste di Bologna," in *I monasteri femminili come centri di cultura fra Rinascimento e Barocco*, ed. Gianna Pomata and Gabriella Zarri (Rome: Edizioni di Storia e Letteratura, 2005), 3–26. ASB,

Demaniale 120/1460 (San Giovanni in Monte), "Miscellanea di Notizie diverse del monastero," letter from the prioress of San Lorenzo dated April 15, 1578.

9. Quotations from Monson, "Ancora uno sguardo," 7, 9. When not stage-mothering Laura's career, the busy clergyman Giacomo Bovio also found time to sire a son. An eighteenth-century family tree characterized the offspring simply as *spurio* (bastard). BCB, MS Gozz. 73, no. 16.

10. ASB, Demaniale 120/1460 (San Giovanni in Monte), letter from Don Theodosio di Piacenza to Don Arcangelo, abbot of San Giovanni in Monte, dated August 3, 1583. Ibid, "Ordinationes D. Theodosij Placentini P'ris R.me G'nalis Canoni Regulariu' Congreg: Lateran. Ad Moniales S.ti Laurentij Bononia," dated April 3, 1583. For another copy, see AAB, Misc. vecchie 804, fasc. 41.

11. Although the transcript of the investigation offers nothing concerning the interrogatory strategies in confronting witnesses attributed here to the inquisitor, questions posed and answers received were hastily set down in detail in the complete transcript of the investigation. The surviving copy in BCB, MS B1877, fols. 325–87, is frequently illegible because of ink bleed-through and corrosion of the paper, requiring some guesswork in the translation. I am grateful to Gabriella Zarri for bringing it to my attention many years ago.

12. Ibid., prioress Serafina Saldini's testimony, fol. 325–325v.

13. Ibid., subprioress Arcangela Bovia's testimony, fol. 326–326v.

14. Ibid., Angela Tussignana's testimony, fols. 326v–328v.

15. Details appear in Rainer Decker, *Witchcraft and the Papacy: An Account Drawing on the Formerly Secret Records of the Roman Inquisition*, trans. H. C. Erik Midelfort (Charlottesville: University of Virginia Press, 2008), 90–93. See also Battistella, *S. Officio*, 168.

16. A particularly useful refuting of the old view appears in Anne Jacobson Schutte, *Cecilia Ferrazzi: Autobiography of an Aspiring Saint* (Chicago: University of Chicago Press, 1996), 6–9. Schutte explores the topic in greater detail in *Aspiring Saints: Pretense of Holiness, Inquisition, and Gender in the Republic of Venice, 1618–1750* (Baltimore: Johns Hopkins University Press, 2001), esp. 26–41. See also Tedeschi, *Prosecution of Heresy*; Ruth Martin, *Witchcraft and the Inquisition in Venice, 1550–1650* (Oxford: Blackwell, 1989), 9–33; and Decker, *Witchcraft and the Papacy*.

17. BAV, MS Borg. Lat. 71, fol. 165, "1620 fiorenza 1 Agosto." Unfortunates subjected to the strappado could be raised by specific amounts, then be allowed to fall the length of the rope for additional encouragement.

18. An inventory of the inquisitor's quarters and their layout is described in Battistella, *S. Officio*, 30–33. Andrea di Bartolo's *Last Supper* now hangs in the Pinacoteca Nazionale di Bologna, which lists the quarters of the Inquisition as its original provenance. The Inquisition's rooms at San Domenico are closed to the public.

19. BCB, MS B1877, Don Livio da Bologna's testimony, fol. 329–329v; Don Ambrosio da Bologna's testimony, fols. 329v–330.

20. Information concerning Ghislieri comes from Pompeo Scipione Dolfi, *Cronologia delle famiglie nobili di Bologna* (Bologna: Giovanni Battista Ferroni, 1670; Bologna: Forni Editore, n.d.). For Semidea Poggi, see Giovanni Fantuzzi, *Notizie degli scrittori bolognesi* (Bologna: Stamperia di S. Tommaso d'Aquino, 1789; Bologna: Forni editore, n.d.), 7:73. Donna Semidea had received the monastic habit in 1579, together with her sister, who took the name Cleria.

21. Battistella, *S. Officio*, 70. On difficulties between Paleotti and Maestro Eliseo, see Paolo Prodi, *Il cardinale Gabriele Paleotti*, vol. 2 (Rome: Edizioni di Storia e Letteratura, 1967), 234–35.

22. BCB, MS B1877, fol. 336–336v.

23. The listing of nuns who knew nothing, BCB, MS B1877, fol. 345v. Donna Florentia Campanacci's testimony, fol. 357. Donna Flaminia Berò's testimony, fol. 369. Donna Ester's testimony, fol. 343–343v. Donna Ester's remark is quoted in Adriano Prosperi, "Dalle 'divine madri' ai 'padri spirituali,'" in *Women and Men in Spiritual Culture*, ed. Elisja Schulte van Kessel (The Hague: Netherlands Government Publishing Office, 1986), 71.

24. The complete incantation of the white angel appears in Donna Fulvia Tussignana's testimony (ending "revellatemi la verita," BCB, MS B1877, fol. 354v) and in Maestro Eliseo's list of questions (fol. 335). Donna Erminia Ghisliera's testimony, fol. 350. Donna Perpetua Theodosio made a virtually identical claim (fol. 359v). An extended discussion of the esperimento dell'inghistera appears in Martin, *Witchcraft*, 114–18; on 101–39 she describes many of the same spells that turn up at San Lorenzo. On Sixtus V and the angel prayer, see Matteo Duni, *Under the Devil's Spell: Witches, Sorcerers, and the Inquisition in Renaissance Italy* (Florence: Syracuse University in Florence, 2007), 61.

25. Margaret Rosenthal, *The Honest Courtesan: Veronica Franco, Citizen and Writer in Sixteenth-Century Venice* (Chicago: University of Chicago Press, 1992), 200–201. For the similar Venetian spell invoking the white angel, probably in 1587, see Guido Ruggiero, *Binding Passions: Tales of Magic, Marriage, and Power at the End of the Renaissance* (Oxford: Oxford University Press, 1993), 119, and 249 n. 64, for evasiveness regarding specific invocation of the devil. Donna Flaminia Berò's testimony, BCB, MS B1877, fol. 344.

26. Donna Maria Maddalena's testimony, BCB, MS B1877, fol. 350; Donna Florentia's testimony, fol. 358v. In the *Key of Solomon* it appears under the heading "How to know whom [sic] has committed a theft." See *Key of Solomon the King (Clavicula Solomonis)*, trans. and ed. S. Liddell MacGregor Mathers (York Beach, ME: Samuel Weiser, 1972), 49. For various British sixteenth- and seventeenth-century examples of the shears and sieve technique, see Keith Thomas, *Religion and the Decline of Magic* (New York: Charles Scribner's Sons, 1971), 212–22, where variations on several other techniques employed at San

Lorenzo also appear. Pomponazzi's use of the spell is mentioned in Ottavia Niccoli, *Prophecy and People in Renaissance Italy* (Princeton, NJ: Princeton University Press, 1990), 129. Uses of the shears and the sieve and similar forms of divination in Brazil are discussed in Laura de Mello e Souza, *The Devil and the Land of the Holy Cross: Witchcraft, Slavery and Popular Religion in Colonial Brazil* (Austin: University of Texas Press, 2004), 93–99.

27. The brief Santa Marta invocation, with somewhat different wording, appears in Martin, *Witchcraft*, 109. Discussion and explanation of various other love spells appears on 135–36. Longer versions of the prayer, including the second invocation, appear in Maria Pia Fantini, "La circolazione clandestina dell'orazione di Santa Marta: Un episodio modenese," in *Donna, disciplina, creanza cristiana dal xv al xvii secolo*, ed. Gabriella Zarri (Rome: Edizioni di Storia e Letteratura, 1996), 45–65, which discusses the circulation of the invocation in detail. Interestingly, the original Italian seems to make the hammered victim feminine ("se la trovate").

28. Suor Antonia's testimony, BCB, MS B1877, fol. 354v. On the Venetian shadowy invocation, see Ruggiero, *Binding Passions*, 123.

29. Donna Cintia Machiavelli's testimony, BCB, MS B1877, fol. 347v. For Count Guido Pepoli's clerical career, which involved the purchase of such positions as protonotary apostolic *participantium* and cleric of the apostolic chamber, see Dolfi, *Cronologia*, 600; see also Salvador Miranda, "The Cardinals of the Holy Roman Church" (http://www.fiu.edu/~mirandas/cardinals.htm). Semidea Poggi and Guido Pepoli were in fact related, sharing the same great-grandfather, the eminent and very prolific Count Guido Pepoli (d. 1505).

30. Fra Mauro da Soresina's testimony, BCB, MS B1877, fol. 381v. On similar invocations of biblical holiness to do, or undo, love's work, see Duni, *Under the Devil's Spell*, 57.

31. Donna Arcangela Bovia's testimony, BCB, MS B1877, fol. 337v; Donna Gentile's testimony, fol. 361; Donna Costantia's testimony, fol. 362; Donna Perpetua Theodosio's testimony, fol. 359v; Donna Florentia Campanacci's testimony, fol. 359; Donna Semidea Poggi's testimony, fol. 362.

32. The sequence and details of Angela Tussignana's devilish conjuring have been reconstructed from witnesses' scattered references, in which quotations were often described in the third person. These include (sequentially): Donna Arcangela Bovia's testimony, BCB, MS B1877, fol. 338; Donna Alexandra's testimony, fol. 341; Donna Arcangela Bovia's testimony, fol. 338; Donna Flaminia Berò's testimony, fol. 343v; Donna Cintia Machiavelli's testimony, fol. 347; Donna Virginia's testimony, fol. 348; Donna Angelica Fava's testimony, fol. 351.

33. Donna Angelica Fava's testimony, BCB, MS B1877, fol. 351; Donna Cintia Machiavelli's testimony, fol. 348. For similar moments in other devilish conjuring, see Ruggiero, *Binding Passions*, 92 (darkened room) and 123–24 (undressing,

the devil's terrifying voice); and Schutte, *Aspiring Saints*, 103 (removing scapulars [small cloth squares worn by members of confraternities or religious orders]).

34. Donna Virginia's testimony, BCB, MS B1877, fol. 348; Ascanio Trombetti's testimony, fol. 376v; Donna Virginia's testimony, fol. 348.

35. Donna Arcangela Bovia's testimony, BCB, MS B1877, fol. 338; Donna Angelica Fava's testimony, fol. 351.

36. Donna Florentia Campanacci's testimony, BCB, MS B1877, fol. 386–386v.

37. Prioress Judith's testimony, BCB, MS B1877, fol. 337–337v. The scribe's orthography for "little girls" looks closer to "puttane" than "puttine," but it seems improbable that the prioress would have defended her own actions by describing the young nuns as "whores." Perhaps the scribe recorded what he was thinking, not what he heard. The subsequent quotation appears in Niccoli, *Prophecy and People in Renaissance Italy*, 194.

38. Niccoli, *Prophecy and People in Renaissance Italy*, 194–95.

39. Donna Arcangela Bovia's testimony, BCB, MS B1877, fol. 337. On Capis's struggles with Bolognese patricians, see Dall'Olio, *Eretici e inquisitori*, 385–89.

40. On the reading of sentences from the organ loft or cemetery in the 1600s, see Battistella, *S. Officio*, 32. The use of a stage outside San Domenico in 1700 appears in Decker, *Witchcraft and the Papacy*, 181–82.

41. BCB, MS B3567, entry for 1590, "adi 21 Sett.re."

42. ASB, Demaniale 120/1460 (San Giovanni in Monte), "Ordini del R.mo P're Don Camillo Rettor G.nale della Congreg.ne lateranense fatti alle Canoniche Regolari di san lorenzo di Bologna . . . alli 2 di Marzo 1589."

43. *La Calliope religiosa di Donna Semidea Poggi, monaca in S. Lorenzo di Bologna* (Vicenza: Francesco Grossi, 1623), 3 (Signor Cavaliere R.P.'s poem), 38–39 (excerpts from *Consiglio spirituale*), 57 (*Al Santissimo Crocifisso*). *Al Santissimo Crucifisso* also appears in Elisabetta Graziosi, "Scrivere in convento: Devozione, encomio, persuasione nelle rime delle monache fra cinque e seicento," in *Donna, disciplina, creanza cristiana dal xv al xvii secolo*, ed. Gabriella Zarri (Rome: Edizioni di Storia e Letteratura, 1996), 322.

CHAPTER THREE

1. On the archbishop of Naples and pet dogs, see ASV, VR, sez. monache, 1635 (marzo–dicembre); on the overweight Neapolitan abbess, see ibid., 1644 (luglio–dicembre). The documents relevant to the fire at San Niccolò di Strozzi and its investigation survive ibid., 1674 (gennaio–aprile).

2. Details on Diego Strozzi, his founding of San Niccolò di Strozzi, and the relevant history of Reggio Calabria, its syndics, and archbishops derive chiefly from Domenico Spanò Bolani, *Storia di Reggio di Calabria da' tempi primitivi sino all'anno di Cristo 1797* (Naples: Stamp. del Fibreno, 1857). See also Francesco Arillotta, *Reggio nella Calabria spagnola, storia di una città scomparsa (1600–*

1650) (Rome-Reggio: Casa del Libro Editrice, 1981); the final decades of the convent's existence are discussed in Antonio de Lorenzo, "Note Varie VIII: Le Domenicane di S. Nicolò di Strozzi in Reggio," *Rivista Storica Calabrese* 6 (1898): 161–71.

3. Strozzi's description appears in Arillotta, *Reggio nella Calabria spagnola*, 238; 235–38 offer the most complete and accurate discussion of Diego Strozzi and correct several errors in other sources. See also Lorenzo, "Note Varie VIII: Le Domenicane," 163. On Strozzi's family alliances, see also Francesco Russo, *Storia dell'archidiocesi di Reggio Calabria*, vol. 2 (Naples: Laurenziana, 1962), 211.

4. I have reconstituted the Monsolino clan of unmarried women from Arillotta, *Reggio nella Calabria spagnola*, particularly the "Genealogia dei Monsolino ricostruita sulla base di atti notarili rogati tra fine '500 e primi '600."

5. Maria Padiglia's extended stay at San Niccolò is mentioned in Russo, *Storia dell'archidiocesi di Reggio Calabria*, 2:212.

6. Both inscriptions appear in Francesco Russo, *Storia dell'archidiocesi di Reggio Calabria*, vol. 3 (Naples: Laurenziana, 1965), 189–90.

7. Details of Reggio's cityscape, history, environment, and natural disasters appear in Spanò Bolani, *Storia di Reggio di Calabria*; Lucio Gambi, *Calabria,* vol. 16, *Le regioni d'Italia* (Turin: Tipografia Sociale Torinese, 1965); Russo, *Storia dell'archidiocesi di Reggio Calabria*, vol. 2; and Demetrio de Stefano, *I Terremoti in Calabria e nel Messinese* (Naples: Edizioni Scientifiche Italiane, 1987).

8. Russo, *Storia dell'archidiocesi di Reggio Calabria*, 2:44.

9. On Reggio's various brigands and bandits, see Giusi Currò and Giuseppe Restifo, *Reggio Calabria* (Rome: Laterza, 1991), 61; and Russo, *Storia dell'archidiocesi di Reggio Calabria*, 2:67, where the original Italian quotation appears.

10. ASV, VR, sez. monache, 1674 (gennaio–aprile), di Gennaro's letter and summary of May 16.

11. Ibid., trial transcript, Suor Girolama Monsolino's testimony, fol. 3.

12. Ibid., Suor Girolama Monsolino's testimony, fol 4.

13. Ibid., Suor Orsola Ricca Monsolino's testimony, fol. 5–5v.

14. Ibid., Madre Maria Maddalena Monsolino's testimony, fols. 6v–7.

15. Ibid., Suor Chiara Monsolino's testimony, fols. 8v–9.

16. Ibid., Francesca Bettula, conversa's testimony, fol. 12–12v.

17. Ibid., Lavinia Cannizzano, conversa's testimony, fols. 13v–14.

18. Ibid., Madre Maria Maddalena Monsolino's testimony, fol. 7.

19. Ibid., letter of May 15 from Francesco Domenico Barone to the Sacred Congregation.

20. For an excellent introduction to silk and silk raising, see John Feltwell, *The Story of Silk* (New York: St. Martin's Press, 1990). For details of the commercial business throughout Italy, see Luca Molà, *The Silk Industry of Renaissance Venice* (Baltimore: Johns Hopkins University Press, 2000). For sericulture in Reggio, see Arillotta, *Reggio nella Calabria spagnola*, 137–43.

21. ASV, VR, sez. monache 1674 (gennaio–aprile), letter of May 15 from Francesco Domenico Barone.

22. Ibid., letter of May 22 from Giovanni Filippo Oliva, Coretto Oliva, and Giuseppe Laboccetta to the Sacred Congregation.

23. Ibid., letter of May 23 from Giovanni Domenico Bosurgi and Giovanni Filippo Battaglia, syndics of Reggio, to the Sacred Congregation.

24. Details of the conflicts between Archbishop di Gennaro and the citizens and clergy of Reggio appear in Spanò Bolani, *Storia di Reggio di Calabria*; Arillotta, *Reggio nella Calabria spagnola*; and especially Russo, *Storia dell'archidiocesi di Reggio Calabria*, 3:189–98. The Vatican pronouncement appears on 191; the two subsequent quotations appear on 195.

25. The fullest account of di Gennaro's career, travails, and good works appears in Russo, *Storia dell'archidiocesi di Reggio Calabria*, 3:189–98. For the quotation describing the archbishop's benevolence, see 191.

26. ASV, VR, sez. monache, 1674 (gennaio–aprile), trial transcript, fol. 11; Suor Chiara Monsolino's testimony, fol. 9–9v; Madre Maria Maddalena Monsolino's testimony, fol. 7v.

27. Ibid., Madre Maria Maddalena Monsolino's testimony, fol. 7v; Francesca Bettula, conversa's testimony, fol. 12v; di Gennaro's letter of May 16, 1673, to the Sacred Congregation.

28. Documents relevant to the nuns of San Niccolò after Archbishop di Gennaro presented his case appear in ASV, VR, reg. monial. 21 (1674); ASV, VR, sez. monache, 1674 (agosto); ASV, VR, sez. monache, 1676 (gennaio–aprile); ASV, VR, reg. monial. 23 (1676); ASV, VR, sez. monache, 1680 (aprile); ASV, VR, reg. monial. 27 (1680).

29. ASV, VR, sez. monache 1674 (gennaio–aprile), undated letter from Giovanna and Anna Monsolino to Cardinal Santa Croce, the appointed cardinale ponente.

30. Tarabotti's treatise is published in Francesca Medioli, *L'"Inferno monacale" di Arcangela Tarabotti* (Turin: Rosenberg e Sellier, 1989). Another work available in English is Arcangela Tarabotti, *Paternal Tyranny*, trans. and ed. Letizia Panizza (Chicago: University of Chicago Press, 2004). Tarabotti's "Women Are of the Human Species" appears in Theresa M. Kenney, trans. and ed., *"Women Are Not Human": An Anonymous Treatise and Responses* (New York: Crossroad, 1998).

31. Di Gennaro's monument is pictured in Ercole Lacava, *La basilica cattedrale di Reggio Calabria: Immagini e storia* (Reggio: Edizioni Comunione, 2005), 48–49. The chronicler's comment is cited in Russo, *Storia dell'archidiocesi di Reggio Calabria*, 2:99.

32. ASV, VR, sez. monache, 1674 (agosto), Abbess Maria Padiglia's letter.

33. Prioress Giovanna Monsolino's petition appears ibid., 1676 (gennaio–aprile); the new archbishop's letter of April 30, 1676, appears ibid. (maggio–luglio).

34. Ibid., 1680 (aprile); ibid., 1674 (gennaio–aprile), Archbishop di Gennaro's letter of May 16.

35. Details of the convent's final decades derive from Lorenzo, "Note Varie VIII: Le Domenicane," 167–71.

CHAPTER FOUR

1. A shorter, preliminary version of this chapter appeared as Craig A. Monson, "The Artistic Heyday (Brief, but Turbulent) of Santa Maria Nuova in Bologna," in *Florilegium musicae: Studi in onore di Carolyn Gianturco*, ed. Patrizia Radicchi and Michael Burden (Pisa: Edizioni ETS, 2004), 697–712, reprinted by permission of Edizioni ETS. Carlo Cesare Malvasia, *Le pitture di Bologna, 1686*, ed. Andrea Emiliani (Bologna: Edizioni ALFA, 1969), 148 [102]; on the bologna-shaped candies, see Mario Fanti, *Abiti e lavori delle monache di Bologna in una serie di disegni del secolo xviii* (Bologna: Tamari, 1972), 62.

2. See Gabriella Zarri, "I monasteri femminili a Bologna tra il xiii e il xvii secolo," *Deputazione di Storia Patria per le Province di Romagna: Atti e Memorie*, n.s., 24 (1973): 208–9.

3. The data for 1574 appear in ASV, VR, posiz. 1588, A-B, and AAB, Misc. vecchie 808. The statistics for 1639 appear in BUB MS 770, vol. xxviii (1639–44), 55. The figures from 1679 appear in ASV, VR, sez. monache, 1680 (maggio–agosto).

4. ASB, Demaniale 167 bis/734 bis (Santa Maria Nuova), "Scelta di racordi piu importanti per le monache, tanto priore, come badesse."

5. The details on the Malvezzi nuns' family relations derive from Giuseppe Fornasini, *Breve cenno storico genealogico intorno alla famiglia Malvezzi* (Bologna, 1927), esp. 76–77. See also BCB, MS B921, 6, 60.

6. See Fornasini, *Breve cenno storico genealogico*, 77.

7. ASV, VR, reg. regular. 34 (1625), fol. 312–312v. On Vittoria Felice Malvezzi's prolonged illness and eventual recovery, see also ibid., 35 (1626), 36 (1627), 39 (1628). ASB, Demaniale 171/2084 (Santa Maria Nuova), 378–79; Cardinal Antonio Barberini served as papal legate in Bologna in 1629 and 1642. See Luciano Meluzzi, *I vescovi e gli arcivescovi di Bologna* (Bologna: Collana Storico-ecclesiastica, 1975), 433, 438.

8. For Varese, ASV, VR, reg. episc. 10 (1586/I), fols. 220v–221. For Guastalla, ibid., sez. monache, 1644 (luglio–dicembre).

9. The extremely popular and prolific Giovanni Francesco Barbiere (1591–1666), nicknamed il Guercino ("the Squinter") because he was cross-eyed, retains the renown he enjoyed in his day, while his contemporary G. B. Bolognini is much less familiar.

10. The acquisition of the painting, thanks to the generosity of Donna Fulvia Maria Bianchi, is recorded in ASB, Demaniale 171/2084 (Santa Maria Nuova), 290, which characterizes it as "S. Domenico . . . Ritratto in atto d'Agonizante unitamente con altri Santi." Carlo Cesare Malvasia missed the painting in his

seventeenth-century guidebook. A Bolognini painting of Saint Dominic and the specified saints was still at Santa Maria Nuova in the nineteenth century, according to Michael Bryan, *Dictionary of Painters and Engravers, Biographical and Critical*, ed., rev., and enl. Robert Edmund Graves (London: George Bell, 1886), 149.

11. A valuable discussion of convent arts, including needlework, appears in K. J. P. Lowe, *Nuns' Chronicles and Convent Culture in Renaissance and Counter-Reformation Italy* (Cambridge: Cambridge University Press, 2003), 318–94.

12. For the 1605 exception, see ASV, VR, reg. regular. 6 (1605), fol. 109v. For Vittoria Felice's licenses, see ASV, VR, reg. monial. 1 (1646); ASV, VR, sez. monache, 1648 (gennaio–giugno); ASV, VR, sez. monache, 1655 (settembre–dicembre); ASV, VR, reg. monial. 7 (1655).

13. The official ban appears in BUB, MS It. 206II, no. 5. Ludovisi's notification to Rome of his action appears in ASV, Sacra Congregazione del Concilio, Visite ad Limina 136A, fol. 65; another copy survives in BUB, MS It. 206II, no. 2.

14. Details of about a dozen services with lavish music at San Guglielmo appear in ASB, Demaniale 80/815 (San Guglielmo). The general ban, published on February 11, 1651, appears in ASB, Demaniale 84/3233 (Santi Vitale ed Agricola); ASB, Demaniale 48/4891 (Sant'Agostino); ASB, Demaniale 75/3686 (Santissima Trinità); and ASB, Demaniale 17/4798 (Santissima Concezione).

15. References to the various Malvezzi musical services appear in ASB, Demaniale 167/734 (Santa Maria Nuova). The supposed transfer of Saint Eutichio's body is mentioned in Antonio di Paolo Masini, *Bologna perlustrata* (Bologna: Erede di Vittorio Benacci, 1666), 553. The specific nature of Costanza Virgilia Malvezzi's donation appears in ASB, Demaniale 171/2084 (Santa Maria Nuova), 317. Costanza Virgilia, daughter of Marc Antonio Malvezzi, marchese di Castel Guelfo, was born in 1610, professed at Santa Maria Nuova in 1633, and died in 1686, according to Fornasini, *Breve cenno storico genealogico*, 52. Given that the Malvezzi relation and former archbishop Niccolò Albergati Ludovisi had been appointed vicar of San Lorenzo in Damaso in the 1630s, perhaps he had a hand in acquiring Saint Eutichio's body part. See Meluzzi, *Vescovi e gli arcivescovi di Bologna*, 443.

16. Biographical information from Fornasini, *Breve cenno storico genealogico*, 77.

17. ASV, VR, sez. monache, 1657 (settembre-dicembre), petition "Per li Monasterij e Monache della Città di Bologna." Ibid., vicar-general Antonio Ridolfi's response of November 14.

18. ASB, Demaniale 171/2084 (Santa Maria Nuova), 286. Malvezzi's initial petition to the Sacred Congregation, dated August 3, 1657, appears in ASV, VR, sez. monache, 1657 (agosto).

19. ASB, Demaniale 171/2084 (Santa Maria Nuova), 286–87; ASV, VR, sez. monache, 1657 (agosto); additional information on the rebuilding appears ibid., 1680 (maggio–agosto).

20. ASV, VR, sez. monache, 1657 (settembre–dicembre).

21. Boncompagni's remark appears in ASB, Demaniale 171/2084 (Santa Maria Nuova), 287. The nuns' complaints appear in ASV, VR, sez. monache, 1660 (settembre–dicembre).

22. The formal payment of the sisters' dowries is recorded in ASB, Demaniale 119/686 (Santa Maria Nuova); the date of their profession appears in BCB, MS B921, 111.

23. *Messe a tre voci, con sinfonie, e ripieni à placito, accompagnato da motetti, e concerti di Giulio Cesare Arresti* (Venice: Francesco Magni, 1663).

24. Craig A. Monson, *Disembodied Voices: Music and Culture in an Early Modern Italian Convent* (Berkeley: University of California Press, 1995); and Robert L. Kendrick, *Celestial Sirens: Nuns and Their Music in Early Modern Milan* (Oxford: Clarendon Press, 1996), both discuss nun composers' uses of such phrases to support their musical endeavors.

25. The details of the Malvezzi decorations are from ASV, VR, sez. monache, 1680 (maggio–agosto), and from ASB, Demaniale 171/2084 (Santa Maria Nuova), 316, where Maria Anna Ratta's cushions are mentioned.

26. For the Ratta family's earlier convent charity, see Pompeo Scipione Dolfi, *Cronologia delle famiglie nobili di Bologna* (Bologna: Giovanni Battista Ferroni, 1670; Bologna: Forni Editore, n.d.), 641; and Gail Feigenbaum, "Catalogo dei dipinti," in *Ludovico Carracci*, ed. Andrea Emiliani (Bologna: Nuova Alfa Editoriale, 1993), 92–94, 123–24. Maria Anna Ratta's profession and infection are mentioned in ASB, Demaniale 145/712 (Santa Maria Nuova), "Aumento di livello di Ratta" (December 15, 1664).

27. ASV, VR, sez. monache, 1680 (maggio–agosto), Maria Anna's petition, dated September 15, 1679. A pallium is a band with pendants in front and back, worn over the chasuble to denote episcopal authority.

28. Ibid., Antonio Rodolfi's order of May 16, 1679, notarized May 30, 1679; ibid., an undated petition from Maria Anna Ratta.

29. Ibid., Maria Vinciguerra's petition, marked June 9, 1679; ibid., Archbishop Boncompagni's summary, marked November 21, 1679.

30. Ibid., Maria Vinciguerra's petition marked June 9, 1679 (original emphasis).

31. Ciotti's book was translated into English and published by William Barley in 1596 as *A Booke of Curious and Strange Inventions, Called the First Part of Needleworkes, Containing Many Singular and Fine Sortes of Cut-workes, Raisde-workes, Stiches, and Open Cutworke . . . Newlie Augmented. First Imprinted in Venice, and Now Again Newly Printed in More Exquisite Sort, for the Profit and Delight of the Gentlewomen of England.* These verses appear in Ann Rosalind Jones and Peter Stallybrass, *Renaissance Clothing and the Materials of Memory* (Cambridge: Cambridge University Press, 2000), 140. Bolognese social critic Camillo Baldi's comments appear in Mario Fanti, "Le classi sociali e il governo di Bologna all'inizio del secolo xvii in un'opera inedita di Camillo Baldi," *Strenna Storica*

Bolognese 11 (1961): 154. Venetian nuns' attitudes are described in Mary Laven, *Virgins of Venice: Broken Vows and Cloistered Lives in the Renaissance Convent* (New York: Viking, 2002), 8.

32. ASV, VR, sez. monache, 1680 (maggio–agosto), Maria Anna's petition marked October 2, 1679.

33. Ibid., Boncompagni's summary, marked November 21, 1679.

34. ASB, Demaniale 171/2084 (Santa Maria Nuova), 316. The additional donations from Ratta and Pulica are listed in ASV, VR, sez. monache, 1680 (maggio–agosto), Boncompagni's summary, marked November 21, 1679.

35. The Malvezzi nuns' death dates and accomplishments are listed in the copy of the convent necrology in BCB, MS B921, 54, 57, 60, 66, 67, 75. See also Fornasini, *Breve cenno storico genealogico*, 52, 77, 79.

CHAPTER FIVE

1. ASV, VR, sez. monache, 1675 (aprile). Santa Maria degli Angeli was near modern Piazza Dante. The church of Santi Gervasio e Protasio, reputedly Pavia's oldest church, still survives, though it was rebuilt in the early 1700s. Much of the cloister was pulled down in 1805. See Elia Giardini, *Memorie topografiche dei cambiamenti avvenuti e delle opere state eseguite nella città di Pavia* (Pavia: Fusi, 1830), 91. The nuns' Carmelite superiors occupied Santa Maria del Carmine, one of Pavia's most important surviving Lombard Gothic edifices.

2. http://it.wikipedia.org/wiki/Lista_dei_Monasteri_di_Pavia (consulted October 31, 2009).

3. The bishop's document setting quotas is transcribed in Virginio Luigi Bernario, *La chiesa di Pavia nel secolo xvi e l'azione pastorale del cardinal Ippolito de' Rossi (1560–1591)*, Quaderni 7–8 (Pavia: Seminario di Pavia, 1972), 361. For comparison, the quotas for other convents ran as follows: 60 or more (2), 40–50 (3), 30–40 (4), 20–30 (9), 10–20 (4), 10 or fewer (2).

4. The subsequent events are reconstructed from the episcopal investigation preserved in ASV, VR, sez. monache, 1652 (gennaio–maggio).

5. Ibid., transcript of investigation, fol. 9v, Suor Paula Emilia Torta's testimony; fol. 30v, Giovanna Balcona's testimony. The events are also variously described by the lay witnesses from next door.

6. Ibid., fols. 6 and 5v, respectively, Prioress Ottavia Marianna Tolentina's testimony.

7. Ibid., fol. 1v, Madre Giovanna Hyacinta Porcellina, abbess of San Gregorio's testimony; fol. 1v, Carlo Albertari, protector of the convent of San Gregorio's testimony.

8. Ibid., fol. 1v, Suor Angela Aurelia Mogna's testimony; fol. 32, Giovanna Balcona's testimony.

9. Ibid., fol. 1v. Suor Angela Aurelia's testimony; fol. 31, Giovanna Balcona's testimony.

10. Ibid, fols. 2v–3, Suor Angela Aurelia's testimony.

11. Ibid., fols. 3v, 34v, 35v, 3v, all Giovanna Balcona's testimony.

12. Ibid., fol. 4, 35, 35v, all Giovanna Balcona's testimony.

13. Ibid., fol. 3, Suor Angela Aurelia's final testimony.

14. Jane Tibbetts Schulenberg, *Forgetful of Their Sex: Female Sanctity and Society, ca. 500–1100* (Chicago: University of Chicago Press, 1998), 350, 519 n. 178, provide the original Latin and a slightly different translation.

15. The song appears in Cosimo Bottegari's lutebook in the Biblioteca Estense in Modena (MS C 311). See Carol MacClintock, ed., *The Bottegari Lutebook* (Wellesley, MA: Wellesley College, 1965), 37.

16. [Desiderius Erasmus], *The Colloquies of Erasmus*, trans. Craig R. Thompson (Chicago: University of Chicago Press, 1965), 108.

17. Details of the Bolognese visitations appear in ASB, Demaniale 51/3918 (Santa Margarita), and BUB, MS It. 206/12, fol. 77, respectively. The examples from Conversano and Pescia appear in ASV, VR, sez. monache, 1665 (gennaio–aprile), and 1658 (giugno–agosto), respectively.

18. ASV, VR, sez. monache, 1652 (gennaio–maggio), fol. 10–10v, Suor Paula Emilia Torta's testimony; ibid., from summary of investigation; fol. 7v, Prioress Ottavia Marianna Tolentina's testimony.

19. Ibid., fols. 21, 18v, Suor Francesca Geronima Finali's testimony; fol. 22v, Suor Francesca Margarita Bertolasia's testimony.

20. Ibid., fol. 22, Suor Francesca Margarita Bertolasia's testimony; fols. 37, 38, Giovanna Balcona's testimony.

21. On lay views, particularly English ones, of same-sex convent relations, including Helena's comment, see Frances E. Dolan, "Why Are Nuns Funny?" *Huntington Library Quarterly* 70 (2007): 525–26. The Casanova and Diderot examples are cited in Ros Ballaster, " 'The Vices of Old Rome Revived': Representations of Female Same-Sex Desire in Seventeenth and Eighteenth Century England," in *Volcanoes and Pearl Divers: Essays in Lesbian Feminist Studies*, ed. Suzanne Raitt (New York: Harrington Park Press, 1995), 21–22. On Bartolomea Crivelli and Benedetta Carlini, see Judith C. Brown, *Immodest Acts: The Life of a Lesbian Nun in Renaissance Italy* (Oxford: Oxford University Press, 1986).

22. ASV, VR, sez. monache, 1652 (gennaio–aprile), fol. 21v, Suor Francesca Margarita Bertolasia's testimony; fol. 10v, Portinara Paula Emilia Torta's testimony; fol. 26, Catterina Villana's testimony.

23. Ibid., fol. 38v, Giovanna Balcona's testimony.

24. Adapted from *The Complete Works of Saint Teresa of Jesus*, trans. and ed. E. Allison Peers (London: Sheed and Ward, 1946), 2:17.

25. ASV, VR, sez. monache, 1652 (gennaio–maggio), bishop of Pavia's letter of November 10, 1652.

26. The bishop of Pavia's letter and the trial transcript appear in ibid.; the Sacred Congregation's response appears in ASV, VR, reg. monial. 5 (1652), fol. 42v.

27. The nuns' complaint appears in ASV, VR, sez. monache, 1652 (gennaio–maggio). Saint Teresa's stipulations for punishment from her Constitutions are adapted from *Complete Works of Saint Teresa of Jesus*, 3:233–38.

28. ASV, VR, sez. monache, 1657 (gennaio–aprile).

29. Ibid., 1658 (settembre–dicembre), petition from the nuns; ibid., 1659 (giugno–luglio), vicar-general's letter.

30. Ibid., 1668 (gennaio–marzo), Suor Anna Domitilla Chini's petition; ibid., bishop of Pavia's letter.

31. Ibid., nuns of San Martino del Leano's letter of August 28, 1668; ibid., "Informatione intorno la Monaca Chini Carmelitana proposta d'accettarsi nel Monistero Leano di Pavia," submitted by the nuns of San Martino del Leano. The convent of San Martino happened also to be home to the nun composer Bianca Maria Meda, who published music in the 1690s.

32. Ibid., 1652 (gennaio–maggio), investigation transcript, fol. 35, Giovanna Balcona's testimony; emphasis added.

33. Ibid., 1668 (agosto–settembre), nuns of San Martino del Leano's letter of August 28; ibid., conclusion to "Informatione intorno la Monaca Chini."

34. On the suppression of small religious houses, see Emanuele Boaga, *La soppressione Innocenziana dei piccoli conventi in Italia* (Rome: Edizioni di Storia e Letteratura, 1971).

35. ASV, VR, sez. monache, 1675 (agosto–settembre).

CHAPTER SIX

1. On Clement XI's ban, see Howard Smither, *A History of the Oratorio* (Chapel Hill: University of North Carolina Press, 1977), 1:160. For oratorio statistics during the ban, see Victor Crowther, *The Oratorio in Bologna (1650–1730)* (Oxford: Oxford University Press, 1999), 115. Ironically enough, shortly after the lifting of the papal ban in 1708, San Domenico was forbidden on March 7 to perform oratorios in future because a recent performance had lasted until close to midnight and attracted inordinate crowds. See BCB, MS Gozz. 185, fol. 275v.

2. The description of Bolognese carnival relies heavily on Lodovico Frati, *La vita privata di Bologna dal secolo xiii al xvii* (Bologna: Zanichelli, 1900; repr. Rome: Bardi Editore, 1968), esp. 147–86, unless otherwise noted.

3. Giovanna Ferrari, "Public Anatomy Lessons and the Carnival: The Anatomy Theatre of Bologna," *Past and Present* 117 (November 1987): 50–106.

4. On maskers' "dimanda . . . sproposita" to perform at convents, see ASB, Demaniale, 17/4798 (Santissima Concezione), letter from the nuns' vicar of February 1, 1676. On "vicars of carnival" at San Guglielmo, see ibid., 80/814 (San Guglielmo), particularly entries from the 1650s. On the abbess marriage broker, see AAB, Misc. Vecchie 804, no. 23; for the play at San Guglielmo, see BCB, MS Gozz. 185, fol. 275v. For a thorough and insightful discussion of Italian convent theater, see Elissa B. Weaver, *Convent Theatre in Early Modern*

Italy: Spiritual Fun and Learning for Women (Cambridge: Cambridge University Press, 2002).

5. Volterra: ASV, VR, sez. monache, 1673 (giugno–luglio); Amelia: ibid., 1630 (febbraio–marzo). For a discussion of carnival diversions in Venetian convents, see Mary Laven, *Virgins of Venice: Broken Vows and Cloistered Lives in the Renaissance Convent* (New York: Viking, 2003), 137–44.

6. Details on the Bolognese stage since 1700 derive chiefly from Corrado Ricci, *I teatri di Bologna* (Bologna: Successori Monti, 1888), esp. 133–35; the quotation is on 135. Details of opera performances and revivals are from Claudio Sartori, *I libretti italiani a stampa fino al 1800* (Cuneo: Bertola e Locatelli, ca. 1990–94).

7. The pope's order survives in ASV, VR, reg. monial. 50 (1706), unnumbered entry of September 24, 1706. An expanded version, with the Bolognese nun's vicar's response to it in 1708, survives in AAB, Misc. Vecchie 820, no. 17.

8. Details of Christina Cavazza's violation of clausura and her discovery are reconstructed from ASV VR, sez. monache, 1718 (marzo–aprile) unless otherwise specified. The date of July 1, 1708, for Cavazza's discovery is specified in BCB, MS Gozz. 184, fol. 67. I have recreated the sequence of events from various scanty second- and third-hand reports, which leave much to the imagination.

9. On the thieves' invasion, see Ugo Capriani, "Chiesa e convento di Santa Cristina della Fondazza in Bologna: Ipotesi di ricerca e recupero" (Degree thesis, University of Bologna, 1987–88), 32.

10. Details from BCB B921; ASB, Demaniale 33/2894 (Santa Cristina); ibid., 23/2884 (Santa Cristina); ASB, Archivio Boschi, no. 260; ASV, VR, sez. monache, 1718 (marzo–aprile); Pompeo Scipione Dolfi, *Cronologia delle famiglie nobili di Bologna* (Bologna: Giovanni Battista Ferroni, 1670; Bologna: Forni Editore, n.d.), 193–94.

11. The eighteenth-century complaints about the Compagnia del Piombo's gardening negligence appear in Capriani, "Chiesa e convento," 83. The back gate appears on Joan Blaeu's *Theatrum civitatum et admirandorum Italiae* (1663). Filippo Gnudi's *Pianta iconografica* (1702) is drawn from a slightly different angle.

12. The scanty, often conflicting details of Giacomelli's capture and trial survive in BUB, MS 626IX, 217–18; BCB, MS B83, 458; BCB, MSS B3666–67; BCB, MSS Gozz. 184, 185; BUB, MS 486VIII; and BUB, MS 3879, where the quotation appears under April 3, 1709.

13. The description of the Cavazza-Giacomelli friendship appears in BCB, MS Gozz. 184, fol. 67.

14. For a fascinating and illuminating discussion of sixteenth- and seventeenth-century priest-nun relationships, with special reference to Venice, see Mary Laven, "Sex and Celibacy in Early Modern Venice," *Historical Journal* 44 (2001): 865–88. See also Laven, *Virgins of Venice*, esp. 167–85.

15. *The Complete Works of Saint Teresa of Jesus,* trans. and ed. E. Allison Peers (London: Sheed and Ward, 1946), 3:237.

16. ASV, VR, sez. monache, 1718 (marzo–aprile), Boncompagni's summary letter of July 22, 1713. Additional sources regarding efforts to transfer Cavazza include ibid., reg. monial. 53 (1709), March 14, 1709; 55 (1711), September 27, 1711; 57 (1713), June 23, 1713; 57 (1713) September 1, 1713.

17. ASV, VR, sez. monache, 1718 (marzo–aprile) undated petition from Christina Cavazza. Boncompagni's recommendation appears ibid., dated January 13, 1712.

18. Additional sources regarding Cavazza's rehabilitation include ASV, VR, reg. monial. 58 (1714), September 28, 1714; 60 (1716), February 7, 1716; 60 (1716), December 18, 1716; 61 (1717), August 13, 1717; 62 (1718), April 29, 1718.

19. ASV, VR, sez. monache, 1718 (marzo–aprile), summary of the affair by the secretary of the Sacred Congregation. The fugitive nun's attempt to escape from Santa Catterina is chronicled in BCB, MS B3666, 375.

20. ASV, VR, sez. monache, 1718 (marzo–aprile), undated petition by nuns of Santa Cristina.

21. BUB, MS It. 170, no. 54, fols. 251–252v, Christina Cavazza's letter, dated May 24, 1718.

22. ASV, VR, sez. monache, 1718 (marzo–aprile), Cavazza's undated and unsigned petition to the Sacred Congregation. Additional sources regarding Cavazza's transfer to Lugo include BUB, MS It. 170, no. 54, fols. 251–252v; ASV, VR, reg. monial. 63 (1719), April 21, 1719; 63 (1719), May 22, 1719; 63 (1719), July 21, 1719; AAB, Misc. Vecchie 262, "All'Emo e R'mo Pr'pe Il Sigr Card'le Lambertini . . . per l'Arciprete D. Gian' Franc:co Rondinelli di Lugo."

23. ASV, VR, sez. monache, 1718 (marzo–aprile), brief petition from Cavazza to the Sacred Congregation. The revised, longer petition includes the brief quotation as well as further insertions such as "with payment of another, new dowry, either to the convent in Lugo or to Santa Maria Maddalena" and "neither would the petitioner decline to employ an appropriate dowry at the other convent in Lugo if Your Eminences would instead transfer her to this one in Lugo rather than to that one of the Magdalene in Bologna."

24. ASV, VR, reg. monial. 63 (1719), July 21, 1719. Cavazza's transfer to Lugo is described in AAB, Misc. Vecchie 262, "All'Ilmo e Rmo Prpe Il Sigr Cardle Lambertini . . . per l'Arciprete D Gian' Franc.co Rondinelli di Lugo."

25. ASV, VR, reg. monial. 77 (1734), February 26, 1734. Other sources for Christina Cavazza's misadventures in Lugo include AAB, Misc. Vecchie 262, I/615/11b; ASV, VR, reg. monial. 77 (1734), February 26, 1734; BUB, MS Ital. 635, vol. 5, "Lettere al Card. Prospero Lambertini," no. 76; ASV, VR, reg. monial. 77 (1734), September 3, 1734; 77 (1734), October 1, 1734; 77 (1734), December 10, 1734; 78 (1735), March 18, 1735.

26. BUB, MS Ital. 635, vol. 5, "Lettere al Card. Prospero Lambertini," no. 76.

27. AAB, Misc. Vecchie 262, I/615/11b, investigation of Cavazza's flight from Lugo, 1735, unnumbered pages, Christina Cavazza's testimony. Ibid., "All'Ilmo e Rmo Prpe Il Sigr Cardle Lambertini . . . per l'Arciprete di Gian' Franc.co Rondinelli di Lugo."

28. AAB, Misc. Vecchie 262, I/615/11b, investigation of Cavazza's flight from Lugo, 1735, unnumbered pages, Christina Cavazza's testimony.

29. ASI, Demaniale I/8590 "Denari che si sono impiegati in spese diverse per la nuova fabrica da mè D. Cristina Teresa Cavazza sindica li anni 1721 e 1722." Several receipts acknowledging Cavazza's payments on June 7, 1721, are also bound into the volume. My thanks to Candace Smith for ferreting out these documents in the remnants of Sant'Agostino's archive.

30. Girolamo Bonoli, *Storia di Lugo ed Annessi* (Faenza: Stampa dell'Archi, 1732), 310–11.

31. Luisa Bedeschi, "La povertà ritrovata: Brevi cenni sulle monache Agostiniane di Lugo," *Studi Romagnoli* 48 (1997): 76–77.

32. ASB, Misc. Vecchie 262, I/615/11b, investigation of Cavazza's flight from Lugo, 1735, unnumbered pages, Christina Cavazza's testimony.

33. H. J. Schroeder, O.P., trans. and ed., *Canons and Decrees of the Council of Trent* (St. Louis, MO: Herder, 1941), 228. Sources concerning Cavazza's determination to return to Santa Cristina include ASV, VR, reg. monial. 77 (1734), September 3, 1734; 77 (1734), October 1, 1734; 77 (1734), December 10, 1734; 78 (1735), March 18, 1735; AAB, Misc. Vecchie 262, I/615/11b.

34. ASV, VR, reg. monial. 77 (1734), September 3, 1734; October 1, 1734; December 10, 1734.

35. Details of subsequent events derive from AAB, Misc. Vecchie 262, I/615/11b.

36. Ibid., investigation of Cavazza's flight from Lugo, unnumbered pages, testimony of Francesco Veronesi, Maria Constanza Filippini, and Fortunata Lodini, conversa.

37. Ibid., Christina Cavazza's testimony.

38. Ibid., testimony of Christina Cavazza and Valeria Rondinelli.

39. Ibid., Valeria Rondinelli's testimony.

40. Ibid., exchange between nuns' vicar Bernardino Mariscotti and Christina Cavazza.

41. Ibid., nuns' vicar Mariscotti's final entry. Final details of Cavazza's reintegration at Santa Cristina and resolution of the case in Lugo appear in ASV, VR, reg. monial. 78 (1735), November 18, 1735; December 23, 1735; ASV, VR, sez. monache, 1735 (novembre–dicembre); AAB, Misc. Vecchie 262, "All'Em'o e R'mo Prpe Il Sig Cardle Lambertini . . . per L'Arciprete D: Gian' Franc.co Rondinelli di Lugo."

42. BCB, MS B3667, 376; ASV, VR, sez. monache, 1735 (novembre–dicembre); Luisa Bedeschi, "Povertà ritrovata," 70.

43. BCB, MS B3667, 376–77.

44. BUB MS 225VII, fol. 180v.
45. Roberta Zucchini, "Santa Cristina della Fondazza: Storia architettonica e storico artistica" (Degree thesis, University of Bologna, 1987–88), 108–9.
46. BCB B921, 264.

CHAPTER SEVEN

1. By the eighteenth century Semidea Poggi's *I desideri di Parnaso* was known in name only, but her *La Calliope religiosa* (Vicenza: Francesco Grossi, 1623), quoted in chapter 2, still survives. See Elizabetta Graziosi, "Scrivere in convento: Devozione, encomio, persuasione nelle rime delle monache fra cinque e seicento," in *Donna, disciplina, creanza cristiana dal xv al xvii secolo*, ed. Gabriella Zarri (Rome: Edizioni di Storia e Letteratura, 1996), 320–22; also Elizabetta Graziosi, "Arcipelago sommerso: Le rime delle monache tra obbedienza e trasgressione," in *I monasteri femminili come centri di cultura fra Rinascimento e Barocco*, ed. Gianna Pomata and Gabriella Zarri (Rome: Edizioni di Storia e Letteratura, 2005), 159. Alfredo Testoni's allusions to Christina Cavazza appear in *Il cardinale Lambertini* (Bologna: Nicola Zanichelli, 1906), 147 and 212. In 1934 Testoni's popular play became a film, directed by Parsifal Bassi. A second film, directed by Giorgio Pàstini, appeared in 1954, and a television version was made in 1963. For Ricci's embroidered versions of the story, see Corrado Ricci, *I teatri di Bologna nei secoli xvii e xviii* (Bologna: Successori Monti Editori, 1888), 138–40 (which misdates Donna Christina's trips to the opera to 1719 but gets the date of her return to Santa Cristina right), and *Una illustre avventuriera (Cristina di Nortumbria)* (Milan: Fratelli Treves, 1891), 21 (the source of the quotation). Giuseppe Cosentino, *Il teatro Marsigli-Rossi* (Bologna: Tipografia A. Garagnani, 1900), 21, on the other hand, offers a version of the tale in which Donna Christina flees to Lugo right after the curtain falls at Teatro Malvezzi and remains there until 1735, which is how another early chronicler had recorded her adventures. In the 1980s Carlo Vitali expressed some doubt about the truth of Cavazza's attractive legend, given such glaring inconsistencies in early manuscript accounts. See Apostolo Zeno and Carlo Francesco Pollarolo, *Il Faramondo*, ed. Carlo Vitali, Drammaturgia musicale Veneta 9 (Milan: Ricordi, 1987), xxvii.
2. Palazzo Malvezzi, now part of the University of Bologna, stands at Largo Trombetti number 4; another Malvezzi palace (better known recently as Palazzo Revegnan) is in via Zamboni, numbers 26 and 28, opposite the Teatro Comunale; Palazzo Malvezzi-Campeggi is at via Zamboni, number 22; Palazzo Malvezzi de' Medici, now seat of the provincial government, is at via Zamboni, number 13. Archbishop di Gennaro's tomb is illustrated in Ercole Lacava, *La basilica cattedrale di Reggio Calabria: Immagini e storia* (Reggio Calabria: Edizioni Comunione, 2005), 49. See also http://www.cattedralereggio calabria.it/la-cattedrale/monumenti-e-sacelli.

3. A description of the convent in decay, written before its recent restoration, appears in Craig A. Monson, *Disembodied Voices: Music and Culture in an Early Modern Italian Convent* (Berkeley: University of California Press, 1995), 239–46.
4. The literature on medieval and early modern women negotiating this contested spiritual territory has expanded significantly in recent decades. Particularly relevant are various discussions in Gabriella Zarri, *Le sante vive: Profezie di corte e devozione femminile tra '400 e '500* (Turin: Rosenberg e Sellier 1990); Gabriella Zarri, ed., *Finzione e santità tra Medioevo ed età moderna* (Turin: Rosenberg e Sellier, 1991); E. Ann Matter and John Coakley, *Creative Women in Medieval and Early Modern Italy: A Religious and Artistic Renaissance* (Philadelphia: University of Pennsylvania Press, 1994); Daniel Bornstein and Roberto Rusconi, eds., *Women and Religion in Medieval and Renaissance Italy* (Chicago: University of Chicago Press, 1996); Beverly Mayne Kienzle and Pamela J. Walker, eds., *Women Preachers and Prophets through Two Millennia of Christianity* (Berkeley: University of California Press, 1998); Lucetta Scaraffia and Gabriella Zarri, eds., *Women and Faith: Catholic Religious Life in Italy from Late Antiquity to the Present* (Cambridge, MA: Harvard University Press, 1999); Anne Jacobson Schutte, Thomas Kuehn, and Silvana Seidel Menchi, eds., *Time, Space, and Women's Lives in Early Modern Europe* (Kirksville, MO: Truman State University Press, 2001); Anne Jacobson Schutte, *Aspiring Saints: Pretense of Holiness, Inquisition, and Gender in the Republic of Venice, 1618–1750* (Baltimore: Johns Hopkins University Press, 2001); Elizabeth Makowski, *"A Pernicious Sort of Woman": Quasi-Religious Women and Canon Lawyers in the Later Middle Ages* (Washington, DC: Catholic University of America Press, 2005).
5. For a compelling examination of seventeenth-century priestly sexual misbehavior, all too similar to bad behavior that has come to light in recent decades, see Karen Liebreich, *Fallen Order: Intrigue, Heresy, and Scandal in the Rome of Galileo and Caravaggio* (New York: Grove Press, 2004), which concludes with a discussion of the current state of the matter.
6. See, for example, Rodney Stark and Roger Finke, *Acts of Faith: Explaining the Human Side of Religion* (Berkeley: University of California Press, 2000), esp. 186–90. Pages 179–82 make the interesting point that in the aftermath of Vatican II, when female religious vocations otherwise began to decline markedly, they continued to rise, then held their own, in religiously conservative Spain and Portugal until the demise of the dictatorships of António de Oliveira Salazar and Francisco Franco in the mid-1970s.
7. For the archdiocese's official description of the matter, see http://www.arch stl.org/index.php?option=com_content&task=view&id=523&Itemid=1.
8. "U.S. Nuns Facing Vatican Scrutiny," *New York Times,* July 1, 2009, http://www .nytimes.com/2009/07/02/us/02nuns.html?pagewanted=2&emc=eta1. The Web site for the apostolic visitation, due to conclude in 2011, is http://www .apostolicvisitation.org/en/index.html.

9. http://www.arch_no.org/News.php?mode=read&id=362&title=A+Statement+from+the+Archdiocese+of+New+Orleans.

10. http://asv.vatican.va/home_it.htm.

11. Time-honored—in the eyes of some, "timeworn"—musicological paradigms such as archival studies began coming under attack from the late 1960s, especially with Joseph Kerman, *Contemplating Music: Challenges to Musicology* (Cambridge, MA: Harvard University Press, 1985). The "new musicology" of the 1990s further shifted scholarly attention into wider-ranging fields. For one entertaining take on the phenomenon, see Charles Rosen, "The New Musicology," in *Critical Entertainments: Music Old and New* (Cambridge, MA: Harvard University Press, 2000), 255–72.

12. ASV, VR, sez. monache, 1628 (febbraio–maggio), 1646 (novembre–decembre), and 1647 (aprile–maggio); on the tarantella and tarantism in Apulia, see Ernesto De Martino, *La terra del rimorso: Contributo a una storia religiosa del Sud* (Milan: Saggiatore di Alberto Mondadori Editore, 1961); for a brief discussion of tarantism in English, see Michael P. Carroll, *Madonnas That Maim: Popular Catholicism in Italy since the Fifteenth Century* (Baltimore: Johns Hopkins University Press, 1992), 77–82. ASV, VR, sez. monache, 1651 (settembre–dicembre), 1660 (aprile–luglio), 1664 (marzo–maggio), 1703 (novembre–dicembre), 1722 (aprile).

FURTHER READING

Baernstein, P. Renee. *A Convent Tale: A Century of Sisterhood in Spanish Milan.* New York: Routledge, 2002.

Bilinkoff, Jodi. *The Avila of Saint Teresa: Religious Reform in a Sixteenth-Century City.* Ithaca, NY: Cornell University Press, 1989.

Bornstein, Daniel, and Roberto Rusconi, eds. *Women and Religion in Medieval and Renaissance Italy.* Chicago: University of Chicago Press, 1996.

Brown, Judith C. *Immodest Acts: The Life of a Lesbian Nun in Renaissance Italy.* Oxford: Oxford University Press, 1986.

Davis, Natalie Zemon. *The Return of Martin Guerre.* Cambridge, MA: Harvard University Press, 1983.

Evangelisti, Silvia. *Nuns: A History of Convent Life, 1450–1700.* Oxford: Oxford University Press, 2007.

Ginzburg, Carlo. *The Cheese and the Worms: The Cosmos of a Sixteenth-Century Miller.* Translated by John Tedeschi and Anne C. Tedeschi. Baltimore: Johns Hopkins University Press, 1980.

Harline, Craig. *The Burdens of Sister Margaret: Inside a Seventeenth-Century Convent.* Abridged ed. New Haven, CT: Yale University Press, 2000.

Hills, Helen. *The Invisible City: Architecture of Devotion in Seventeenth-Century Neapolitan Convents.* New York: Oxford University Press, 2004.

Kendrick, Robert L. *Celestial Sirens: Nuns and Their Music in Early Modern Milan.* Oxford: Clarendon Press, 1996.

King, Margaret. *Women of the Renaissance.* Chicago: University of Chicago Press, 1991.

Laven, Mary. *Virgins of Venice: Broken Vows and Cloistered Lives in the Renaissance Convent.* New York: Viking, 2003.

Lowe, K. J. P. *Nuns' Chronicles and Convent Culture in Renaissance and Counter-Reformation Italy.* Cambridge: Cambridge University Press, 2003.

Matter, E. Ann, and John Coakley, eds. *Creative Women in Medieval and Early Modern Italy: A Religious and Artistic Renaissance.* Philadelphia: University of Pennsylvania Press, 1994.

Monson, Craig A. *Disembodied Voices: Music and Culture in an Early Modern Italian Convent.* Berkeley: University of California Press, 1995.

————, ed. *The Crannied Wall: Women, Religion and the Arts in Early Modern Europe.* Ann Arbor: University of Michigan Press, 1992.

Pomata, Gianna, and Gabriella Zarri, eds. *I monasteri femminili come centri di cultura fra Rinascimento e Barocco.* Rome: Edizioni di Storia e Letteratura, 2005.

Reardon, Colleen. *Holy Concord within Sacred Walls: Nuns and Music in Siena, 1575–1700.* Oxford: Oxford University Press, 2002.

Scaraffia, Lucetta, and Gabriella Zarri, eds. *Women and Faith: Catholic Religious Life in Italy from Late Antiquity to the Present.* Cambridge, MA: Harvard University Press, 1999.

Schutte, Anne Jacobson. *Aspiring Saints: Pretense of Holiness, Inquisition, and Gender in the Republic of Venice, 1618–1750.* Baltimore: Johns Hopkins University Press, 2001.

Weaver, Elissa B. *Convent Theatre in Early Modern Italy: Spiritual Fun and Learning for Women.* Cambridge: Cambridge University Press, 2002.

Zarri, Gabriella. "Monasteri femminili e città (secoli xv–xviii)." In *Storia d'Italia: Annali,* vol. 9, *La chiesa e il potere politico dal Medioevo all'età contemporanea,* ed. Giorgio Chittolini and Giovanni Miccoli, 359–429. Turin: Giulio Einaudi, 1986.

————, ed. *Finzione e santità tra Medioevo ed età moderna.* Turin: Rosenberg e Sellier, 1991.

INDEX

Chini Langosca, Anna Domitilla, xv,
132–34, 142, 143, 145–51, 223nn30–33
choirboys, 15
choir nuns, 16
choirs / choral singing, 14–16, 160;
Council of Trent mandates on,
29–30; novelty of female voices
in, 15–16, 208nn12–13; polyphony
in, 14–15. *See also* forbidden music;
permitted music
Ciotti, Giovanni Battista, 120, 219n31
Cipri, Giovanni, 210n3
clausura. *See* enclosure rules
Clement VIII, Pope, 99, 184
Clement X, Pope, 81
Clement XI, Pope, 153–54, 156, 158–59,
222n1, 223n7
clergy child abuse scandals, 199, 227n5
cloisters, 11–12
Coeli et terrae of 1586 (Sixtus V,
Pope), 44
Colombina, Domenica (La Fuggatina), xvi, 191–94
"Complete Poems: The 1554 Edition
of the Rime" (Stampa), 208n13
composing, 114, 219n24
Congregation for the Doctrine of the
Faith, 199–200
Congregation on the State of the
Clergy, 150
conjuring, 37–39
"Consiglio spirituale da fuggire il
vano . . ." (Poggi), 59–60
Constitutions for Discalced Carmelites (Saint Teresa), 143–44, 171,
223n27
*Contemplating Music: Challenges to Mu-
sicology* (Kerman), 228n11
contested spaces, 9, 12–14, 16, 158–61,
208n10. *See also* enclosure rules
convent life: aristocratic daughters in,
8–10, 66–67; carnival celebrations

in, 156–57, 222n4, 223n7; choice of
religious names in, 99–100; choral
singing in, 14–16, 29–30, 208nn12–
13; contested public spaces of, 12–
14, 16, 158–61, 208nn12–13; love and
sexuality in, 135–44, 170, 222n21,
223nn13–14; male pets in, 63, 78,
205–6, 214n11; menial labor in, 17,
119–21; musical performance in,
96–98, 101, 103–6, 113–18, 158–59,
163–65, 195, 198, 218nn13–14; necrologies and burials in, 123, 151,
220n35; private interior spaces of,
11–12; punishments and prisons
in, 143–44; quotas in, 126, 220n3;
refined pursuits in, 16–18, 208nn13–
15; religious vocation in, 17–18,
66–67, 198; sacristan roles in, 106–7,
112; transition and acceptance into,
10–11, 66. *See also* enclosure rules
converse nuns, 17, 75–76, 119–21
Convertite convents, 16, 45, 148–49
Corpus Domini convent (Bologna),
28, 109
Cortellini, Camillo (Il Violino), 32
Coryat, Thomas, 15–16, 208n13
Cosentino, Giuseppe, 226n1
Costantia (of San Lorenzo), 213n31
Council of Ten, 25, 209n1
Council of Trent, 25; convent reforms
of, 29, 96, 156–57; implementation
of decrees of, 85; on profession,
11, 188
countertenors, 15
Crivelli, Bartolomea, 139, 222n21
*Cronologia delle famiglie nobili di Bolo-
gna* (Dolfi), 162–63

Dainotto, Colomba, 93
dance, 156, 204, 228n12
Davis, Natalie, 22
I desiderj di Parnaso (Poggi), 59, 226n1